# PILL
# POLITICS

# PILL
# POLITICS

## DRUGS AND THE FDA

STEPHEN J. CECCOLI

LYNNE
RIENNER
PUBLISHERS

BOULDER
LONDON

Published in the United States of America in 2004 by
Lynne Rienner Publishers, Inc.
1800 30th Street, Boulder, Colorado 80301
www.rienner.com

and in the United Kingdom by
Lynne Rienner Publishers, Inc.
3 Henrietta Street, Covent Garden, London WC2E 8LU

**Library of Congress Cataloging-in-Publication Data**
Ceccoli, Stephen J., 1968–
   Pill politics : drugs and the FDA / Stephen J. Ceccoli
      p.   cm.
   Includes bibliographical references and index.
   ISBN 1-58826-241-3 (alk. paper)
   1. Pharmaceutical policy—United States.  2. United States. Food and Drug
Administration.  I. Title.
RA401.A3C435    2003
362.1'782'0973—dc21                                            2003047045

**British Cataloguing in Publication Data**
A Cataloguing in Publication record for this book
is available from the British Library.


Printed and bound in the United States of America

      The paper used in this publication meets the requirements
  ∞   of the American National Standard for Permanence of
      Paper for Printed Library Materials Z39.48-1992.

   5  4  3  2  1

*To my parents,*
*John and Denise Ceccoli,*
*and family*

# CONTENTS

# TABLES AND FIGURES

## Tables

## Figures

# ACKNOWLEDGMENTS

The completion of this book marks the culmination of a long journey in which I have devoted considerable time, traveled countless miles, and met many people along the way. Though all errors are of course my own, the book could not have been written without the assistance and support of a number of special people.

The seed for this book was planted at Washington University in St. Louis, where Andy Sobel, Bill Lowry, Fiona McGillivray, and Itai Sened challenged me to expand my thinking, were extremely generous with their time, and always led by example. I owe a special debt of gratitude to Andy Sobel, who oversaw this project from its inception and has always provided stimulating conversation, thoughtful advice, and lots of encouragement. Thanks, Andy. I benefited greatly from many conversations with Itai. The same is true with Bill, and I especially enjoyed the ones at Lambert's.

At Rhodes College, I appreciate the support and encouragement from my departmental colleagues (past and present) and owe special thanks to department chairs Andrew Michta, Frank Mora, and Karl Kaltenthaler. Brenda Somes, Kenan Padgett, and a variety of student assistants, especially Jill Reifstek, provided excellent research assistance. I also appreciate the feedback from students in my courses, who have always given me much to think about. This work would not have been possible without the research support of Dean Robert Llewellyn, Margaret Handwerker, and the Faculty Development Committee at Rhodes. The same is true of Marcia Brasel and the generous support provided by the J. S. Seidman Research Fellowship.

John Bing and Mike Nelson read the entire manuscript and provided thoughtful comments. John first introduced me to political science as an undergraduate at Heidelberg College and has taught me valuable lessons about teaching and learning ever since. Mike has been a terrific colleague at Rhodes and sets the bar high for the rest of us.

A special thanks goes to Randy Glean and Robert Klotz, whom I will always consider close friends, as well as to Kevin and Kathy Corder, Jim Davis, Pauline Farmer, Barbara Hoffman, Bill Olbrich, Mary Olson, Jonathan Rapkin, Jan Rensing, Bob Salisbury, Richard Smith, John Sprague, and Andrew Whitford. At various stages throughout this project, Bob and Amy Bunger, John Copper, Betty Fields, John and Joan Groce, John Hansen, Bill Hixon, the late Frank Horvay, John King, Jay and Disa Mason, Fr. Maurice Nutt, Skip Oliver, Hazel and Clifford Paris, Mabel Rea, Harry Stone, Robert Taylor, George and Jackie Ullrich, Chuck and Donna Wagner, and Cindy and Lyle Weldon provided wonderful inspiration, conversation, and a meal or two along the way.

I am proud to be part of a publishing team that includes Leanne Anderson, Lesli Athanasoulis, Deborah Knox, and Lynne Rienner. Leanne recognized the merits of this project early on and provided superb editorial guidance throughout the process. Several anonymous reviewers also helped to greatly improve the final product.

My family has been especially supportive throughout this journey. My grandparents, Edith and the late Domenic Tavoletti and Jacqueline and the late Marino Ceccoli, have always provided inspiration, warmth, and loving encouragement. Ditto for my four brothers, Dave, Chris, Mike, and Joe, and their families. Stacia Wagner has always been a considerable and unwavering source of support, encouragement, and patience, and I will always treasure her love. Finally, this book is dedicated to my parents, Denise and John Ceccoli, whose love, sacrifice, and generosity has been absolutely unbelievable. A person could not ask for more wonderful parents and living role models.

# 1

## Putting the FDA into Perspective

> D octors pour drugs of which they know little, / To cure diseases
> of which they know less, / Into human beings of whom they
> know nothing.
>
> —*Voltaire*

The United States is the most highly medicated society in the world. According to the National Association of Chain Drug Stores, more than 3 billion prescriptions were dispensed in the United States in 2002.[1] Americans depend on prescription drugs in many ways and for a variety of reasons. For curative purposes, prescription medicines are dispensed to heal wounds, cure infections, and eradicate diseases. Other medicines are prescribed to enhance the quality of life of individuals suffering from conditions for which a medical cure has yet to be found. For cancer, diabetes, mental health, or AIDS patients, prescription medicines can not only prolong but also greatly improve life. For physically and mentally healthy individuals, so-called lifestyle drugs are being increasingly prescribed to enhance the quality of life in a much different context. In this case, prescription medicines can be used for purposes ranging from the treatment of male pattern baldness to the enhancement of sexual performance.[2]

The increasing medication of Americans is an important component of the nation's overall health profile. Spending on prescription drugs now accounts for approximately 9.4 percent of all health care expenditures in the United States.[3] In monetary terms, spending on outpatient prescription drugs in retail outlets in the United States exceeded $154 billion in 2001 (NIHCM, 2002). Such medicines enable Americans to lead happier, healthier, and ultimately longer lives. This latter point is no cliché. During the course of the therapeutic revolution in the twentieth century, the average life expectancy for Americans increased from 47 years in 1900 to 68 years in 1950 to an average of 76.7 years in 1999. Clearly, pharmaceutical products play a vital role in maintaining a higher quality of life for many Americans.

With such commercial success, the pharmaceutical industry is generally regarded as both the fastest growing and the most profitable legitimate industry in the United States (Garrett, 2001). The pharmaceutical industry remains highly competitive and its profitability often hinges on its ability to consistently provide new and successful drugs. Pharmaceutical firms have been largely successful over the years in seeking to develop the next "blockbuster" drug. Blockbuster drugs are superior selling drugs whose revenues ensure a continual stream of company profits. In 2000, for instance, the top twenty prescription drugs in the United States (based on sales revenues) *each* netted U.S. sales in excess of $1 billion.[4] Five of these drugs surpassed the $2 billion mark. Such revenues allow pharmaceutical companies to develop other drugs in the research pipeline with the hope that some of these will also reach blockbuster status. Given their profit-driven nature, pharmaceutical firms have considerable incentives to develop drugs for specific demographic markets. Particularly, firms seek to produce innovative products aimed at relatively wealthy consumers.

Coinciding with the increasing medication habits of Americans has been the dominant growth of the worldwide pharmaceutical industry. Global pharmaceutical sales totaled nearly $364 billion in 2000, and the industry perennially ranks among the most profitable in industrialized countries (Tan, 2000). North America, Europe, and Japan are currently the three largest markets for prescription drug products in the world. Of these three, North America is the world's largest prescription drug market and within North America the United States is clearly the dominant player.[5] Collectively, the European Union ranks second. In the twelve months following March 2000, pharmaceutical sales totaled a combined $50.7 billion in the five largest individual European pharmaceutical markets.[6] Japan, the world's third largest pharmaceutical market, was worth $50.4 billion in 2001. In 2001 the U.S. market exceeded the size of the European and Japanese markets combined.

The increasing reliance on prescription medicines by Americans and the emergence of a powerful global pharmaceutical industry does not come without a social and political cost, however. Medication habits rest on an implicit assumption that such products will be safe and will work as advertised. In a perfect world, all new medicines would be safe and effective and there would be no need for government to play a regulatory role. Yet we do not live in a perfect world. In the absence of what economists refer to as "perfect" markets, regulation is necessary to protect consumers against potentially harmful products. In an imperfect market, there may be incentives for companies to avoid the full disclosure of relevant information about a particular product and, in extreme cases, firms may find it in their interest to produce and sell unsafe or ineffective products. As such, the regulation of new medicines remains a critical function of the federal government. In this capacity, the Food and Drug Administration (FDA), the nation's lead drug regulatory authority, remains one of the most important regulatory agencies in Washington.

## What Is the FDA and What Does It Do?

Dating back to its nineteenth-century origins in the Bureau of Chemistry, the FDA has been influenced heavily by its dual law enforcement and consumer protection mandates.[7] The agency's initial mandate was to protect consumers from the dangers of fraudulent, impure, or mislabeled substances. Since that time, federal drug safety laws have become increasingly more stringent and highly centralized. Today, the FDA's primary role is to enforce the 1938 Food, Drug and Cosmetic Act (FDCA), the cornerstone legislation governing the introduction of new medicines in the United States. The law requires manufacturers to demonstrate the safety and efficacy of a drug to the FDA as a condition of obtaining licensing approval.[8]

In its enforcement of the FDCA, the FDA maintains a vast regulatory jurisdiction. The regulation of human medicines is only one aspect, albeit a highly critical one, of the agency's overall regulatory responsibility. Consider for a moment that the agency is charged with regulating human drugs and biotechnology products, medical devices (from tongue depressors to pacemakers), foods (except meat and poultry), cosmetics, and animal drugs. It also monitors imported pharmaceutical products, licenses the nation's blood banks, oversees clinical investigations, and inspects food and drug manufacturing facilities on a biennial basis.

The FDA also regulates other health-related products that may not be immediately apparent given the agency's name. Few Americans realize, for example, that the FDA shares with the Federal Communications Commission (FCC) the responsibility for regulating wireless telephones (i.e., cell phones). Because the FDA's mandate includes the regulation of the nation's radiological health, the agency monitors the health effects of wireless phones by maintaining a set of performance standards. Other popular radiation-emitting electronic products subject to the provisions of FDA regulation include x-ray machines, radar detectors, microwave ovens, sun lamps, and television receivers.

In addition to the agency's wide regulatory product range and varied regulatory mandates, FDA authority extends to a number of distinct industry actors. FDA-regulated firms range from small biotech companies with fewer than ten employees to huge multinational conglomerates with portfolios including everything from chemicals to agricultural products to manufacturing plastics and with annual research and development budgets ranging into the hundreds of millions of dollars.

The broad range of industries regulated by the FDA in addition to the varying types of firms and practices subject to FDA regulation reflects the tremendous scope of the agency's regulatory responsibility. A frequently accepted estimate is that the FDA is responsible for regulating products accounting for approximately 20 to 25 cents of every dollar spent by U.S. consumers (Burkholz, 1994). This amounts to over $1 trillion annually. In short, the FDA has an enormous scope of regulatory jurisdiction. Whether many Americans realize it or not, the agency plays a significant role, directly or indirectly, in their everyday lives.

Because an act of Congress originally created the agency, it is Congress that oversees most aspects of the agency's operation. Through the FDCA, Congress directs the agency to protect consumers from potentially harmful products and, in order for the FDA to carry out this mandate, supplies the agency with budgetary and other resources. Given its vast array of responsibilities, the FDA operates with relatively modest resources. Today, the agency employs more than 9,000 people in both its suburban Washington headquarters and more than 150 field offices around the country.

The agency operates on an annual budget in excess of $1.4 billion.[9] Of the agency's total budget, more than one-third of the resources are dedicated to human drug programs. Such drug programs include the review of prescription medicines, over-the-counter (OTC) medicines, and generic medicines, as well as the postapproval monitoring of drugs that are currently available to U.S. consumers ($353 million in FY 2002). In addition to these drug programs, the agency devoted $156 million to biologic programs during the 2002 fiscal year. Biologic programs include the FDA's regulation of the nation's blood supply, human gene therapy products, vaccines, allergenic products, and human tissues intended for transplantation. The remaining resources support a wide range of programs for the regulation of products including cosmetics, medical devices, animal feed and drugs, and radiation-emitting products, as well as to administrative and construction costs.

Given the size of its regulatory jurisdiction, the FDA is divided into six centers in order to carry out its regulatory responsibilities. They are the Center for Drug Evaluation and Research, the Center for Biologic Evaluation and Research, the Center for Veterinary Medicine, the Center for Food Safety and Applied Nutrition, the Center for Devices and Radiological Health, and the National Center for Toxicological Research. Each of these centers has teams of physicians, chemists, microbiologists, biochemists, pharmacologists, medical statisticians, and other professionals who perform the agency's regulatory review activity. However, the FDCA directs the agency to undertake a variety of regulatory approaches. For example, new drugs and biologic products must be demonstrated to be safe and effective (by the manufacturer) prior to marketing. In addition, drug and biologic products are subject to FDA monitoring once they are made available to consumers. Alternatively, products such as cosmetics, vitamins, food additives, and dietary supplements do not require premarket approval. These products are subject to FDA regulation only after their manufacturers market them. Still other products are subject to a combination of premarket and postmarket regulatory standards. Certain medical devices, particularly the more complex ones (e.g., pacemakers) require the agency's premarketing approval while others (e.g., bed sheets) do not.

FDA offices and laboratory facilities represent another important element of agency resources. Recently, the federal government started construction on a new $600 million facility for the FDA in White Oak, Maryland. The move is highly symbolic of past shortcomings in agency resources. As Orrin Hatch, the one-time ranking Republican on the Senate Labor and Human Resources Committee once lamented during a committee hearing, the FDA is scattered among thirty-two different buildings at eleven sites in Washington, including one lab that was "a converted chicken-coop built in 1933" (U.S. Senate, 1991: 3). Plans call for the new facility to be completed in 2007.

## FDA Politics and Life in the "Goldfish Bowl"

In its role as the nation's gatekeeper for approving new medicines, the FDA does not operate in a political vacuum. The Institute of Medicine (IOM), an affiliate of the National Academy of Sciences, perhaps best summarized this observation. Created in 1970, the IOM conducts policy studies on health issues and provides advice to government agencies on scientific and technical matters. The IOM acknowledged in a 1992 report that the "FDA operates in an environment of intense public scrutiny. Its actions are closely followed by the general public, Congress, the press, the regulated industries, and the financial community. It, as much as any federal agency, functions in a goldfish bowl" (IOM, 1992: 108).

The agency's proverbial life in the fish bowl is briefly, though pointedly, depicted in the following account. In March 2002, hearings were held before the U.S. House of Representatives' Committee on Energy and Commerce. The committee's Health Subcommittee was meeting to discuss the five-year reauthorization of an important piece of FDA legislation—the Prescription Drug User Fee Act (PDUFA). In opening the hearing, Republican congressman Michael Bilirakis of Florida, who chairs the Health Subcommittee, noted in his prepared statement that "PDUFA has been so successful because it is a partnership between the agency, the industry, and patients" (U.S. House, 2002: 3). Bilirakis's characterization of this relationship as a "partnership" is an interesting, though not trivial, word choice in this context. In effect, he is suggesting that the agency naturally works together with the pharmaceutical industry and patients in making new drugs available for U.S. consumers.

Later, during that same hearing, Congressman Sherrod Brown, an Ohio Democrat, criticized acting FDA commissioner Lester Crawford for calling the industry its "customer" and bragging about FDA performance in relation to industry competitiveness. Consider Brown's admonition of Crawford:

> I hear some of your people calling industry its customer, and I heard . . . about the launch of new products into the market. Industry uses the term launch, but the FDA using that term concerns me. Discussing the success of PDUFA, in terms of changes in the U.S. drug industry's market share, I guess I grew up thinking the FDA was there to protect safety and not to play a role in enhancing the U.S. market share. I just didn't know that that was the mission of this government agency to help U.S. companies' enhance market share. You are a regulatory body, and you are not a subsidiary of the drug industry. I am not accusing you of that. But I just wondered where the separation is. I mean, I wonder where is the separation, and who is in control? Is the FDA in control or is the industry that it regulates in control? (U.S. House, 2002: 36–37)

Public scrutiny of the agency, its performance, and its top officials is not uncommon. This public criticism is simply a reflection that the agency is not immune to public scrutiny, controversy, and occasional political turmoil. A number of factors create opportunities for such scrutiny and criticism.

First, FDA-regulated products affect most Americans in one way or another. Moreover, due to the highly personalized nature of prescription medicines—and because many are designed to be ingested—approved products occasionally cause serious injury and even death to those who take them.

The FDA's approval of thalidomide for the treatment of Hansen's disease (leprosy) in 1998 illustrates this occasionally fine line between therapeutic effectiveness and product safety. Prior to 1998 thalidomide had never been marketed in the United States. In fact, the sedative became a rallying point for the agency's reputation as a staunch protector of public health during the 1960s and 1970s. Approved and marketed throughout Europe during the late 1950s and early 1960s, thalidomide was blamed for causing several thousand birth defects after it had been revealed that the drug was being prescribed to help pregnant women get a good night's sleep. The FDA's refusal to approve thalidomide in the 1960s contributed to the widely held perception that its drug safety standards were among the highest in the world. Thus, although thalidomide's approved usage is now heavily monitored and restricted, the symbolism associated with the drug's 1998 approval raised a number of fundamental public health concerns.

Second, the approval or rejection of certain classes of prescription medicines—such as birth control products—can occasionally spark ethical debates and even moral outrage among large segments of the U.S. population. For instance, in 2000, the agency approved the controversial abortion pill, mifepristone. Commonly known as RU-486, mifepristone was first made available in France over a decade earlier. Yet the FDA had long resisted approving the drug for use in the United States. Shortly after mifepristone's approval, the 2000 presidential candidates—George W. Bush and Al Gore—publicly reacted to the agency's decision and used the opportunity to outline their positions on abortion. In a country highly divided over issues such as abortion and birth control, agency decisions in these areas routinely stir contention.[10] Even now, many antiabortion activists would like to see mifepristone's approval revoked by the agency.

In addition to the approval and rejection of new medicines, FDA decisions on medical procedure may also infringe on sensitive ethical matters. For instance, the FDA plays a significant role in determining which patients are eligible to receive experimental medicines and under what conditions such drugs may be taken. Such procedures are part of the agency's broader efforts to help determine standards for preclinical testing (e.g., the testing of substances in animals), as well as standards for clinical testing (i.e., the testing of substances in humans).

Third, the agency regulates powerful industry actors who can mobilize political opposition to the expansion of regulatory authority. The FDA nearly turned the tobacco industry—as well as the roughly 46 million Americans who smoke—upside down in 1996 when it claimed regulatory authority over tobacco and tobacco products.[11] The agency adopted a rule allowing cigarettes to be regulated as "drug delivery" devices. The agency's rationale asserted that nicotine was a drug and that cigarettes were actually medical devices used for the purpose of "delivering" the effects of the drug. Since then, the issue has been tied up in the appellate courts.[12] In addition to the tobacco industry, the pharmaceutical industry maintains one of the most influential voices in Washington. In 2001, the primary trade association of brand name drug manufacturers—the Pharmaceutical Research and Manufacturers Association (PhRMA)—ranked twenty-fourth on the list of *Fortune* magazine's "Power 25," the magazine's annual list of Washington's most powerful lobbying groups.[13]

Fourth, as a consumer protection agency, the FDA functions within the context of the larger regulatory bureaucracy in Washington. Agency decisions and the behavior of FDA officials are subject to congressional oversight. In addition, FDA resources are subject to annual congressional appropriations. Therefore, it is not unusual for top agency officials to be called to testify before a congressional panel when controversial matters arise. In some respects, this point illustrates the fact that FDA actions are often political issues. Such actions involve the allocation of scarce resources, as well as the career concerns of legislators, bureaucrats, and others.

In a similar vein, the agency's decision processes themselves are likely to showcase occasional controversies. For example, factors such as media coverage, freedom of information laws, and the Internet ensure that the agency's operations remain transparent to outside observers. As the former acting FDA commissioner, Michael Friedman, once acknowledged before a House panel, "No area of FDA's responsibility has been more closely scrutinized by Congress, industry, health professionals, and the public than the approval process for new drugs, or more specifically, the speed with which new therapies of proven effectiveness and safety are made available to those who need them."[14]

Thus, even though the agency's role in drug review is a highly specialized and technically sophisticated process, FDA decisions are not insulated from political scrutiny and public criticism.

The FDA's December 2001 rejection of ImClone Systems' application for Erbitux, a colorectal cancer drug, illustrates the nature of this openness. Erbitux was touted as a future blockbuster drug, and some Wall Street investment houses projected that the drug's annual sales would eventually exceed $1 billion (Schultz, 2002). Yet, the agency's decision to "refuse to file" the application on the basis of incomplete clinical evidence amounted to a rejection of the application.

To compound the matter, the FDA's decision also ignited a tremendous financial and political fallout. ImClone's founder and then-CEO, Sam Waksal, was accused of tipping off family members and close associates about the FDA's rejection shortly before the official announcement (White and Gillis, 2002). ImClone's stock, which had peaked above $70, plummeted. Investors subsequently lost millions of dollars on the company. Martha Stewart, whom one newspaper referred to as "America's diva of domestic perfection," was one of Waksal's close associates implicated in the insider trading and securities fraud investigation (Usborne, 2002). Waksal later pleaded guilty to securities fraud, bank fraud, and conspiracy to obstruct justice, and was sentenced to seven years in prison. These events became a prominent symbol for the substantial business implications of FDA drug approvals, including stock price volatility, the shaking of investor confidence, and even securities fraud.

Beyond the business implications of the FDA's decision, the FDA was taken to task for its handling of the application. A subsequent congressional hearing by the House Energy and Commerce Committee's Oversight and Investigations Subcommittee was held to sort out the matter and several top agency officials were aggressively questioned. Moreover, several national media outlets heavily criticized the agency's handling of the case. An investigative report by *U.S. News and World Report,* for example, leveled the following claims: "The FDA's system for bringing lifesaving drugs to market . . . utterly collapsed." "The biotech division of the FDA . . . was manifestly not up to the task." "The communication that should have taken place between the FDA and the drug maker . . . simply didn't happen" (Schultz, 2002). As the ImClone case illustrates, FDA decision processes can occasionally showcase controversies involving the transparency of public policy debate and formation.

Finally, as some of the above examples illustrate, the FDA is a consumer protection agency at its most fundamental level. In regulating new medicines the agency is charged with making decisions that protect the public interest and promote public health along a number of different dimensions. By its very nature as a regulatory body, agency decisions will inherently please some constituents and displease others. It should be of little surprise, then, to see that the agency often finds itself in the middle of political controversy.

## A Model for Examining the Politics of New Drug Approvals

The notion that political factors influence the behavior of regulatory agencies is not a novel concept in the political science literature on regulation.[15] Building on this relatively straightforward theoretical premise, a simple descriptive model can be used to help demonstrate some of the difficulties associated with the politics of new drug approvals.[16] A drug must meet certain safety, efficacy, and quality criteria before it can gain regulatory approval and eventually be sold to consumers. Prior to marketing a drug, pharmaceutical manufacturers must prove safety, efficacy, and quality—demonstrating that the drug is safe for human consumption, performs in accord with its therapeutic claims, and is produced with a high degree of manufacturing consistency.

Four possible outcomes may occur when a government regulatory agency decides whether or not to license a product. The possible outcomes result in some combination of two underlying dimensions: (1) the decision of the regulatory agency and (2) the ultimate safety and efficacy of the drug under consideration.

On the first dimension is the regulatory agency's decision about whether the product is efficacious and safe for public consumption. For instance, the agency can grant a product license, enabling the drug to be freely marketed into society, or it may reject the application on the grounds that the drug presents a potentially serious public health risk to consumers.[17]

The second dimension affecting the final outcome hinges on the drug itself. This is the "state of the world" or "state of nature" dimension. In this case, the drug will either be safe and effective for its intended usage or it will not. Unfortunately, since regulatory judgments are made on the basis of the drug's performance in clinical trials, decisions often have to be made on the basis of incomplete information (e.g., limited duration of clinical trial, small sample size, or extraneous factors). There is no way that the regulator can ascertain the true "state of the world" with complete certainty at any time during the decisionmaking process. Nonetheless, regulatory decisions must be made in the presence of incomplete information.

The four basic outcomes in the regulatory process are a product of whether the drug is accepted or rejected and whether it is safe and effective or not. These four potential outcomes are represented in Figure 1.1. In an ideal situation, the regulatory agency would approve the effective drugs and reject the ineffective ones. However, in the presence of incomplete information, decisions on new drug approvals inherently contain a certain level of risk and uncertainty. Given this theoretical juxtaposition of possible outcomes, the potential dilemmas confronting drug-licensing agencies are analogous to the problem of Type I and Type II errors facing any decisionmaker in a routine decision situation. William McPhee once insightfully described this abstract decision dilemma as "the wheat and the chaff problem." In separating wheat from the chaff, he noted, "any process that eliminates chaff also loses wheat and any process that holds wheat also retains chaff" (1963: 29).

Generally speaking, a Type I error occurs when a decisionmaker rejects a product that falls within the predetermined limits of acceptability. In this case, the product should have been accepted given the preestablished decision criteria (i.e., the wheat goes out with the chaff). In the drug approval process, a Type I error occurs if the regulatory authority rejects the application of a drug that is safe and effective. While the presence of Type I errors likely plague all drug approval agencies, the direct and immediate consequences of such errors may not appear to be very severe.

Figure 1.1  A Model of New Drug Approvals

State of the World

|  |  | Drug Is Safe and Effective | Drug Is Unsafe or Ineffective |
|---|---|---|---|
| Regulatory Decision | Accept | Correct decision | Type II error |
|  | Reject | Type I error | Correct decision |

*Source:* Grabowski and Vernon (1983).

Essentially, a Type I error can go completely unnoticed by a vast majority of the U.S. population who remain largely unaware of FDA activity.

Conversely, a Type II error is said to occur when a faulty or defective entity is accepted, even though it does not satisfy the preestablished decision criteria (i.e., the chaff is retained). In terms of drug approvals, a Type II error occurs when the regulatory agency approves a drug that is eventually found to be unsafe or ineffective. Type II errors pose serious and highly visible consequences, as the public risks exposure to unsafe or ineffective drugs.

In the absence of either a Type I or Type II error, it can be safely argued that an appropriate regulatory decision has been made.

The basic four-way decisionmaking schema depicted in Figure 1.1 provides an accurate and economical portrait of the much broader and more complex political situation facing the FDA and other drug regulatory agencies. Due to their scientific expertise, most drug regulatory agencies are given considerable discretion in the administration of national drug statutes. In an ideal world, all drug regulatory agencies would use their discretion to approve the good drugs and reject the bad ones. Unfortunately, this scenario is impossible given the many complexities associated with drug development and testing. Clearly, the scientific prowess and technical capabilities of leading regulatory authorities and multinational pharmaceutical firms are of world-class caliber. Yet complexities easily arise when considering the massive amounts of data that require careful analysis, the almost incalculable reaction of different drugs that may occur in different individuals, drug interactions, and the potentially unforeseen long-term effects of a drug.

In addition to the actual approval or rejection decision, there are many instances where lives hinge on whether patients can gain access to certain drugs in a timely fashion. Thus, agencies often face external pressure to perform tasks expediently. Though it is difficult to get an accurate measurement of regulatory costs in terms of lost lives, it has been argued that regulatory delays can be equally as harmful as defective drugs (Ward, 1992). According to one observer's estimate, one year of bureaucratic delay in drug development could cost as many as 32,000 to 76,000 lives per decade, a number likely surpassing the rate of deaths occurring as the result of unsafe or ineffective drugs (Gieringer, 1985). In the event of delays, governmental agencies are not insulated from the public and political pressure urging them to act in a timely fashion. In some cases the time it takes to reach an approval decision is as critical as the decision itself.

## The Influence of
## Political Factors on Regulatory Behavior

Given the immediate possibilities of Type I and II errors occurring, regulators are forced to make difficult decisions in the face of incomplete information. Even in this difficult decision environment, empirical evidence suggests that some degree of variation exists in regulatory decisionmaking both across time and across national boundaries. This raises an interesting question: Why do regulatory agencies accept more risk during some periods than others? Stated another way, what factors contribute to an agency's propensity to avoid committing Type I and Type II errors?

This book examines how differing political environments have affected the design and performance of the Food and Drug Administration. Understanding answers to the questions about the risk acceptance and varying performance of regulatory agencies is significant not only from the perspective of a political scientist but also for those affected by the fundamental tradeoffs inherent in this important (though largely understudied) regulatory function.

This book makes three arguments. First, it seeks to demonstrate that the FDA is an inherently political actor. Though the agency enforces federal drug safety laws, it has some degree of administrative autonomy in enforcing these laws. Second, the book argues that political factors have significantly influenced the design of the FDA. Because Congress is the primary architect of the nation's drug safety laws, it is important to examine carefully the institutional structures Congress has created, as these institutions largely guide FDA behavior and performance. Given that the FDA is a political actor and that political factors have influenced the design of the agency, the third argument is that drug regulation in the United States has entered a new period. That period, described in more detail below, is distinct from earlier ones that prevailed during the twentieth century. In this latest regulatory period, the FDA has rebalanced its traditional risk-benefit analysis in a way that places an increased relative emphasis on promoting public health and the benefits associated with making new drugs available to the U.S. public sooner.

Due to its nature as a regulatory authority, the FDA is an inherently political actor. Given the FDA's consumer protection and law enforcement origins, its primary concern has traditionally been to avoid approving drugs that should not be approved. Moreover, as one might imagine, the political ramifications of committing Type I and Type II errors vary immensely. In their study of the effects of regulation on drug development, Henry Grabowski and John Vernon made this point explicitly clear:

> It can be plausibly argued that [the U.S.] regulatory structure does not have a neutral stance between Type I and II errors. The mandate to the FDA is drawn in very narrow terms—to protect consumers against unsafe or ineffective drugs (that is, to avoid Type II errors). There is no corresponding mandate to avoid Type I errors or to compel equal concern with new drug innovation and improved medical therapy. In point of fact, the institutional incentives confronting FDA officials strongly reinforce the tendency to avoid Type II errors at the expense of Type I errors. (1983: 10)

Risk-averse behavior by the FDA simply reflects the reality that it is quite easy to identify victims who suffer adverse reactions to unsafe drugs (Seidman, 1977). As Sam Kazman points out, "Incorrectly approving a drug can produce highly visible victims, highly emotional news stories, and heated congressional hearings" (1991: 18). Alternatively, though this risk-averse behavior gradually lessened largely in response to the intense political pressure by AIDS activists seeking to get new drugs approved more rapidly, it is generally far more difficult to identify individuals suffering as the result of their inability to obtain effective treatments because they are legally unavailable. Kazman concludes, "Incorrectly delaying a drug will produce invisible victims and little more. The ultimate issue continues to be one of asymmetry in public perception and in institutional incentives" (18–19). Because the costs to the agency for committing a Type II error are obviously quite high, historically there were few, if any, institutional penalties for failures of omission by the agency.

As an administrative agency, the FDA is charged with enforcing federal drug safety laws enacted by Congress. Yet in carrying out a highly specialized task, the FDA operates with some degree of administrative autonomy. As John Ferejohn has noted: "Though administrative agencies may be charged with the pursuit of some legislated end, the means they choose in this pursuit—their actions—are largely determined internally. That these actions can be consequential we take for granted" (1987: 441). In this case, agency behavior can be viewed in the context of Type I and Type II errors.

Second, the book argues that political factors have influenced the design of the FDA in distinct and profound ways. Making this argument

requires an examination of agency design and the corresponding institutional structures. These factors can be examined by analyzing the
landmark laws creating the regulatory structure. In the history of U.S.
drug regulation, analysts typically point to three landmark laws: (1) the
1906 Pure Food and Drugs Act, (2) the 1938 Food, Drug and Cosmetic
Act, and (3) the 1962 Amendments to the Food, Drug and Cosmetic Act
(also known as the 1962 amendments or the Kefauver amendments).
Examining these landmark institutional structures discloses a great deal
about agency behavior and regulatory performance.

Three initial points about agency design and institutional structures
are also instructive. First, the occurrences of drug-related tragedies
throughout the twentieth century in the United States and around the
world have provided important catalysts for drug regulation. Drug-
related tragedies create dramatic, powerful, and lasting images in the
minds of both consumers and policymakers. These images help create
what John Kingdon (1984) has described as a "policy window" and can
be used to mobilize the political forces required for policy change. Such
major regulatory changes, it could be argued, would be highly unlikely
in the absence of these types of catalysts.

A second important consideration is that reactions to drug tragedies
have not always been the same in different countries. Experience suggests that the United States has been more likely to overhaul its regulatory apparatus dramatically in response to major drug-related tragedies.
As a consequence of such episodes, U.S. drug law was transformed considerably in 1906, 1938, and 1962. Alternatively, responses to drug-
related tragedies in some European countries led to the gradual modification of the existing regulatory framework. The British government's
initial response to the thalidomide tragedy in the 1960s, for example,
did not significantly disrupt the existing regulatory framework in the
United Kingdom.[18] Ultimately, these incongruities provide important
insights into societal tolerances toward risk and reward.

A third point is that for most of the twentieth century, many
national drug regulatory bodies failed to agree on fundamental regulatory standards that have significant implications for Type I and II errors.
Specifically, national drug authorities have yet to establish a mutually
agreeable standard for determining a given drug's efficacy during the
review process.[19] While safety standards are generally globally consistent, efficacy standards have not been harmonized. Nations sometimes
pursue markedly distinctive regulatory approaches in evaluating new
drugs. As a result of the limitations on information and the time constraints imposed on the decisionmaking process, efficacy decisions are

closely intertwined with the commission of Type I and Type II errors. Thus, decisions by national regulatory authorities (such as the FDA) in the face of incomplete information reflect an important interaction between institutional structure and the agency as a political actor.

Finally, this book argues that drug regulation in the United States has now entered a new period that is distinctive from the previous periods initiated by each of the three landmark institutional structures mentioned above. Beginning in the late 1980s, the agency gradually broadened its interpretation of "consumer protection" to take account of the perils of delay in approving new drugs. The new regulatory period, created with the passage of the 1992 Prescription Drug User Fee Act, is characterized by the agency's expanded definition of promoting public health, as well as expeditiousness in the drug review process (i.e., balancing the risks of Type I and II errors).

The fundamental philosophical shift brought about by the PDUFA entails a rebalancing of the agency's traditional risk-benefit analysis. The drug review process has inched away from an orientation that emphasized risk and was heavily focused on avoiding the premature release of unsafe products to the market. Instead, the new orientation places a greater relative emphasis on the benefits of making new drugs available to the public sooner. While substantial centralized controls obviously remain in place, many critical controls have been gradually lessened in order to accommodate a public intent on gaining access to new medicines.

In addition, this regulatory transformation reflects a convergence with European and Japanese regulators. Many other European regulatory agencies (e.g., Swiss, French, British, and German authorities) have long sought to avoid committing errors of the Type I variety. Historically, more drugs have been made accessible to European consumers and at an earlier stage in their development process. This strategy does not come without potentially sizable costs, however. In seeking to avoid Type I errors, regulators become more susceptible to committing Type II errors by prematurely releasing new medicines.

Analyzing factors such as agency design and institutional structure in a broader context discloses a great deal about agency behavior and regulatory performance (Zegart, 1999). A look at historical data reveals discernible differences in the regulatory performance both within the U.S. context and within the context of other global drug regulatory authorities. The U.S. approach has clearly emphasized strong centralized controls, particularly since the passage of the FDCA. Consequently, during the 1960s and 1970s the FDA was heavily criticized for taking a longer time than some of its foreign counterparts in reviewing new drug applications. By the mid-1990s, however, the agency had undergone a regulatory transformation in responding to such criticisms.

## Description of Data and Method

Before developing the argument further, it is necessary to clarify two methodological points: one theoretical and one empirical. Theoretically, this book attempts to add to the literature on regulation, public policy, and policy change. Two predominant theoretical perspectives will become evident to the reader.

First, I take as a starting point the assumption that the nature of state institutions plays a critical role in shaping regulatory policy and behavior (Skocpol and Finegold, 1982; Skowronek, 1982; Moe, 1989). In the regulation of new medicines, institutional structures greatly constrain the actions of regulators and regulated, as well as the behavior of policymakers, consumers, and other pertinent actors. Since the 1980s, a substantial body of social science literature considering the effect of institutions on political outcomes has developed. Different strands in this body of thought have emphasized the significance of institutional change and the political economy of institutions.[20] Political institutions both constrain the opportunities of actors in the policy subsystem and dictate the realm of feasible alternatives.

Second, this study affords the opportunity for a closer examination of key actors in the policy subsystem. At the surface level, the relevant actors share a common regulatory concern, as each wants to provide patients with the best drugs in the timeliest manner. At a deeper level, however, disparate actors in the regulatory process include legislators, administrative agents, patient activists, and industry executives. Each actor possesses preferences that are generally easily definable and often divergent. For example, the true objectives of government actors (e.g., maximization of votes, agency resources, bureaucratic authority) generally differ from those of industry actors (e.g., increased market share and profit maximization). Collectively, such preferences are instrumental in designing and implementing regulatory institutions, and they create opportunities for bargaining and mutual adjustment by those involved in the policy process (Lindblom, 1965; Peacock, 1984).

Alternately, from an empirical standpoint, this book attempts to add to our understanding of the regulation of new medicines. As such, the explanations developed are based on a combination of primary and secondary sources. Much of the primary source data is derived from original documents such as congressional testimony and committee reports. Interviews by the author with key persons involved in the regulation of new medicines also provide a unique and rich source of primary data. The author has conducted interviews with dozens of industry executives, regulatory officials, and industry analysts in Washington, London, and elsewhere over the past few years.[21] For the purposes of ensuring the anonymity of those interviewed, interviewees will be referred to in the text by generic descriptions such as industry executive or FDA official.[22] Such primary data are supplemented with related quantitative and qualitative data reported by various national governments and other sources. Secondary sources include historical references such as medical and pharmaceutical journals and other sources on medicines and regulation. These documents offer a rich historical perspective on both regulatory institutions and regulatory behavior.

## Outline of the Book

The book is organized as follows. Chapter 2 provides a discussion of the politics of assessing drug risk and effectiveness. The chapter reviews several leading theories of regulation and then develops a principal-agent framework emphasizing the significance of transactions between relevant actors in the policy arena and the costs such transactions generate. It is argued that the design of institutional structures provides important decisionmaking guidelines and defines patterns of agency interaction. Once established, the institutional structures governing the regulation of new medicines are relatively difficult to change and significantly constrain agency behavior. An understanding of such institutional structures greatly helps explain why the FDA has traditionally sought to avoid Type II errors while other national regulatory authorities have adopted somewhat differing approaches. The primary theme and the basis of the argument throughout this and subsequent chapters is that agency design, regulatory structure and process, and the corresponding regulatory philosophy toward risk and reward significantly affect regulatory behavior.

After having considered the fundamental significance of regulatory structures and processes, Chapter 3 places U.S. drug regulation in a historical context by reviewing the history of drug safety legislation in the United States as it evolved alongside an emerging pharmaceutical industry. This examination requires a careful consideration of policy change and the actors responsible for implementing such change. Oftentimes, policy change is brought about by a shock (or a "punctuation") to the existing regulatory regime (Baumgartner and Jones, 1993). Consequently, specific regulatory institutions and distinctive regulatory approaches characterize each regulatory period. The chapter concludes by examining the first two periods of drug regulation in the United States, 1906–1938 and 1938–1962.

Chapter 4 begins by considering the effect of the thalidomide tragedy in Europe and the shift to a third regulatory period with the passage of the 1962 Kefauver amendments to the Food, Drug and Cosmetic Act. These amendments greatly centralized the regulatory structure. Shortly following the amendments, however, it was often pointed out that the FDA approved fewer drugs and approved drugs less rapidly than many of its European counterparts, especially the United Kingdom. The chapter considers FDA behavior during this time with respect to the possibility of committing Type I and Type II errors. Critical differences between U.S. and European regulatory structures and processes—factors often overlooked in discussions of regulatory performance—are emphasized. In looking at such structures, this chapter considers the drug lag phenomenon and the accompanying public debate in the United States throughout the 1970s and 1980s over the regulation of new medicines.

Chapter 5 examines important changes in the policy subsystem and argues that a regulatory transformation occurred at the FDA during the early 1990s. Significant domestic pressures (from consumer activists, industry leaders, and ultimately Congress) led to the modification of long-established institutional structures in U.S. drug regulation. The analytical focus of this chapter centers on the influential role played by participants in the regulatory policy arena. This chapter argues that a new (now fourth) regulatory period is present in U.S. drug regulation. This fourth period has seen the expansion of the government's role in drug regulation from simply protecting public health (by avoiding the premature release of new medicines) to also promoting public health (by making more drugs available to the public and making them available in a rapid fashion).

Chapter 6 identifies several critical issues facing the FDA in this new regulatory period. Several of the issues have important implications for consumers. During this new regulatory period, the FDA leadership remains a prominent issue. In addition, agency relations with the pharmaceutical industry and with worldwide regulatory agencies remain critical. Above all, this chapter considers the most important issue in the current regulatory era, drug safety. The issues of drug safety and risk management will ultimately define the current regulatory period.

Finally, Chapter 7 reviews the primary arguments made in the book and further argues that the policy shift that took place over the course of the 1990s has critical implications for both the protection and promotion of public health in the United States. The FDA's early emphasis on protecting public health produced a relatively cautious regulatory approach. Yet the agency now recognizes the significance of promoting public health by enabling consumers to access new and effective therapies in a timely manner. In effect, the pendulum of public health and safety has begun to move in the other direction.

# 2

## THE POLITICS OF ASSESSING DRUGS

Bureaucratic structure emerges as a jerry-built fusion of congressional and presidential forms, their relative roles and particular features determined by the powers, priorities, and strategies of the various designers. The result is that each agency cannot help but begin life as a unique structural reflection of its own politics.

*—Terry Moe, professor of*
*political science, Stanford University*

Identifying and focusing attention on factors such as agency design and institutional structure are imperative for understanding the rationale behind the U.S. approach to regulating new medicines. Although the intricacies of regulatory structure and process rarely receive adequate media attention, these details have become increasingly significant to social scientists (McNollgast, 1999; Zegart, 1999). In the licensing of new medicines such factors reflect inherent regulatory philosophies toward risk and reward.

In this book I argue that politics plays an important role in drug licensing. Perhaps nowhere is this more evident than in the design of regulatory structures and processes. The Constitution vests the lawmaking powers of the federal government with the U.S. Congress. Among the "expressed" powers the Constitution bestows on Congress is the power to regulate commerce. If pharmaceutical manufacturers seek to sell products to consumers, they must do so in accordance with the regulatory apparatus constructed by the legislative branch.

Congress is the principal architect of the regulatory structures and processes discussed in this chapter. Three simple assumptions are to be taken into consideration when looking at the congressional design of regulatory institutions. First, as Terry Moe points out, "structural politics is

21

interest group politics" (1989: 269). In the creation of regulatory structures and processes, interest groups are assumed to pressure the enacting coalition, the specific mix of legislators responsible for enacting the legislation. Interest groups—reflecting the concerns of business, consumers, and a variety of other public and private interests—participate in order to influence the creation of structures and processes that will produce favorable outcomes to those constituencies. Second, the enacting coalition seeks to make the legislation as durable as possible (Horn, 1995). Lawmakers attempt to construct legislation that will endure long after the dissolution of the enacting coalition. This assumption is based on the premise that because the legislation delivers a specific set of benefits to particular interests, the durability of the legislation ensures that such benefits will continue long into the future. Third, despite that the enacting legislation is intended to be as durable as possible, it is important to consider how and under what circumstances changes are made to existing regulatory structures and processes (see, for example, Eisner, Worsham, and Ringquist, 2000). Since the mix of political interests can be fluid and enacting coalitions may change over time, an understanding of policy change is critical (Baumgartner and Jones, 1993). Thus, considering the dynamics of regulatory structures and processes requires a careful understanding of the relationship between the relevant political interests and the existing institutional arrangement.

Congress enacts drug safety laws that are presumably consistent with the prevailing public sentiment of the time. In constructing an institutional framework designed to protect U.S. consumers from the potentially harmful effects of unsafe medicines, Congress' predominant concern has been to avoid Type II errors. In the event that a Type II error occurred, causing widespread or systematic harm to the U.S. public due to the premature release of unsafe medicines, highly visible victims would emerge and significant political costs would be imposed on both the legislature and the regulatory bureaucracy. In effect, the commission of Type II errors may likely undermine the public trust in the federal government's regulatory role. Thus, in enacting and implementing federal drug safety laws, Congress and the FDA have concentrated on avoiding Type II errors. Historically, this emphasis has led the FDA to be highly cautious in the risk-benefit assessment of new medicines. The tradeoff, of course, is that the risk-averse approach may on some occasions tend to discount the notion of expediting patient access to new drugs. In seeking to protect public health by minimizing instances of prematurely releasing unsafe medicines, the regulatory agency may have a higher propensity to commit Type I errors, failing to approve safe and effective medicines to those who need them.

The remainder of this chapter proceeds as follows. In the next section, I characterize the relationship between Congress and a regulatory agency such as the FDA as a principal-agent relationship. Next, several leading theories of regulation are considered. One set of these theories, known as organic theories, treats the regulatory agency as a unitary, rational actor. Alternatively, structural theories focus on the critical role played by political principals in creating structures and processes that ensure agency compliance with the intentions of the principal. The explanation developed here extends these structural theories and considers their relevance in the context of drug regulation. Finally, I identify one specific structural and one procedural aspect of FDA regulation. Examining these elements of structure and process reveals fundamental insights into the nature of drug regulation, particularly in balancing the avoidance of Type I and Type II errors.

## Regulatory Tradeoffs and Congressional Delegation

The regulation of new medicines requires highly detailed and careful scientific analyses. In this context, drug licensing represents what William Gormley (1986) has referred to as a "high complexity" regulatory issue. Given the inherent complexities, and considering that such analyses are beyond the competence of the average elected politician, legislators must delegate important decisions to regulatory administrators who possess the required scientific and technical expertise. In one sense, the delegation of decisionmaking responsibility reflects the expertise and other informational advantages that administrative agents possess relative to legislators. Due to the nature of legislative behavior, it is much easier for legislative actors to pass relatively vague legislation that shifts the responsibility of regulatory administration and implementation to the bureaucracy.[23]

In addition to the information asymmetries, the decision to delegate medicine reviews involves a substantial political tradeoff between risk and reward. The risks in this case, equivalent to the Type I and Type II errors described in Chapter 1, are sizable. The rewards, however, are more diffuse and less visible. In comparable terms, David Epstein and Sharyn O'Halloran frame the issue of airline safety as one that offers few direct tangible rewards to legislators, yet brings potentially tremendous costs. They note that:

> Policymakers will get little credit if things go well and no airline disasters occur, but they will have to withstand intense scrutiny when things go wrong. Airline regulation is an issue with only a political downside, and failures tend to be spectacular and well-publicized. Furthermore, legislative and executive preferences on this issue will tend to be almost perfectly aligned: have fewer accidents rather than more as long as the costs to airlines are not prohibitive. (1999: 8)

Essentially, this is the same logic that applies to the regulation of new medicines. The preferences of legislators, administrative agents, consumers, and pharmaceutical industry officials are generally aligned: each would prefer to have expedient access to new medicines, provided that such medicines are safe and effective. In practice, most drugs are approved with relatively little fanfare, and coverage of drug approvals receives only modest attention in the media (Klotz and Ceccoli, 2002). Yet administrative failures—particularly Type I and II errors—can be highly costly to all relevant actors: legislators, regulatory agencies, consumers, and the drug's sponsor. Such failures are especially costly in regulatory terms because drug licensing is a "highly salient" regulatory issue; that is, it "affects a large number of people in a significant way" (Gormley, 1986: 598).

Because information asymmetries and significant political risk are so great, it is necessary to look closely at the interaction between the relevant actors in the policy arena. This interaction is akin to a fundamental social contract. The legislature retains the constitutional responsibility to enact laws that regulate commerce and effectively protect public health. Yet, because of the associated risk and information complexities, the legislature often has an incentive to delegate important decisions to administrative agents. Meanwhile, interested third-party actors, such as consumers and officials from the regulated industry, have distinct incentives to influence such decisions in a way that coincides with their broader interests. Implicitly, each of the relevant political actors must contend with a series of important exchanges or transactions.

The most fundamental transaction involves the legislature's decision to delegate responsibility to the administrative agent. Legislative statutes such as those directing regulatory agencies are often deliberately written with vague and ambiguous language (Quirk, 1981). This ambiguity allows the regulatory agency a considerable amount of discretion in administering regulatory policies, implementing rules, and making decisions on specific matters (Fritschler, 1989). For example, the FDCA asserts that a new drug cannot be approved for marketing until it has been satisfactorily demonstrated to be "safe" and "effective." Determinations of exactly what evidence, or how much evidence, is necessary to demonstrate safety and efficacy, however, have long been the subject of debate. Such decisions often hinge on the inherent risk-benefit calculation involved in medicines licensing (Lowrance, 1976). Unfortunately, safety and efficacy are "relative" rather than "absolute" concepts, and no new drug product offers assurances of being completely without risk (Hancher, 1990: 121). In the absence of specific direction by the legislature, the regulatory interpretation of the safety and efficacy provisions ultimately remains in the hands of the administrative agency.[24]

## Bureaucratic Control and the Principal-Agent Problem

The relatively recent analytical focus on the contractual nature of societal relations has led political scientists to borrow heavily from ideas originating in microeconomics (see, for example, Moe, 1984; Mitnick, 1980, for reviews), economic history (North, 1981, 1990), organization theory (Perrow, 1993), and industrial organization (Williamson, 1975, 1985).[25] Collectively, the term *new institutionalism* describes a number of important analytical concepts related to the study of political institutions and their effect on economic and social behavior. By extension, principal-agent theory (or agency theory) has emerged as an important explanatory heuristic for studying political behavior. In such a relationship, the principal (the elected official or legislature as a whole) seeks to influence the behavior of the agent (the bureaucratic organization) in accord with the principal's preferences. The political economy literature has advanced our understanding of the principal-agent relationship considerably by modeling one of the most pressing (and perplexing) questions for social scientists: How do principals control agents?[26]

Before relating the principal-agent model specifically to the relationship between legislators and administrative agents, it will be useful to briefly review the core assumptions of agency theory. The principal-agent model has at least three fundamental assumptions (Perrow, 1986, 1993).[27] First, both principals and agents are assumed to act in a rational, self-interested manner. That is, individual actors are assumed to possess a set of well-defined goals or objectives and their behavior reflects an attempt to maximize such goals. Naturally, the interests of principals and agents may not always be congruent. To bridge the gap between these incongruities, a contract or exchange provides an important linkage between the actors and their behavior. This linkage leads to the theory's second assumption that societal relations are characterized by a series of exchanges or contracts between actors. Contracts, which may be formal or informal, generally obligate the agent to deliver a good or service to the principal in return for some compensation. Because the principal is perceived to be the "buyer" of goods or services provided by the agent, the exchange specifically stipulates what is expected of both the agent and the principal. The principal then provides the compensation or reward to the agent on delivery of the goods or services.

At times, however, this exchange can be problematic. Problems arise because of the agent's significant advantage in information and expertise. Such advantages may lead the agent to "shirk" his or her responsibility. As a result, the third tenet of the theory is that the principal must monitor such exchanges. Monitoring is necessary because in the face of divergent self-interests the principal has no way of ensuring that the agent will deliver on the contract in a manner that is consistent with the principal's preferences. As Charles Perrow notes, "the relationship is fraught with the problem of cheating, limited information, and bounded rationality" (1993: 224). Put another way, "disjunctures" arise between the principal and the agent over time (Wood and Waterman, 1994). In light of the agent's information advantage, his or her actions may deviate from the principal's preferences. Consequently, principals need to monitor the agent's behavior. Unfortunately for the principal, however, monitoring can be costly, inefficient, and difficult to achieve successfully (McCubbins and Schwartz, 1984). As a result of the disjuncture between principals and agents, the principal must strive consistently to minimize the possibility that the agent will "shirk" its responsibility.

In sum, agency theory provides a useful heuristic for the study of regulatory behavior because of the assumptions it makes about rationality, the nature of transactions, and the monitoring of such agreements. In addition, agency theory can also be quite instrumental in helping us better understand how these institutional arrangements change over time. Such transactions are executed based on the rational interests of both principals and agents. These transactions ultimately create a highly specific mix of regulatory structures and processes. Yet, as time passes, political interests may change, and the set of actors in the policy subsystem may also change. In addition, it can be assumed that principals and agents constantly learn from their accumulation of experiences while engaged in the specific transaction. These dynamics presumably alter the preferences of both principals and agents over time. Consequently, the requirements for principals and agents will also gradually change over time. If so, the existing contractual arrangements will need to be updated and we should expect such regulatory arrangements to be replaced with new structures and processes that better reflect the preferences of the actors in the policy subsystem. The linking of agency theory to policy change in the context of FDA drug regulation will be discussed in more detail in the following chapter.

## Leading Theories of Regulation

Several theories of regulation can be used to explain the behavior of a regulatory agency such as the FDA in its broader context. In an insightful review essay, Roger Noll (1985) places theories of regulatory behavior into two broad categories: organic theories and structural theories. Noll defines organic theories as those that consider the agency as the primary unit of analysis. Such theories typically explain regulatory behavior by assuming that regulatory agencies act rationally. Specifically, the agencies are thought to operate in a rational manner by (1) having a set of clear regulatory preferences or goals and (2) operating in a way that maximizes such preferences. In essence, organic theories of regulation assume the "coherency" of the regulatory agency. Organic theories dominated early conceptualizations of regulatory behavior, and two organic theories—public interest and regulatory capture—were once dominant paradigms in the study of regulation. A third—the external signals theory of regulation—was created as an extension of the first two. These three organic theories of regulation are given brief consideration below.

### Regulation in the Public Interest

Early conceptualizations of the public bureaucracy's role in society were highly normative. For instance, proponents of the public interest theory argued that the role of the regulatory agency was to protect the public from private behavior that may be harmful to society. Regulation in the public interest was thought to be required particularly in cases where market failures occurred and inefficiencies arose as a result of natural monopolies. The contributions of Harold Hotelling (1938) and others became the seminal work on which future studies of regulation in the public interest were based.

In the context of regulating new medicines, regulatory agencies play an important gatekeeping role in allowing or preventing new drugs to enter the consumer marketplace. This normative approach is consistent with David Easton's definition of politics as the "authoritative allocation of values for a society" (1965: 50). Government officials are presumed to share common concerns about the safety and quality of new drugs and the bureaucracy's gatekeeping role is to provide patients with the best conceivable drugs in a timely manner.

Yet this conceptualization has a number of limitations. First, it assumes that the bureaucracy (and the government in general) operates as a unitary actor. The theory ignores the multitude of governmental actors and interests that play important roles in shaping public policy. For instance, regulatory actors may have core preferences that fundamentally conflict with the preferences of consumers, legislators, or other actors. Classic accounts of bureaucratic behavior suggest that bureaucrats may seek a variety of organizational or even personal goals. William Niskanen (1971), for example, argued that bureaucrats seek to maximize agency resources and expand bureaucratic authority. It has also been assumed that bureaucrats attempt to maximize personal objectives, ranging from furthering their own personal fortunes to insulating themselves from criticism and political pressure applied by their political superiors.

Second, the notion of regulation in the "public interest" implicitly assumes that a singular public interest exists and can be identified. This premise ignores both the multitude of interests in a pluralist society and the difficulties inherent in aggregating individual preferences into a collective whole. In his study of insurance regulation, Kenneth Meier suggests: "Regulation is a political process, and, as such, it is concerned with the distribution of political and economic power. Individuals seek to be regulated or have others regulated because they are dissatisfied with the current distribution of economic or political power" (1988: 181). Unfortunately, public interest explanations of regulatory behavior virtually ignore the premise that regulation is an inherently political process. This omission suggests that public interest explanations cannot account for the differing objectives on the part of individual governmental actors that may lead to conflicting policy goals and ultimately produce disparate views of regulatory behavior.[28]

## Regulatory Capture

Regulatory capture theories emerged in the 1960s as an extension of public interest explanations. Since regulation generally imposes significant costs and constraints on private actors, the regulated actor has an interest in developing a mutually beneficial relationship with the regulatory agency. This relationship may include the sharing of information, the movement of personnel from the agency to the organized constituency (and vice versa), and the reduction of political costs to the point where synergy occurs between the regulator and the regulated over time. This mutually beneficial relationship eventually causes regulatory preferences to become virtually synonymous with industry preferences. When such regulatory and corporate interests become entwined, industry actors are able to use regulation to limit both the amount and nature of competition from other private actors and, thus, maximize profits. In a general sense, capture leads to regulation that serves as an effective barrier to market competition and further entrenches the position of the well-organized constituency.[29]

Since the 1960s, no single capture theory has emerged, and scholars have been unable to identify one universal mechanism used by groups to capture executive agencies. Consequently, explanations of regulatory capture have emerged along a number of different strands. Marver Bernstein's "life cycle" theory of regulatory commissions provided one of the more prominent early explanations of regulatory capture. Bernstein argued that regulatory commissions experience four stages of growth during their life cycle from gestation to old age. The latter stage, he suggested, is characterized by "passivity" and the "loss of vitality" as the regulatory agency seeks to maintain the status quo as the "recognized protector of the industry" (1955: 92). Thus, one rationale for regulatory capture is that regulatory agencies, in their "old age" stage, need the support of industry in order to maintain (or prolong) their existence.

Scholars during the 1950s looked to apply theories of regulatory capture to some of the nation's earliest independent regulatory commissions, such the Interstate Commerce Commission. For example, in explaining the "marasmus" of the Interstate Commerce Commission, Samuel Huntington argued that if agencies are to remain viable, they must adapt to changing political pressures. "If the agency fails to make this adjustment," he wrote, "its political support decreases relative to its political opposition, and it may be said to suffer from administrative marasmus" (1952: 470). Yet, as an alternative to the life cycle–based approach to regulatory capture, Gabriel Kolko argued that those who were being regulated—in this case, the nation's railroad interests— "were the most important single advocates of federal regulation" in leading up to the passage of the Interstate Commerce Act (1965: 3). Moreover, "The crucial point is that the railroads, for the most part, consistently accepted the basic premises of federal regulation since only through the positive intervention of the national political structure could the destabilizing, costly effects of cutthroat competition, predatory speculators, and greedy shippers be overcome" (5). In this latter sense, regulatory capture became an important avenue for organized constituencies to protect their interests during the creation of independent regulatory commissions.

In an earlier work examining the competing economic and political interests during the Progressive Era in the United States, it was Kolko who perhaps best summarized the logic of regulatory capture as an alternative to Bernstein's and Huntington's life-cycle approach. Kolko suggested, "Federal economic regulation was generally designed by the regulated interest to meet its own end, and not those of the public or the commonweal" (1963: 59).[30] Kolko's argument about the benefits of federal regulation to industry was later echoed by George Stigler, who wrote, "As a rule, regulation is acquired by industry and is designed and operated primarily for its benefit" (1971: 2). Thus, notions of regulatory capture picked up where earlier public interest theories of regulation failed, and capture theories then provided the basis for a number of important economic analyses of market failure regulation (Peltzman, 1973, 1976; Posner, 1974; Becker, 1976). With such logic at hand, capture theories became widely used to explain the pro-industry bias by independent commissions and other executive agencies, particularly in the areas of transportation regulation (e.g., Kolko, 1965; Stigler, 1971; Behrman, 1980) and utilities regulation (e.g., Stigler and Friedland, 1962; Gormley, 1983).

Pharmaceutical manufacturers have long argued that the highly centralized nature of drug regulation greatly increases both the cost of drug development and the length of time it takes to develop a new drug (see, for example, Grabowski, 1976; Helms, 1975; and Peltzman, 1974). For firms, centralized regulation is readily measured in economic terms. One estimate suggests that a firm can lose as much as $19 million per year on a single drug as a consequence of regulatory delay (DiMasi, Hansen, and Grabowski, 1991). While the pharmaceutical industry has been known to lament the high costs of drug development and the perils of regulatory delay, drug manufacturers at the same time have a substantial incentive to participate in the regulatory decisionmaking environment. Though the high costs of drug development and regulatory delays adversely impact profits, such costs may also serve as barriers to newer and smaller firms seeking to enter the market. This notion of regulatory capture suggests that larger and well-established firms may have an incentive to use regulation as a barrier to entry for newly emerging firms.

In the case of pharmaceutical regulation, the available empirical evidence of regulatory capture remains mixed at best. On one hand, John Abraham (1995) has argued that U.S. and, to a greater extent, British regulators are captured by the pharmaceutical industry as each authority exhibits "corporate bias" in licensing new medicines. In contrast, the special counsel of an independent FDA review panel found "no significant evidence of industry domination of FDA," following an extensive review of agency personnel and operations (Review Panel, 1977). Paul Quirk (1981) and others have also dismissed claims of regulatory capture at the FDA. A novel argument emerging in more recent formal and empirical work by Daniel Carpenter (2001) suggests that in the case of regulatory drug approvals, "protection without capture" can occur in certain circumstances. Specifically, Carpenter demonstrates that although firms submitting more drugs for regulatory approval tend to receive shorter approval times and that early entrants to the market receive shorter approval times as well, such results can occur under circumstances where there is little evidence of industry dominance of the agency. Thus, Carpenter's work shows that such empirical discrepancies in firm performance may exist in the absence of traditional notions of regulatory capture.[31]

Regulatory capture also presents theoretical inadequacies on several grounds. First, many of the economic models (including those described above) have a tendency to overlook important political considerations. The focus on the economic effect of regulation tends to treat political institutions as "black boxes" and ignores the important underlying political motivations of legislators, administrative agents, and other interested actors. Second, accounts of regulatory capture by political scientists have unsuccessfully attempted to correct for this limitation by placing considerable analytical focus on an exclusive group of political actors in the policymaking arena. This exclusive group, formerly referred to as an "iron triangle," comprised the particular regulatory agency, the relevant congressional committees, and powerful interest groups representing the regulated industry. The confluence of such actors served to close the policy arena to outside interests (see Heclo, 1978; Ripley and Franklin, 1984). Capture theories imply that the powerful interests are able to persuade the regulatory body to protect the interests of the regulated industry. Such accounts, however, largely ignore the prominent roles played by other political actors—in this case, consumers, consumer protection groups, and the medical profession, among others—as well as the influence of political institutions (Moe, 1987; Wood and Waterman, 1994).

Third, in practical terms, the regulation of medicines requires considerable scientific and technical prowess. Safety is ostensibly the dominant concern. Pharmaceutical firms and regulatory agencies each have significant reputational factors to consider. For instance, FDA approval of a new drug has long been considered the "gold standard" for the pharmaceutical industry. Certain variations of regulatory capture theories imply that regulatory agencies are willing to risk their reputations in exchange for the benefits received from the regulated industry. This account tends to neglect the long-term, repeated nature of the interaction between regulator and regulated. Firms also have significant reputational considerations. Failed drug approvals likely diminish consumer confidence in the particular firm, and weakened confidence will surely produce a detrimental effect on industry profits. Thus, for a number of analytical and political reasons, regulatory capture theories offer limited explanatory power.[32]

## External Signals Theory of Regulation

The external signals theory of regulation represents a third type of organic theory of regulation described by Noll. This framework, originally developed by Paul Joskow (1974), posits that regulatory agencies are responsive to their surrounding political environment. Specifically, the theory suggests that agencies respond to "signals" in their respective political environments. Noll argues: "Agencies try to serve the public interest but have difficulty identifying it, because the public interest is such an elusive concept. Consequently, agencies judge the extent to which their decisions satisfy the public interest by observing the responses of other institutions to their policies and rules" (1985: 41). In effect, the theory presumes that rationally behaving agencies respond to positive and negative feedback supplied by other actors in the political setting.

While the external signals model possesses great intuitive appeal, the notion that agencies respond to "signals" in the political environment is an extremely general one. In fact, the notion is so general that it offers relatively little explanatory power. In claiming that agencies respond to signals, the theory does not explicitly state what types of signals agencies respond to, how agencies respond to different signals, or why they might respond to signals in certain circumstances and not others. Additionally, many of the existing empirical applications of this model are relatively limited. On balance, then, while the external signals theory has much allure at the surface level, its relative underdevelopment as a theory of regulatory behavior and the relative dearth of empirical applications significantly limit the theory's utility.

The most notable exceptions to this general criticism, however, are the empirical applications of the model by Mary Olson in the context of FDA behavior. Olson's analyses incorporate the influence of external signals on FDA regulation and competition among the brand-name drug, generic-drug, and medical device industries (1995), FDA enforcement activities (1996), and the effect of firm-specific characteristics on regulatory approvals (1997). In effect, certain firm-specific characteristics (e.g., firm size, industry type) can provide an important signal to regulatory decisionmakers operating with relatively limited information.

Each of these three organic theories of regulation—public interest, capture, and external signals—uses the agency as the primary unit of analysis and assumes that agencies behave in a rational, self-interested manner. Yet each theory is plagued by a number of explanatory limitations.

Additionally, the three theories have a number of collective limitations consistent with specific criticisms outlined by Noll (1985). Generally speaking, given that organic theories treat the agency itself as the principal unit of analysis, little attention is characteristically paid to the formulation of agency goals. Agency goals are assumed to be given, and, as a result, it is difficult to discern exactly how various agency preferences are derived in the first place. Analytically, this is especially problematic when considering Herbert Simon's contention in *Administrative Behavior* (1957) that most organizations are oriented around a particular goal that gives purpose to organizational decisions and activities. Moreover, it is not uncommon for regulatory agencies to suffer from goal *uncertainty,* which may reflect "the absence of a clear legislative mandate" (Hult and Walcott, 1990) or failure to comprehend the "organizational objective" (Simon, 1957). In using the agency as the principal unit of analysis, organic theories cannot account for these critical initial conditions.

In the absence of such information, it is also difficult to discern which constituency (if any) agency objectives represent. A related confounding factor is that organic theories often ignore how structural phenomena influence regulatory behavior. That is, they generally cannot account for the effect of political institutions in shaping regulatory out-comes. Though it is plausible to assume that regulatory agencies oper-ate in complex political environments with a variety of competing pres-sures, organic theories cannot inform us *how* such tensions affect agency behavior. The external signals theory attempts to do this, but as of yet the theory remains far too underdeveloped. By failing to account for the structural constraints imposed by political institutions, organic theories lack important causal mechanisms that we would expect to see in a highly compelling explanation of regulatory behavior.

## Structural Theories of Regulation

Structural theories of regulation pose an alternative to organic theories by beginning with a narrower unit of analysis and an entirely different set of core assumptions. Specifically, structural theories examine agen-cies "as collections of individuals with conflicting objectives whose behavior is coordinated by a selection of rules, hierarchies, and com-munication" (Noll, 1985: 15). The rules, hierarchies, and patterns of interaction provide structural and procedural mechanisms to influence individual (and hence agency) behavior (Eggertsson, 1990; Miller, 1992). Thus, rather than imputing rationality at the agency level, struc-tural theories focus on the critical microanalytic mechanisms that pat-tern regulatory behavior. In doing so, they enable the observer to isolate the influence of structural, procedural, and environmental conditions in evaluating the performance of a regulatory agency. In filling this signif-icant void created by organic theories, structural explanations have gen-erated a renewed scholarly attention to the intricate details of adminis-trative law (see, for example, Mashaw, 1985; Schuck, 1994; Robinson, 1991; and Rosenbloom, 2000). As one scholar has noted, "Each agency's behavior reflects its distinctive history, statutory scheme, policy prob-lematic, legislative politics, bureaucratic culture, judicial review pat-tern, private interests, and specialized bar" (Schuck, 1994: 5).

The most influential structural theories in the political economy lit-erature focus on both administrative "structure" and "process." Matthew McCubbins, Roger Noll, and Barry Weingast define structure as "the allocation of resources and decisional authority among agencies and within an agency" (1989: 431–432). Using this definition, an under-standing of agency structure becomes critical in the explanation of reg-ulatory behavior for at least three reasons. First, by emphasizing resource allocation and decisional authority, structure helps define pat-terns of interaction both within and outside the agency. In this sense, the agency is placed within the context of the governing hierarchy, and structure formally defines the agency's role in the extant political environment. Second, agency resources generally provide the lifeline of an agency. Substantial agency resources can provide administrative agents with valuable political capital, as well as insulation from external political pressure. Moreover, we would expect variable behavior from agencies with ample resources compared to those struggling to acquire resources. Finally, by formally defining resource allocation and decisional authority, structure provides the political principal with a "hammer" to leverage or change the behavior of the agent, if necessary. Principals retain the capacity to modify agency structure if the agent does not live up to its end of the contract, and such modification would be expected to increase the flow of benefits to the principal.

In addition to an understanding of regulatory structure, regulatory process is defined as "the rules and standards that apply to policy decisions by an agency and guide judicial review" (McCubbins, Noll, and Weingast, 1989: 431). The analytical focus on process addresses an important causality gap left by organic theories. Structural theories do not assume that rules and standards are given. Instead, these elements ultimately reflect the process of political bargaining and negotiation. In this context, process is important for three reasons. First, process provides a basis or set of guidelines for agency decisionmaking. By extension, process limits the range of options available to administrative agents by defining the set of feasible alternatives. Second, because process presents a clear guideline for agency behavior, it becomes the basis for the monitoring of the agent by the principal. The detection of deviations from rules and standards enables principals to intervene and possibly punish agents. Finally, because these rules and standards are developed and imposed by the principal, they are subject to change at a later time at the principal's discretion. Thus, principals have an inherent interest in process because clear regulatory guidelines generally reduce transaction costs and increase efficiencies.

Structural theories of regulation are analytically appealing because they take into account the effect of regulatory structure on the content and direction of regulatory policy. Terry Moe, a leading theorist of structural politics, has argued: "Structural choices have important consequences for the content and direction of policy, and political actors know it. When they make choices about structure, they are implicitly making choices about policy. And precisely because this is so, issues of structure are inevitably caught up in the larger political struggle" (1989: 268). Moe emphasizes the significance of the ex ante agreements between political actors. In terms of the principal-agent relationship, the critical challenge for the principal lies in the design of an effective incentive structure (Moe, 1984, 1989). That is, principals can design (and modify) institutional structures that best serve their long-term interests. The emphasis on regulatory structure provides an opportunity to examine the role of several prominent political actors involved in creating the structure. Ultimately, a better understanding of the rules and standards should shed considerable light on the behavior of regulatory agencies.

Two structural theories stand out in this context. First, the "administrative procedures" hypothesis developed by McCubbins, Noll, and Weingast (1987, 1989) remains one of the most influential structural theories in the political economy literature. This theory places considerable emphasis on the ex ante control of regulatory agencies (in the form of structure and process) established by the enacting legislature. The arrangements precisely specify what the principal expects of the agent, what the rewards to the agent will be, and finally, what the punishment will be should the agency deviate from the specified contract. In effect, structure and process are critical for enabling principals to exert control over their agents. McCubbins, Noll, and Weingast assert that "the potential for agency deviations from intended policies that are difficult for politicians to punish or correct leads them to devise institutions that limit an agency's ability to deviate" (1989: 443). In other words, principals have the advantage of being able to "stack the deck" in their favor with respect to agents.

Second, Murray Horn's "structure hypothesis" is significant in this context because it develops a transaction cost approach to explain the choices of legislators during the design of institutional frameworks for regulatory agencies.[33] Essentially, Horn argues that focusing analytical attention on the relationship between legislators and constituents is critical to understanding institutional design. A specific mix of legislators takes on the role of the "enacting coalition" in adopting regulatory standards. The goal for the enacting coalition, he argues, is to make the legislation as durable as possible so that it will endure long after the dissolution of the enacting coalition. Specifically, he asserts, "institutional choices that determine the character of administrative organization are important in part because they influence 'who gets what' out of the political process" (1995: 3). This approach recognizes the politics shaping the contract between principals and agents.

Individually, then, structural theories of regulation offer several advantages in explaining regulatory behavior. The emphasis on ex ante institutional arrangements by the administrative procedures hypothesis offers important insights into the motivations of both principals and agents. Moreover, the notion that policies are devised to minimize agency deviations is a highly intuitive one. Also, Horn's structure hypothesis focuses critical attention on the specific transaction between the principal and agent. This transaction entails the exchange of significant political resources, and, as Horn argues, understanding the relationship between the enacting coalition and constituents is central to enhancing the durability of the legislation.

Examining critical elements such as agency design (i.e., structure) and institutional rules (process) can help explain the cross-temporal and cross-national differences in regulatory philosophy. These elements also reflect the prevailing attitudes toward risk and reward (e.g., the commission of Type I and II errors). Therefore, examining regulatory behavior requires focusing attention on the institutions themselves, as well as on the coalition of political actors (i.e., the enacting coalition and private interests) responsible for shaping regulatory policies. In the remainder of this chapter, I identify and analyze one specific aspect of the design of the FDA (structure) and one particular set of institutional rules (process). Together, these factors provide a useful starting point for beginning to explain the FDA's regulatory behavior.

## The FDA and Congress: Agency Design and Structure

Over the years a number of actors—ranging across the ideological spectrum and including the president, Congress, the courts, interest groups, private industry, the media, and the general public—have influenced the FDA and its design. However, due to its role as the chief architect of the nation's primary drug safety law—the 1938 Food, Drug and Cosmetic Act and its subsequent amendments—and as a result of its appropriations and oversight powers, Congress has a substantial impact on the structure of the agency and its subsequent behavior. Congress' critical role in the regulatory transaction is evident along a number of dimensions, including providing the agency with resources, legislative oversight, and a level of regulatory transparency.

### Agency Resources

The annual congressional appropriation to the FDA is a primary indicator of agency resources. Congressional appropriations to the agency are illustrated in Figure 2.1. The figure illustrates that agency appropriations can be roughly divided into three distinct periods. FDA appropriations during the 1960s were relatively flat, as annual appropriations never exceeded $100 million. As will be seen in the following chapter, this period is significant because it represents the period immediately following one of the major amendments to the 1938 Food, Drug and Cosmetic Act in 1962 (later known as the Kefauver amendments). Appropriations to the agency increased appreciably between 1972 and 1982 and then began to level off in the Reagan era during the mid-1980s. Appropriations then began to rise significantly during the late 1980s and into the early 1990s. It was at this point when the designation of "serious" and "life threatening illnesses" (with HIV/AIDS eventually becoming the most salient example) captured the attention of both Congress and the agency. (This focus will be seen in Chapters 4 and 5.) Finally, the leveling off of appropriations during the mid-1990s coincides with the passage of the Prescription Drug User Fee Act in 1992. PDUFA supplemented agency appropriations with user fees provided by the pharmaceutical industry. (The impact of PDUFA and its effect on agency resources is discussed further in Chapter 5.)

The number of agency staff members, as measured by full-time equivalents (FTEs), represents a second prominent indicator of agency resources. The number of FTEs at the FDA is illustrated in Figure 2.2. During the 1960s, agency staff levels increased amid heightened concerns

Figure 2.1  FDA Congressional Appropriations, 1960–1999 (in $ millions)

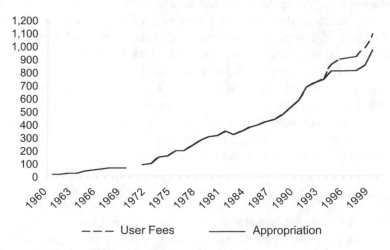

Source: *Congressional Quarterly Almanac* (1960–2000).

Figure 2.2 FDA Staff Levels, 1960–1998 (full-time equivalents)

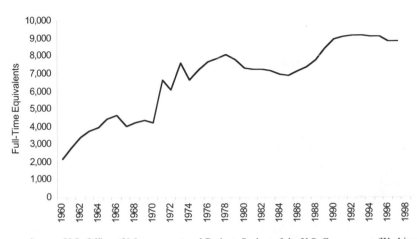
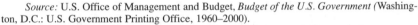

*Source:* U.S. Office of Management and Budget, *Budget of the U.S. Government* (Washington, D.C.: U.S. Government Printing Office, 1960–2000).

of drug safety, especially regarding the revelations of the thalidomide disaster in Europe, and the passage of the 1962 Kefauver amendments. Figure 2.2 also illustrates an increase in FDA personnel during the 1970s. Around 1980, however, agency staff increases would begin to stagnate, and this would continue for much of the decade. This can be attributed largely to the efforts of the Reagan administration in reducing the size of the federal bureaucracy. The size of the agency then steadily increased during the late 1980s, along with agency appropriations, during the administration of George H. W. Bush. Significant legislative changes in the early 1990s (especially PDUFA in 1992) directly led to the hiring of several hundred additional agency reviewers during the early 1990s. FDA staff levels then remained flat during the remainder of the Clinton administration.

## Legislative Oversight

In addition, congressional oversight in the form of congressional hearings and the establishment of independent review panels has historically precipitated changes in agency operating procedure and behavior. A fragmentation of authority combined with a mix of political supporters and detractors characterizes congressional control over the agency. As Table 2.1 illustrates, a number of congressional committees have jurisdiction

Table 2.1  Congressional Committees with FDA Responsibilities

Senate
  • Committee on Appropriations, Subcommittee on Agriculture, Rural Development, and
    Related Agencies
  • Committee on Agriculture, Nutrition, and Forestry
  • Committee on Commerce, Science, and Transportation
  • Committee on Governmental Affairs
  • Health, Education, Labor and Pensions Committee

House of Representatives
  • Committee on Appropriations, Subcommittee on Agriculture, Rural Development, Food
    and Drug Administration, and Related Agencies
  • Committee on Agriculture
  • Committee on Energy and Commerce
  • Committee on Government Reform
  • Committee on Resources
  • Committee on Science
  • Committee on Small Business

in areas that correspond with FDA responsibilities. This fragmentation provides multiple avenues for agency critics in Congress to undertake oversight activities ranging from launching investigations to holding hearings.

Congressional oversight extends from the top of the agency with the commissioner's office on down. Beginning with the tenure of Commissioner David Kessler in 1990, the position of FDA commissioner is now subject to Senate confirmation. In considering the notion that the FDA, as well as its commissioner, operates in the midst of a highly politicized atmosphere, one agency official explained, "The commissioner is a political animal. He has to be."

In recent years there have been a number of congressional oversight hearings pertaining to drug approvals and the drug approval process. In slightly over a decade and a half between January 1980 and December 1995 the top agency officials were summoned to Capitol Hill for congressional hearings over 400 times.[34] In addition to congressional oversight, the Department of Health and Human Services' Office of Inspector General also conducted numerous inquiries during this same period (USHHS, 1991). This type of oversight generally applies to the broader operation and direction of the agency. Congressional oversight at lower levels of the agency, however, such as at the division level where drug approvals are done, is a much more difficult task. Because of the scientific and highly technical nature of the approval process, one former agency official remarked, "Politicians cannot get into drug evaluations."

From this standpoint, agency reviewers have some degree of political autonomy.

For most of the post–World War II period, congressional criticism of the FDA was in the direction of exerting pressure on the agency toward product disapprovals and negative action. The tone of agency criticism vis-à-vis new drug approvals changed in the latter years of the twentieth century, however. Over the course of the 1990s, the primary tone of congressional criticism was to chastise the agency for moving too slowly in the drug approval process. This type of criticism, originally spearheaded by a number of Republicans critical of the agency for acting overly cautious and moving too slowly in the drug approval process, eventually gained widespread acceptance. Former House Commerce Committee chairman Thomas Bliley was fond of remarking that the agency acted as "an unnecessary speed bump" in the approval process and created the potential danger of "paralysis by analysis."[35] Bliley's views are not uncommon among Republicans on Capitol Hill. According to one Senate staff member speaking at a time when significant FDA reform legislation was being considered, "We estimate that 90 percent of the problems at FDA are attitudinal problems. Unfortunately, you can't legislate good attitudes, and you can't legislate good management." This comment points to the relative autonomy of the FDA as an administrative agent.

In reflecting on the tone of this criticism, consider the contrasting roles and responsibilities of the agency and Congress. This contrast was well described by the same staff member: "FDA has the luxury in speaking of 'public health' in the broadest of senses. Congress does not have that luxury since we see things in terms of constituents; in terms of people waiting for drugs. This is about politics. We've got to be responsive." While Congress clearly thinks in terms of representation and responsiveness, one House staffer warned against overstating the political divide between the FDA as a protector of public health and the congressional role of representing constituents: "Remember, almost nobody pulls the lever on this one [FDA reviews]. Almost no one bases their vote choice on how the FDA is doing in drug review." This reality is what makes drug regulation much like airline safety. Policymakers get little credit when regulatory systems function properly. Yet those same policymakers may pay a severe political cost in the event that harmful drugs are released onto the market.

Not all congressional members reflect the harsh criticism of FDA leveled by Bliley and other Republicans. As one former House staff member explained, there are several different perspectives in Congress regarding the FDA and new drug approvals. First, there are those who feel that all drugs proposed may be harmful. This attitude is character-istic of legislators who were part of the enacting coalition of the 1960s drug amendments. Public health, for those holding this view, continues to be defined as keeping unsafe drugs out of the hands of unsuspecting consumers.

Second, others in Congress feel the approval process should move much more quickly. Those holding this position are generally sympa-thetic toward industry views that regulation impedes drug development. This group feels that if reviews can be expedited, as they were in the case of AIDS drugs during the 1990s, then drug licensing could also be accelerated in the case of non-AIDS drugs.

Finally, some legislators are content with the regulatory status quo. They are confident in the current levels of safety standards yet take a highly cautious approach when FDA reform is considered because they do not want the approval process to move too fast. In short, this group also seeks to preserve the durability of the enacting legislation. They have little to gain politically by altering the status quo.

Legislative oversight of FDA activity remains a constant presence. Such oversight places continual demands on agency resources and on the time of top agency officials. The agency falls within the jurisdiction of at least eleven different congressional committees and subcommit-tees. In this sense, the FDA as an administrative agent has to satisfy the wishes of several political principals.

## Transparency and Access to Information

In addition to agency resources and legislative oversight, the relative transparency of the agency represents a third aspect of agency design (structure) to consider. By almost any standard, the FDA can be consid-ered a highly transparent agency with respect to its regulatory opera-tions. Approximately 90 percent of the agency's files regarding new drug applications are available to the public (Belcher, 1995). The pri-mary reasons for this transparency can be traced to the emphasis on structure and process formalized by the 1946 Administrative Procedures Act. First, the FDA is subject to the provisions of the Freedom of Information Act (FOIA). Enacted in 1966, the FOIA requires agencies such as the FDA to make a large percentage of information available for public consumption on request. Consequently, the FDA has an entire division devoted to handling requests via FOIA. Thus, any individual can obtain information about any drug, including the results of clinical trials or other information related to the agency's decision. In addition, on the approval of a new drug application (NDA), the agency publishes a Summary Basis of Approval Report that is also made available to the public through the FOIA. In releasing such information, the agency is careful not to release any proprietary information that may be considered sensitive (i.e., proprietary information that may be desirable to other drug manufacturers) or potentially jeopardize the patent of the sponsoring firm.

Second, through congressional hearings and investigations, the agency's commissioner and other top officials frequently appear before Congress in order to answer questions and respond to inquiries about FDA behavior. Third, as a result of the Federal Advisory Committee Act (FACA), advisory committee meetings held to discuss the approval of particular drugs are open to the public. FACA, enacted in 1972, requires that advance notification of the advisory committee meetings be published in the *Federal Register* fifteen days prior to the meeting and that all documents to advisory committee members must be made available to the public prior to the meeting. Such meetings are usually held in a suburban Washington, D.C., hotel and typically provide an open forum for a public audience. Generally, any interested persons can attend these meetings and occasionally participate in the proceedings by asking questions or raising points of information. Public participation by consumers, consumer activist groups, and other interested parties at FDA advisory committee meetings was instrumental in the approval of certain AIDS drugs (Kwitny, 1992).

Fourth, as is typical of agency rulemaking by U.S. regulatory agencies, the FDA allows for a public comment period on almost all agency rulemaking activities. All proposed rules are published weekly in the *Federal Register*. The publication of proposed and full rules and the resulting public comment period also play key roles in shaping agency policy and behavior. Finally, a significant level of information is made available by the agency to the general public. This is done primarily through the agency's Public Affairs Office and Drug Information Branch. The FDA website is also accessible as a growing repository of relevant information. These five factors make the FDA a highly transparent agency. While the level of transparency at FDA is consistent with a democratic vision of government regulation, it also plays a role in affecting the level of political support for the agency. The old military adage suggesting that "you can't hit what you can't see" has a great deal of relevance for the FDA. With greater transparency, the agency potentially becomes more frequently exposed to political scrutiny and criticism.

In summary, an examination of several components of agency structure provides a useful backdrop for explaining the behavior of the FDA in the context of Type I and Type II errors. Elements of agency design—such as agency resources, provisions for oversight, and the transparency of the agency—provide an important consideration for examining the behavior of the agency as an administrative agent. Clearly, the agency has both detractors and proponents in Congress. Consequently, agency resources and levels of oversight have varied over the years. As Commissioner Alexander Schmidt once testified, congressional hearings provide the "greatest pressure" with respect to new drug approvals. In the years prior to the mid-1980s, the agency was heavily criticized for controversial approvals, while disapprovals usually led to no further inquiries. Since then, the FDA has routinely been criticized for the failure to approve new drugs whereas difficult or controversial approvals have seemingly become more acceptable.

## The FDA's "Bottom-Up" Review Style

Complementing the discussion of agency design in the previous section, this section provides a closer look at one agency "process." Process, the rules and standards that apply to policy decisions, further illustrates the nature of regulatory behavior in the context of Type I and II errors.

Examining the FDA's "style" of reviewing new drug applications offers useful insights regarding the use of structural theories of regulation. The FDA traditionally takes a "bottom-up" approach when assessing new drugs. Rather than starting with summaries written by the sponsors of the new drug application and accepting their conclusions, agency reviewers prefer to examine the raw data from the sponsor. Specifically, Section 505 of the Food, Drug and Cosmetic Act requires the agency to examine "full reports of investigations," and the FDA has interpreted this clause to mean virtually the entire gamut of information collected by the sponsoring firm, including the raw data from clinical studies. Raw data generally includes computer data tapes of case report forms, case report tabulations, and narratives of clinical study reports. Based on this vast array of information, the FDA begins its review.[36] (See the appendix for an overview of the agency's drug review process.)

In order to appreciate fully the significance of this regulatory process, it will be useful to frame the discussion in a relative context. Unlike the bottom-up approach traditionally used at the FDA, European regulatory authorities have long preferred "top-down" assessments.

Rather than requiring raw data points, European regulators rely on summary tables of data compiled by the sponsoring firm. In addition, European regulators require sponsoring firms to provide multiple, independently generated executive summaries, known as expert reports, of the drug application. (In Europe, the drug application is known as the dossier.) From these summaries, reviewers then make further inquiries when discrepancies in the dossier arise. According to one European executive, "The philosophy is 'Okay, you [the sponsoring firm] developed the drug; tell us what it's good for and we'll review it.'" This approach sharply contrasts with that employed by the FDA. One long-time FDA official did not conceal his skepticism of the European reliance on the top-down approach to reviews: "Summaries and executive reports are highly subjective documents. That they could be neutral is a European fantasy."

Generally, industry officials find it defensible for the FDA to have access to all the raw data compiled in clinical investigations. They differ, however, on whether supplying all the raw data is necessary for every application, as well as on what the agency does with the data once received. One industry official complained, "I've heard that 60 percent of the time spent by FDA reviewers is spent by checking raw data points. Is it reasonable for FDA to sit around and ask, 'Do all the data precisely match?'? Auditing should be done by auditors, not FDA reviewers." Another lamented, "A number of the health authority people said they are becoming the heads of warehousing departments."

On the other hand, European industry officials and analysts repeatedly echoed the merits of the European top-down approach. One official suggested, "The key to the UK regulatory approach, and in Europe generally, is that the burden of proof is much different. The feeling is that the company presents the dossier and it is okay. The British regulatory authority does not challenge every detail and every table." In much the same vein, another added, "Much more dialogue is inherent in the British system. The assumption is, 'Here is the dossier, read it, let's talk,' and so on. The assumption and subsequent challenge for the Medicines Control Agency [MCA] is not to pick the dossier apart."[37]

In relying on a bottom-up approach, the FDA attempts to reconstruct the raw data presented in the new drug application. The differences are evident in the following comments of two U.S. pharmaceutical industry officials and one U.S. industry analyst: "In the U.S. the assumption seems to be, okay, this product is potentially harmful and it's up to the FDA to show why." "Delay and inaction at the FDA are not the result of a lack of resources, but a way of doing business. FDA is guided by the slow down and wait it out approach." "We don't have the same level of trust to say, 'Whatever is in the expert report is okay.'" These comments clearly reflect the agency's approach with respect to avoiding Type II errors. In this sense, the agency has taken a relatively vague standard from the Food, Drug and Cosmetic Act (i.e., "full reports of investigations") and used its administrative autonomy to forge a strict regulatory interpretation.

In conjunction with the FDA's bottom-up style of review, it is revealing to consider how the agency views its broader role in the process of drug development. The FDA's view in this regard is also particularly revealing when considered in a comparative context. In using bottom-up reviews, the FDA implicitly views assisting industry in the drug development process to be one of its core functions. This practice is certainly not the case in European and Japanese regulatory arenas, however. Instead, foreign drug regulatory agencies generally see their role solely in the capacity of the licensing authority. In practice, this means that the process of drug development is left almost solely in the hands of the pharmaceutical industry.

Several examples can be used to illustrate this difference in regulatory approach. A first example is merely nominal in one sense, but also highly instrumental. The organizational format of the FDA divides the agency into six main centers. The two primarily involved in the licensing of new medicinal products are the Center for Drug Evaluation and Research (CDER) and the Center for Biological Evaluation and Research (CBER). In addition to its core licensing function, an additional function—the task of drug research—is an explicit feature of each center. No such parallel exists at the British MCA, for example. Of the five divisions at the MCA, the Licensing Division is solely responsible for the review of new products. Neither the MCA nor its Licensing Division makes any claims to be involved in drug development or assisting in the process of drug research. One European industry official explained the difference this way: "There is a real difference between cultures here. The FDA believes they can help in drug development, whereas European review agencies do *not* consider themselves to be doing research. The ethos in the U.S. is that the FDA can serve as a partner with companies in drug development. This ethos is not present in Europe at all." This difference in ethos has a significant impact on the size of each agency. While the FDA employs over 2,000 individuals at CDER alone, the entire staff size of the MCA amounts to just over 500.

A second illustration of this difference in regulatory styles can be found in the early stages of the drug review process. For each new drug application submitted to the agency, the FDA conducts extensive "pre-NDA meetings" with the sponsoring firm. During these meetings agency reviewers and representatives of the sponsoring firm discuss various clinical strategies and seek to develop a mutually acceptable protocol for clinical testing and other aspects of drug development. Another European official pointed out this difference: "In theory, the FDA can lead the firm by its hand during drug development. This is not the same in the UK. The MCA doesn't offer such guidelines. They are less interested in drug development, per se."

Finally, the FDA and the MCA remain distinctive in the organization of their review divisions. For instance, FDA review divisions are organized by therapeutic classification. That is, separate divisions exist for reviewing drugs intended to treat various illnesses or physiological functions (e.g., cardiovascular, AIDS, neurological, oncology). The FDA believes that reviewing can best take place if specialists in individual therapeutic areas conduct the reviews. The absence of such an organizing principle remains a typical feature of European review agencies in general and the MCA in particular. Reviewing responsibilities at the MCA are not organized according to therapeutic classification. As one European official stated: "In Europe, we believe a reviewer is a reviewer is a reviewer. We believe that a professional review does not have to be based on therapeutic classification." Accordingly, many reviewing doctors at European regulatory agencies are generalists. The same official also said, "For virtually all regulatory agencies in Europe, there are few specialists." It should be noted, however, that such specialists are called in on occasion to assist on particular drug applications.

In summary, building on the discussion of agency structure in the previous section, this brief glimpse at an important, though perhaps not immediately obvious aspect of regulatory process also provides considerable insight into the agency's approach toward Type I and II errors. Acting as an administrative agent, the FDA chooses to interpret Section 505 of the Food, Drug and Cosmetic Act in a manner that enables the agency to access virtually all available raw data when reviewing new drug applications. Since drug licensing is a highly complex task, the agency is afforded some degree of autonomy to interpret the legislative standard. Historically, this interpretation has been crafted in a manner to minimize the highly costly nature of committing Type II errors. The FDA's "bottom-up" approach reveals substantial differences with European approaches to reviewing new drug applications. These differences are apparent in institutional structure, as well as in attitudes toward risk and reward.

## Conclusion

Noll's (1985) discussion of structural theories of regulation provides the theoretical basis for this chapter. Within this framework, McCubbins, Noll, and Weingast's "administrative procedures" hypothesis and Horn's "structure" hypothesis offer specific insights into the nature of the principal-agent relationship. Each of these arguments emphasizes the ex ante agreements in the principal-agent relationship and the significance of structure and process in shaping agency behavior. The "administrative procedures" hypothesis argues that political principals attempt to create institutional frameworks that help them resolve their agency control problems and emphasize important endogenous factors governing agency behavior. Alternatively, Horn's transaction cost approach emphasizes the significance of the political nature of the transaction between principal and agent.

Analyzing the behavior of the FDA in the context of regulatory structure and process provides a unique opportunity to study the U.S. regulatory system along several dimensions, including agency design, institutional structure, and regulatory philosophy. In order to better comprehend the nature of the institutional structure and process, I have briefly sketched out the role of Congress, the primary actor in the principal-agent relationship, in designing the agency's institutional structure and identified the "style" of FDA reviews as an important regulatory process. Together, these fundamental structures and processes are indicative of the agency's inherent regulatory philosophy toward risk and reward. As the following chapters suggest, this approach has gradually evolved over the course of several distinct regulatory periods.

# 3

## AN EVOLVING REGULATORY BALANCE

No area of FDA's responsibility has been more closely scrutinized by Congress, industry, health professionals, and the public than the approval process for new drugs, or more specifically, the speed with which new therapies of proven effectiveness and safety are made available to those who need them.

—*Michael Friedman,*
*former lead deputy FDA commissioner*

In this chapter, I build on the discussion of agency theory and structural theories of regulation to provide a framework for understanding policy change. I then briefly review the early history of U.S. medicines regulation in the context of this framework. This historical experience provides valuable insights into the varying philosophies toward Type I and II errors and serves as a foundation for understanding contemporary regulatory policies and practices. U.S. medicines regulation can be characterized by several distinct periods over the course of the twentieth century. Each period possesses a distinctive regulatory philosophy, as well as a specific set of institutions designed to shape and constrain individual behavior.

The historical context of drug regulation in the United States is of considerable importance largely because of the evolutionary nature of policy development. Regulatory policy—whether pertaining to environmental protection, securities laws, worker safety, or consumer protection—often emerges in reaction to major events or paradigm-shifting ideas. Drug-related tragedies and developments in pharmaceutical science have played important roles in the development and implementation of pharmaceutical regulation. Widespread drug-related tragedies in the early part of the twentieth century provided the initial impetus for regulation. Such episodes created an initial opportunity for political principals to devise a specific set of regulatory structures and processes to regulate the release of new medicines into the U.S. consumer market. With the passage of time, other drug safety–related tragedies (or near tragedies) would be instrumental in creating a political climate amenable to modifying and, in most instances, strengthening the regulatory apparatus. These episodes provided an opportunity for actors in the policy subsystem to evaluate the existing principal-agent contract and update the nature of the arrangement to better reflect the specific mix of political interests prevailing at the time.

Similarly, rapid technological developments in the pharmaceutical industry necessitated the further development of regulatory policy. Initial advances during the early twentieth century led to the creation of a pharmaceutical "science" and paved the way for a "revolution" in therapeutics. The therapeutic revolution altered cultural norms in U.S. society as more and more consumers ingested medicines to treat a variety of conditions, ranging from psychosomatic maladies to life-threatening illnesses. As these technological changes gradually altered consumer behavior, they would also provide the impetus for political principals to examine the nature of the principal-agent contract. In sum, the nature and the timing of drug-related tragedies and rapid technological advances created important and distinctive policy synergies as regulatory policy was increasingly linked with pharmaceutical science. Consequently, the resulting regulatory arrangements needed to reflect these synergies.

In addition, policy outputs are the product of bargaining and negotiation among the relevant actors in the policy subsystem. Such actors may include Congress, the FDA, the pharmaceutical industry, the medical profession, consumer advocacy groups, and individual consumers. These actors typically reflect a variety of diverse and often competing interests. Consequently, it takes skillful political maneuvering by one or more of these actors to instigate significant policy change. As will be shown, both the medical profession and the pharmaceutical industry were relatively late in developing as powerful political actors. As a result, they did not play especially crucial roles in the shaping of early regulatory institutions. Instead, the maneuvering of various legislators and regulators was the primary force behind major policy change.

The previous chapters have argued that the regulation of new medicines reflects a fundamental societal tolerance toward risk and reward. Consumers want to be assured that the medicines they take are safe. Yet patients suffering from various ailments (and, in fact, virtually all consumers) demand that medicines be made available in a timely fashion.

Because approving medicines that are later shown to be unsafe (or ineffective) can be terribly costly for both Congress and the regulatory
agency, there tends to be a natural preference for avoiding Type II
errors. This suggests that regulatory agencies like the FDA are inherently political actors. Moreover, because the legislative branch created
the FDA and provides the agency with the bulk of its resources and
oversight, this preference toward avoiding Type II errors also suggests
that Congress is able to embed its preferences into the FDA's structures
and processes.

Despite Congress' and the FDA's preference for avoiding Type II
errors, evidence suggests that regulatory performance varies over time.[38]
If regulatory structures and processes are the underlying mechanisms of
agency performance, then it is necessary to account for the nature of
regulatory change. In this case, agency structure and process, as
described in the previous chapter, provides the foundation for understanding the nature of regulatory change.

## Understanding Policy Change

An explanation of policy change is needed to better understand the
changes in structural politics. Theoretical notions about policy change
traditionally center on the importance of agendas and agenda setting
(Kingdon, 1984; Cobb and Elder, 1983). Frank Baumgartner and Bryan
Jones (1993, 2001) extend this emphasis on agendas in a number of
ways. First, they integrate agenda-setting models with the notion of policy subsystems. A policy *subsystem* involves the interrelations of the
central actors in the policy arena, including bureaucratic agents, congressional committees, and related interest organizations (Redford,
1969). Over the years this notion of subsystem has been captured by a
variety of labels including issue networks, iron triangles, and policy tri-
ads. Regardless of the analytical label employed, such subsystems "provide continuing benefits to the same group of privileged elites" (Baumgartner and Jones, 1993: 3). Thus, as long as the policy elites derive
benefits from the policy subsystem and the prevailing policy, we should
not expect much change in the policy agenda. In essence, the policy status quo remains durable and becomes entrenched by the policy elites.
The policy subsystem, then, can be characterized by its stability.

Second, Baumgartner and Jones's empirical emphasis on policy
subsystems sheds considerable light on "policy dynamics" or the evolving nature of public policy and institutional change. The dynamic nature

of policy and policy change assumes that the status quo policy (and the prevailing policy regime) represents stability, if not partial equilibrium. Baumgartner and Jones show this empirically in their examination of nuclear power, pesticides, smoking, and other areas over an extended period of time.

The notion of policy as equilibrium is not a new one, however. David Truman's (1951) classic notion of "disturbance theory" suggested that policy change is often the result of external shocks. Such shocks disrupt the policy equilibrium and lead interest groups to respond by mobilizing in the attempt to influence policy. More recently, Marc Eisner has defined a regulatory regime as "a historically specific configuration of policies and institutions which . . . play a central role in structuring regulatory policies and the relationship between societal interests, the state, and economic actors" (2000: xv). Richard Harris and Sidney Milkis also use the phrase "regulatory regime" to describe "distinct patterns of political intervention throughout American history that have structured business-government relations" (1996: 24).

By extension, one could argue that such regimes are conducive to creating and maintaining stable policy outcomes. Kenneth Shepsle's notion of "structure-induced" equilibrium (1979) demonstrated that institutions and institutional rules create stable policy outcomes. Baumgartner and Jones (1993) use the term *policy monopoly* to characterize how the specific contractual agreement between the principal and agent (i.e., the specific institutional arrangement of regulatory structures and processes) endures over time. Specifically, they assert that policy monopolies ensure long periods of policy stability. Baumgartner and Jones define a policy monopoly as "the monopoly on political understandings concerning the policy of interest, and an institutional arrangement that reinforces that understanding" (1993: 6). In this case, policy monopoly is a critical concept because it provides a clear and direct linkage between the specific mix of political interests, the relevant actors in the policy subsystem, and a particular institutional arrangement (which is the product of the existing principal-agent contract). This linkage suggests that principals and agents maintain a set of shared expectations concerning the existing contract and, to the extent that each benefits from the arrangement, share a common interest in seeing that the contract endures.

The analytical emphasis on policy monopolies (and the linkage between actors, interests, and institutions) also provides the basis for understanding policy change in terms of a "punctuated equilibrium" view of the political system. In this dynamic formulation of policy, some policy change routinely takes place beyond the public purview (general stability) but occurs other times in the midst of widespread public debate (an interruption to the system).[39] During periods of general stability, we may expect to see policy change take place incrementally (Lindblom, 1959), particularly due to budgetary considerations (Wildavsky, 1964; Jones, Baumgartner, and True, 1998; Carpenter, 1996; True, 1999). During these periods of general policy stability, we expect to see relatively little change in the policy subsystem. The stability in the policy subsystem presumably reflects the relative satisfaction with the existing regulatory institutional arrangement.

Alternatively, interruptions to the policy subsystem may be brought about by exogenous factors or "focusing events." Such events act as a catalyst in sparking debate and moving the policy agenda (Kingdon, 1984; Birkland, 1997). In the case of medicines regulation, occurrences of drug-related tragedies throughout the twentieth century in the United States and around the world have provided such exogenous shocks. These shocks occur when unsafe drugs harm large numbers of people. Consequently, drug safety problems on a large scale produce highly visible victims and accentuate the "high saliency" of drug licensing. On occasion, these shocks have led to significant alternations in drug regulation. In effect, such episodes may shake up the prevailing political interests in the policy subsystem and create opportunities to alter the principal-agent contract. As the subsystem changes, consequently, it is possible that the preferences of the principals will change as well. Likewise, as the subsystem changes, the requirements for agents and/or the structures of agents may gradually change. When either of these scenarios arise, it is likely that the principal, the agent, or both will seek to alter the existing structures and processes that govern agent behavior.

Jones, Baumgartner, and James True have nicely captured this phenomenon of "punctuated equilibrium." They argue:

> Complex interactive political systems do not react slowly and automatically to changing perceptions or conditions; rather, it takes increasing pressure and sometimes crisis atmosphere to dislodge established ways of thinking about policies. The result is periods of stability interspersed with occasional, unpredictable, and dramatic change. (1998: 2)

The notion of "dislodging established ways of thinking" is crucial to the principal-agent relationship, the prevailing contract that binds the two, and the more general policy punctuation approach to policy dynamics. Yet, as the above passage implies, the punctuated equilibrium model uses the political "system" as the primary unit of analysis. As a result, the model may not fully realize the role of primary actors in the policy subsystem. This suggests the need to identify the primary actors in the subsystem and consider their primary interests and motivations. In doing so, one can better understand the nature of the relationship between principals and agents.

In a distinct, yet related approach to policy change, Paul Sabatier and Hank Jenkins-Smith argue that "major policy change" requires more than mere exogenous shocks: "Such perturbations provide an opportunity for major policy change, but such change will not occur unless that opportunity is skillfully exploited by proponents of change" (1999: 148). In effect, then, they argue that skillful political maneuvering provides an important catalyst for major policy change. Thus, for a policy punctuation in the regulation of new medicines to occur, we would expect to see exogenous factors accompanied by changing perceptions or conditions. This combination provides a necessary, though not sufficient condition for a policy punctuation. In addition, such factors should be accompanied by skillful political maneuvering within the policy subsystem that ultimately becomes the catalyst for a policy punctuation. Such skillful political maneuvering may also lead to a modification of the existing principal-agent contract.

## Distinctive Regulatory Periods in U.S. Drug Review

The "punctuated equilibrium" model of policy change provides a useful heuristic to explain transformations in the regulation of new medicines (as well as changes in the FDA's regulatory behavior and performance). The punctuated equilibrium model is particularly appropriate because it captures the notion that political systems endure long periods of stability yet are occasionally "punctuated" by dramatic change.

The model is also appropriate because it helps reveal how a new set of political and societal interests (i.e., a "policy monopoly") occasionally emerges to influence the regulation of new medicines. As Baumgartner and Jones point out, a policy monopoly must contain (1) "a definable institutional structure responsible for policymaking" and (2) "a powerful supporting idea associated with the institution" (1993: 7). In the former case, it is clearly evident that both administrative and legislative changes have, on occasion, significantly altered the institutional structure of the agency over the years. By extension, such changes (often found in the form of major pieces of drug safety legislation) tend to influence significantly the FDA's regulatory performance. In the latter case, it can be shown that FDA regulatory politics can be characterized by a series of powerful supporting ideas. The powerful supporting ideas often hinge on the balance between Type I and Type II errors.

In the remainder of this chapter and in the following two chapters, I examine the various periods of policy equilibrium (as well as the subsequent punctuations) that have occurred over the past century. Each punctuation led Congress to enact a landmark piece of drug safety legislation, and such legislation precipitated an institutional change that ultimately enhanced the FDA predisposition toward avoiding Type II errors. These periods of policy stability and change also provide a means to see how agency theory can be used to better understand the manner in which laws enacted by Congress create a particular institutional structure in the regulation of new medicines. This structure involves a specific mix of regulatory structures (i.e., patterns of interaction within and outside the agency, agency resources, political oversight, etc.) and regulatory processes (i.e., rules and standards that apply to policy decisions). Agency theory also can lead to a better understanding of the behavior of the FDA in acting as the agent charged with implementing the regulatory policies enacted by Congress.

## The Historical Context of U.S. Drug Regulation

Grabowski and Vernon (1983) characterize three distinctive periods in the history of U.S. drug regulation. Each period is the product of landmark drug safety legislation that created a definable institutional structure and reflected a powerful supporting idea. First, the period 1906–1938, beginning with the Pure Food and Drugs Act (PFDA) of 1906, was characterized by a predominantly market-oriented approach to drug regulation. Dr. Harvey Wiley—through his group of volunteers in the Department of Agriculture known as the "Poison Squad," his verbal jousting with President Theodore Roosevelt over the harmful effects of food adulteration, and his regular engagements with women's clubs and business and civic groups—provided skillful political maneuvering in demonstrating the dangers of adulterated products. This maneuvering ultimately led to the passage of the 1906 law (Herring, 1936; Young, 1981; Jannsen, 1981). The premise behind the Pure Food and Drugs Act was to correct for the occasional market failure (i.e., a powerful supporting idea). For example, the regulatory apparatus sought to prevent misbranding and the adulteration of drugs by using the court system to punish violators. Ultimately, though the PFDA provided some regulatory centralization, the law was relatively weak.

In response, the 1938 Food, Drug and Cosmetic Act provided an alternative, definable institutional structure, and it signals the beginning of a second regulatory period. Advocates for consumer safety, as well as governmental actors such as Assistant Secretary of Agriculture Rexford Tugwell and Walter Campbell, who oversaw the regulatory agency at this time, provided the skillful political maneuvering. The Food, Drug and Cosmetic Act greatly strengthened and centralized the regulatory apparatus by requiring premarketing proof of safety by the manufacturer. Thus, Grabowski and Vernon's second major period, 1938–1962, featured a "blend" of market mechanisms and elements of centralized control. Despite the introduction of a centralized control mechanism, automatic approvals were granted if the agency failed to act within two months and "most drugs were cleared without major objections by the FDA" (1983: 8).

Third, following the thalidomide disaster in Europe in the early 1960s, major amendments to the 1938 Federal Food, Drug and Cosmetic Act—known as the Kefauver amendments—were passed in 1962. Partially the result of the dogged activism of Tennessee senator Estes Kefauver, the 1962 amendments strengthened and centralized the review process even further and significantly expanded the FDA's regulatory jurisdiction. Since 1962, pharmaceutical manufacturers have been required to get regulatory approval at two major junctures in the drug development process: prior to clinical testing (the testing of the drug in humans) and prior to marketing the drug to the general public. In addition, the burden of proof was placed on the manufacturer to demonstrate that the drug was both safe and efficacious prior to its marketing. In effect, the applicable model for drug review moved away from correcting the occasional market failure to "the presumption of a more pervasive and health-threatening market failure that required extensive codification and enforcement of very stringent standards" (Grabowski and Vernon, 1983: 9).

Grabowski and Vernon's characterization of the various regulatory regimes reveals a systematic pattern of regulatory behavior. In the context of agency theory, each period was the product of a distinct policy monopoly that created a direct linkage between the principal's concern for protecting consumers and a set of institutional structures and processes put in place to shape the behavior of the agent. At the same time, the institutional arrangement was designed to reinforce the interests of those actors in the policy subsystem. On their creation, such institutional structures were meant to be durable. Yet, over time, the effectiveness of the principal-agent contract gradually waned, as interests and actors changed and the existing institutional structures were perceived to no longer be adequate. As a result, exogenous factors, changing perceptions, and political maneuvering became key ingredients leading to institutional change. This is consistent with the assertion by Harris and Milkis that particular "ideas, institutions, and policies" characterize distinct regulatory regimes.

The Food and Drug Administration has since moved toward yet another period in regulating new drugs (1992–present). This time, however, the agency did not move further toward the avoidance of Type II errors, as it had in previous periods. Instead, partially as the result of exogenous shocks stemming from the relative unavailability of new medicines and pressure from political interests intent on approving more new medicines and approving them more rapidly, Congress and the agency actually moved closer toward an approach that emphasizes the promotion of public health and the expedited review of new medicines. In the words of Baumgartner and Jones, changes in the policy subsystem, an exogenous shock, and skillful political maneuvering combined to create another "policy punctuation" and a new policy monopoly.

Thus, the fourth (and current) regulatory period entails a rebalancing of the agency's traditional risk-benefit analysis. The new orientation expands the agency's traditional concern of protecting public health to also include the promotion of public health by placing a greater relative emphasis on the benefits of making new drugs available to the public sooner. In terms of the model presented in Figure 1.1, the agency's shift in the current period reflects the increasing preference of Congress and the agency for avoiding Type I errors. (The nature of this regulatory shift is the subject of Chapter 5.)

Table 3.1 illustrates the confluence of factors necessary to explain the distinctive regimes in the regulation of new medicines. First, as the discussion of the structural aspects of regulatory policy in the previous chapter suggested, regulatory institutions (in the form of landmark laws) provide the basis for understanding regulatory policy. In this case, each regulatory regime features a defining institutional structure that emerged through the enactment of landmark legislation. Such institutional structures ultimately yield distinguishable regulatory outcomes. In addition, the analytical attention of policy change points to the relative significance of factors such as policy subsystems, policy monopolies, and skillful political maneuvering. Consequently, each regime

Table 3.1 Distinctive Regimes in the Regulation of New Medicines

|  | 1906–1937 | 1938–1961 | 1962–1991 | 1992–Present |
|---|---|---|---|---|
| Landmark law | 1906 Pure Food and Drugs Act | 1938 Federal Food, Drug and Cosmetic Act | 1962 Kefauver amendments | 1992 Prescription Drug User Fee Act |
| Regulatory era | Progressive | New Deal | Great Society | New social regulation; deregulation |
| Regulatory regime[a] | Market | Associational | Societal | Efficiency |
| Focusing event | Revelation of unsanitary conditions | "Elixir" tragedy | Thalidomide disaster | AIDS pandemic |
| Fundamental philosophy | Preventing occasional market failure | Blend of pre-market controls and automatic approval | Stringent central-ized controls | Balancing risks of Type I and II errors; expanding definition of public health |
| Regulatory impact | Identifying "sins of commis-sion"; empha-sis on food | Certification role; prevent-ing "bad" actors | Increasing cost of drug devel-opment; dura-tion of review | Increased access; risk-benefit calculation tilted toward benefit |

*Note:* a. After Eisner (2000).

occurs within the context of a distinctive regulatory era, as well as a regulatory period that characterizes the nature of business-governmental relations. The fundamental philosophy associated with each regime reflects the interests of the prevailing policy monopoly.

Thus, Table 3.1 summarizes the landmark laws (i.e., the key institutional structures) shaping the agency's regulatory behavior. Second, to provide a broader context for such regulatory behavior, the table also summarizes the distinctive regulatory eras and regulatory periods that prevailed during each particular time frame. Third, in the specific context of medicines regulation, it summarizes the primary focusing events that served as the precursor to each new regulatory regime (as well as the new policy monopolies) and the fundamental philosophy toward medicines regulation in each period. Finally, it summarizes the impact that the newly formed policy monopoly has had on shaping regulatory behavior.

In the remainder of this chapter, I discuss the nature of the first two periods (1906–1938 and 1938–1962) in the context of the framework described above. Chapter 4 discusses the third regulatory period (1962–1992), and Chapter 5 describes the changes leading to the latest regulatory period.

## The Early Period and the 1906 Pure Food and Drugs Act

U.S. drug law dates back to at least 1820 when the first *United States Pharmacopoeia* (*USP*) was published.[40] The *Pharmacopoeia* (from the Greek *pharmakon,* a drug, and *poiia,* making) is the official compendium of all drug products, their formulas, and other relevant information. The *U.S. Pharmacopoeia* is published annually by a nongovernment organization (of the same name) whose membership is comprised of doctors and pharmacists. The organization establishes drug quality standards and also publishes the *National Formulary* (NF), the companion volume to the *USP,* which is used primarily by pharmacists.

Europeans imported some of the earliest medicinal products into the United States. European chemists at this time had discovered therapeutic effects of various organic substances derived from plants. Among the so-called alkaloid drugs in use during this time were morphine (extracted from opium), caffeine, quinine (extracted from tree bark), and later cocaine.[41] In 1848, the Drug Importation Act prohibited the entry of adulterated drugs from overseas. During this time, as former FDA historian Wallace Jannsen noted, "The United States had become the world's dumping ground for counterfeit, contaminated, diluted, and decomposed drug materials" (1981: 32). Despite the tampering with drug materials, the primary emphasis during the period remained on government control over the adulteration of foods. Such concerns led to the creation of the Division of Chemistry, the forerunner to the Food and Drug Administration, in the Department of Agriculture in 1862.

The Division of Chemistry was for a long time "the only conspicuous and relatively well-equipped laboratory in Washington" (Dupree, 1957: 176). The division focused its efforts primarily on chemical testing and solving problems. As Jannsen notes, "Changes from an agricultural to an industrial economy had made it necessary to provide the rapidly increasing city population with food from distant areas. [Yet] use of chemical preservatives and toxic colors was virtually uncontrolled and . . . sanitation was primitive in the light of modern standards" (1981: 32).

The Division of Chemistry's focus would later change dramatically with the passage of the Hatch Act in 1887. With the development and increasing importance of food-production techniques, the Hatch Act provided federal aid to develop state agricultural experiment stations. The agricultural stations would be attached to a land-grant college in every state. The Hatch Act effectively expanded the Division of Chemistry's role and decentralized scientific and chemical testing on food and other agricultural products.

This expanded role paved the way for the skillful political maneuvering of Harvey W. Wiley. Wiley took over as director of the Division of Chemistry in 1883 and, as James Harvey Young points out, "Wiley had a flair for the dramatic and was something of an innovator" (1961: 232). Wiley's leadership was especially critical given that the Division of Chemistry was based on a discipline, instead of a specific problem (Dupree, 1957). Peter Temin later echoed this point: "The Division of Chemistry was based on a discipline, not a problem, and its organizational survival depended on finding problems to solve" (1980: 27). Wiley concentrated his greatest efforts on the problem of food adulteration (see Anderson, 1958: chap. 4). As a result of its ongoing experimental testing, the division published *Bulletin 13: Foods and Food Adulterants* in 1887. Wiley's biographer, Oscar Anderson, would later point out: "*Bulletin 13* was a significant contribution to the literature of food. It was not the only treatise on adulteration published in America, but it was the most complete, the most thorough, and the most grounded in basic science" (1958: 74). Based on the results contained in *Bulletin 13* and through his work in the Division of Chemistry over the next decade, Wiley began to make the case for national antiadulteration legislation.

In addition to the ongoing work of the Division of Chemistry, the latter half of the nineteenth century witnessed several other significant developments. The origins of the public health movement, the birth of the U.S. drug companies, and the rise of the medical profession are perhaps the most notable in this context (see, for example, Porter, 1997; Duffy, 1979; Liebenau, 1987). For instance, the public health movement in the United States largely emerged in the aftermath of the Civil War. The Civil War created a need for the federal government to tend to the health needs of army and navy servicemen, as well as merchant seamen. The Marine Hospital Service, the forerunner of today's Public Health Service, was dramatically reorganized in 1870 to better meet the health needs of servicemen. The American Public Health Association was formed in 1872. A year later, Baltimore businessman Johns Hopkins bequeathed his fortune of $8 million to found a university and hospital. Hopkins's will stated that the hospital was to "compare favorably with any institution of like character in this country or in Europe." The bequest indicated that the hospital was to treat "the poor of this city and state, of all races." It "gave the chance for a new departure in medical education in the United States" (Dupree, 1957: 257).

It was also during this time that the effects of industrialization would significantly alter the nature of chemical and drug production and the pharmaceutical industry. During the late nineteenth century, the fledgling pharmaceutical industry comprised numerous small- and medium-sized companies, many of which were family owned (Slinn, 1995). The size of these companies generally restricted them from having large research units. As time passed, however, the industry was being transformed by innovative new manufacturing technologies and the mass production of pharmaceutical products. Rapid medical discoveries in German laboratories (e.g., Paul Ehrlich's work on arsphenamine) enabled Germany to be the world's primary pharmaceutical supplier at this time. Eventually, the research and production units of large chemical firms such as Hoechst and Bayer would enable Germany to maintain a considerable pharmaceutical export market. However, the outbreak of war in 1914 abruptly halted the flow of German pharmaceutical products around the world. As a result, the United States had to become more self-reliant in the production of pharmaceuticals (Slinn, 1995).

By the turn of the century, Wiley had been highly active in his pursuit of antiadulteration legislation. He had routinely appeared to testify in congressional hearings and he even verbally jousted with Presidents Theodore Roosevelt and William H. Taft on several occasions over the effects of food preservatives. In perhaps the most dramatic example of Wiley's skillful political maneuvering, he organized a group of a dozen healthy volunteers at the Department of Agriculture in 1902 into what would become known as the "Poison Squad." Over the course of the next five years, the Poison Squad consumed food preservatives—such as borax; salicylic, sulphurous, and benzoic acids; and formaldehyde—to determine their overall impact on health. Wiley used these experiments to demonstrate that food preservatives should only be used when necessary and that burden of proof should fall on the producer (Jannsen, 1981). He also made it apparent that food and drug products need to be clearly and accurately labeled.

Collectively, public concerns about food safety would be instrumental in providing the climate for drug safety legislation. Yet, as Anderson notes, "the effort to pass a general anti-adulteration law was doomed to frustration" and the timing for such a law was not yet right (1958: 78). This climate for legislation was eventually enhanced as a result of changes in medical science and the "revolution" in bacteriology, which greatly expanded the possibilities for medicinal treatments and stemming disease, as well as the transformations of the Progressive era, which provided the social and political conditions for change.

Concerns over preservatives and food safety eventually triggered the passage of the first significant drug safety laws. As in other countries around the world, drug tragedies provided the impetus for landmark drug laws in the United States. Deadly reactions to a diphtheria vaccine in children in Camden, N.J., and St. Louis spurred the passage of the Biological Controls Act of 1902. In addition, turn-of-the-century public concerns persisted over the unsanitary conditions persistent throughout the U.S. meat-packing industry. Such concerns were exemplified in Upton Sinclair's depiction of the Chicago stockyards in *The Jungle* in 1906. This concern over the safety of meats coupled with the political climate of the Progressive era led to the passage of the Meat Inspection Act of 1906. Not coincidentally, Congress passed the Pure Food and Drugs Act on the very same day in 1906. The vote in Congress over this first significant piece of drug safety legislation was quite convincing (241–17 in the House of Representatives and 63–4 in the Senate).

The passage of the 1906 law reflects the skillful political maneuvering of Harvey Wiley, and Wiley's Bureau of Chemistry (so renamed in 1901) was then charged with administering the Pure Food and Drugs Act. Wiley was a "magnificent crusader" and had an uncanny ability to attract a diverse variety of consumer groups in the push for antiadulteration legislation (Silverman and Lee, 1974: 84). For instance, Wiley enlisted the support of the Women's Christian Temperance Union, which was primarily concerned about the problems alcohol was causing to society. Wiley also earned the support of a number of commercial interests, including the American Society for the Prevention of the Adulteration of Food, which represented the interests of grocers. Agricultural interests, especially farmers, sought protection from fraud induced by adulteration. Wiley's contribution to the momentous political achievement of the passage of the 1906 law is perhaps best captured by Young:

> The Pure Food and Drugs Act marks a mighty turning point in patent medicine history. For more than a century, American proprietors had been free to mix whatever they wanted and promote it however they

wished. In such an atmosphere "the toadstool millionaires" had flour-
ished. Now, with Dr. Wiley's law, the concept of control over proprietary remedy promotion was firmly written into national policy.
(1961: 244)

The PFDA focused mainly on food, but it also featured a drug provision that dealt with consumer fraud and safety. The primary questions
about drug substances centered on their purity and labeling in an effort
to eliminate medical quackery. In the 1906 law, Congress gave government regulators the authority to seize adulterated or misbranded products and enabled the regulators to remove unsafe drugs from the market.
In this case, adulterated products were those whose contents deviated
from the formulas listed in the two national formularies, the *U.S. Pharmacopoeia* and the *National Formulary*. Similarly, misbranded products
were those that were sold under a false name or those whose packaging
included false or misleading statements. In effect, the law transformed
the *USP* and *NF* "from private publications into official standards for
drug manufacture" (Temin, 1980: 31). Yet, despite drug safety concerns,
no premarket regulations were included in the 1906 law.

The law also had a significant political impact on the Department of
Agriculture's Bureau of Chemistry. The Bureau of Chemistry had created its own drug-testing lab in 1903.[42] The 1906 law, seen as a political victory for Wiley, led to an increase in the size of the Bureau of
Chemistry. According to Temin, "the bureau's appropriation rose by a
factor of five and its employees by a factor of four between 1906 and
1908" (1980: 32). However, in regulatory terms, the bureau (and later
the FDA) was not given the legal jurisdiction to prevent false advertising for drug products. This failure was perhaps the single greatest weak-
ness of the 1906 law (Jackson, 1970). Enforcement responsibilities for
the Pure Food and Drugs Act were divided among several agencies
including the Departments of Agriculture, Commerce, Treasury, Justice,
and Labor. The task of enforcement against false advertising was left to
the Federal Trade Commission (FTC).

As shown in Table 3.1, the passage of the 1906 Pure Food and
Drugs Act was reflective of the state-societal relations of the Progressive era and a period of national regulatory authority that Eisner refers
to as the "market regime." The late nineteenth and early twentieth cen-
turies were a time when industrialization and urbanization were rapidly
changing the nature of U.S. society. The election of Theodore Roosevelt
in 1900 enhanced the Progressive movement and though Roosevelt's
agenda was generally pro-business, this was also the era in which

antitrust and regulation of business interests expanded dramatically. The period witnessed the enactment of a core of regulatory initiatives—the Interstate Commerce Act (1887), the Sherman Antitrust Act (1890), the Federal Reserve Act (1913), and the Clayton Act (1914)—that would become the cornerstone for the regulation of U.S. business in the twentieth century.

Consequently, the safety and purity of food and drugs provided an important area for the expansion of the regulatory state, but one in which business interests were taken into consideration. In keeping with Eisner's notion of the market regime, "Markets were emphasized because of their economic function as decentralized systems of exchange . . . they symbolized personal independence and local autonomy . . . [and] a return to the market was an affirmation of the economic structure that was being eroded by the changes of the period" (2000: 28). Thus, the food and drug regulation that emerged during this time ensured that "the choices of what drugs should be produced and what drugs should be bought were left entirely in the hands of private producers and consumers" (Temin, 1980: 31).

The underlying premise of the 1906 law was to use market-based forces to expose fraudulent behavior and drive "quacks" out of business. Its focus was largely based on minimizing misrepresentation. Short of imposing premarket regulations, government strategy targeted postmarket activities, such as seizing adulterated products (Bureau of Chemistry) and prohibiting false advertising (FTC). The regulations emanating from the Bureau of Chemistry were geared toward restricting "false" or "misleading" labels.

Over time, the bureau's regulations on the accuracy of therapeutic claims were eventually challenged in the courts.[43] The U.S. Supreme Court ultimately decided that manufacturers could not be prosecuted for making false *therapeutic* claims about a product because in many instances it was impossible to determine whether or not such claims were true. In response to the legal challenges and the Court's decision, Congress enacted the Sherley amendment in 1912 to further define misbranded items as those that were "false and fraudulent." The effect of this amendment was that "the government was saddled with the exceedingly difficult task of proving fraudulent intent in every misbranding case" (Jackson, 1970: 4–5). This turned out to be difficult, according to Temin, "for the simple reason that the producer could always claim ignorance" (1980: 34). Thus, the law was greatly limited in that the burden of proof remained with the government to demonstrate that a given

product was unsafe and the Bureau of Chemistry was unable to effectively challenge potentially dubious claims about therapeutic effectiveness.[44] This flaw in the 1906 law and its 1912 amendment would be
exposed over the following decades.

The impetus of food safety as the primary motivation for early drug
safety laws indicates that the pharmaceutical industry and the medical profession were not yet established as powerful actors in the policy subsystem
in 1906. The worldwide therapeutic armamentarium advanced considerably over the course of the twentieth century. Such advances were driven
largely by landmark discoveries in medical science that were made possible through the expanding use of chemical synthesis. For instance, Paul
Ehrlich coined his discovery of arsphenamine (Salvarsan) in 1911 a
"magic bullet" in the treatment of syphilis (Davis, 2000). Beyond the treatment of syphilis, however, the discovery of arsphenamine was a remarkable example of the fruits of a process of building a "chemically synthesized compound with specific activity against an infectious pathogen
which leaves the infected individual relatively untouched" (Davis, 2000:
38). The discovery of Salvarsan was certainly not accidental and can
largely be attributed to the persistence of researchers like Ehrlich. As John
Davis notes, Ehrlich had studied more than 600 compounds by the time he
had come across the effects of Salvarsan as an anti-syphilis drug. Eighteen
years after Ehrlich's discovery of Salvarsan, Alexander Fleming discovered penicillin as a remarkable antibacterial agent in 1929.

It was also during this period that support for a national health system was increasing in Europe. Similar efforts were under way in the
United States, as the medical profession there was increasing in stature.
By this time, the American Medical Association (AMA), which had
been established in 1847, was only starting to gain political clout
(Porter, 1997). The AMA supported compulsory health insurance, a
position supported in the pages of the *Journal of the American Medical
Association* (*JAMA*) (Duffy, 1979). Unlike in Europe, however, the concept of national health insurance in the United States was met with
"shrill denunciations" of socialism and the perception that "health insurance was the road to bolshevism" (Duffy, 1979: 19). During this time
period, according to John Duffy, "Among the many explanations for the
failure of health insurance are America's preoccupation with the war,
the decline of Progressivism, the opposition of insurance companies and
other vested interests and the charge that its proponents conducted the
campaign on too intellectual a level" (18–19). Thus, most of the debate
over national health insurance had quieted considerably by the 1920s.[45]

The lack of a national health insurance program in the United States was critical for at least two reasons. First, the AMA was not yet a highly powerful political force that could get its wishes on this issue. Despite its failures in pushing for compulsory health insurance at this time, the AMA did play an important role in evaluating new medicinal products. During this time it established its own drug-testing lab in Chicago. The AMA lab would become an important nongovernmental arbiter of new medicinal products because the AMA prohibited the advertisement of drug products in the pages of *JAMA* until the drug gained the organization's seal of approval.

Second, the lack of a centralized health insurance system meant the absence of a key institutional linkage between government and the drug industry. This is not a trivial point, even in the current context of medicines regulation. Unlike the experience in many European countries, the U.S. government does not have a direct, vested interest in the economic success of its pharmaceutical industry. That is, while the U.S. government is a major purchaser of pharmaceutical products, it does not enjoy anything like the monopsony position of governments with centralized, national health services.[46] So whereas many European countries with centralized health systems have long been forced to maintain a balance between promoting the domestic pharmaceutical industry and regulating the products it markets, the U.S. government has been guided by a sole focus—regulating the pharmaceutical industry. Consequently, an increasingly centralized (and formal) regulatory apparatus emerged during the early phases of drug regulation.

## Responding to Tragedy: The 1938 Federal Food, Drug and Cosmetic Act

Though Wiley resigned from the Bureau of Chemistry in 1912, he would continue his lifelong crusade against adulteration by founding the *Good Housekeeping Magazine* Institute for Consumer Protection. Wiley was succeeded at the Bureau of Chemistry by Carl Alsberg, an M.D. by training. According to Jannsen, "Research, education, and cooperation with State and local officials were basic elements in Dr. Alsberg's policy of administration" (1981: 41). In comparing his tenure as bureau chief to the Wiley era, Alsberg once noted, "I have no desire to be known as a great personage, a fighting character or a man who has killed a dragon."[47] Thus, aside from the Sherley amendment, there would be very little changes to federal drug law over the next two decades. As Young (1967: 159) points out, "During the golden glow of prosperity particularly, the political climate had not been conducive to reform."

Despite the lack of congressional modification to federal drug statutes, several administrative reorganizations would soon follow. The Food, Drug, and Insecticide Administration was created in 1927. This administrative reorganization enabled the federal government to separate the roles of agricultural research and law enforcement and to secure more funding for the purposes of law enforcement (Jannsen, 1981). A few years later, in 1931, the agency was renamed the Food and Drug Administration.

In the decades following the passage of the Pure Food and Drugs Act, consumers became increasingly concerned with fraudulent behavior in the food and drug market. The 1906 law was plagued by three serious flaws (Silverman and Lee, 1974). First, though it offered some degree of control over impure foods, it maintained relatively weak control over impure drugs. Second, many people accepted the notion that the mere existence of the 1906 law was an indication that issues of drug impurity had been resolved. Finally, and most important, the 1906 law provided the Bureau of Chemistry with relatively little enforcement capability.

These concerns were epitomized by the publication of two books in the genre that came to be known as "guinea pig" muckraking: Stuart Chase and F. J. Schlink's *Your Money's Worth* in 1927 and Arthur Kallet and Schlink's *100,000,000 Guinea Pigs* in 1933. The former was a best seller and the latter was a Sinclair-like exposé of the food, drug, and cosmetic markets. The latter book proclaimed, "In the eyes of the law we are all guinea pigs, and any scoundrel who takes it into his head to enter the drug or food business can experiment on us" (Jackson, 1970: 17). Kallet and Schlink took aim at the inherent dangers existing in everyday household products, including products such as Kellogg's All-Bran, Pebeco and Pepsodent toothpastes, Ex-Lax, and Bromo-Seltzer.[48] Their first chapter, entitled "The Great American Guinea Pig," begins, "A hundred million Americans act as unwitting test animals in a gigantic experiment with poisons, conducted by the food, drug, and cosmetic manufacturers" (1933: ix). Similar, though less dramatic, concerns about fraudulent behavior also regularly appeared in national magazines such as *Collier's Weekly* and the *Ladies Home Journal,* as well as scientific publications like *JAMA.*

As drug law historian Charles Jackson noted, this 1930s brand of muckraking differed significantly from the muckraking that occurred thirty years earlier in regard to the prevailing view toward government regulation. Whereas the turn-of-the-century muckraking of the Progressive era was supportive of increased government regulation for consumer protection, the 1930s-style muckraking was widely critical of government regulators, especially the Department of Agriculture, which continued to maintain jurisdiction over food and drug regulation. Nonetheless, earlier muckraking failed to generate enough momentum necessary to revise the original drug safety legislation during the second two decades of the twentieth century, and 1930s muckracking ultimately served as a precursor for the second phase of U.S. drug regulation.

The 1930s was a major period for reconsidering and ultimately restructuring drug safety and regulatory policy. World War I had greatly accelerated the evolution of the U.S. pharmaceutical industry. Drug development was increasing rapidly, and the war had led to a greater self-reliance for the domestic pharmaceutical industry. The industry responded by becoming increasingly science-based, experiencing tremendous growth and momentum toward larger firms (Liebenau, 1987). In terms of drug discovery, Duncan Reekie estimated that 61.1 percent of new drug discoveries between 1941 and 1963 originated in the United States (1975: 24).

The onset of World War I also signaled the close of the Progressive period and the market regime. The interwar years and the Great Depression brought about the New Deal period and the "associational" regulatory regime. With millions of Americans out of work and the economy at its nadir, New Deal programs reflected the rise of the welfare state in the United States. Perhaps more important, in the context of regulation of business activities, "This period was responsible for more regulatory initiatives than any other in U.S. history" (Eisner, 2000: 74). Further, unlike the Progressive era's market regime, the New Deal era's prevailing regulatory regime of "associationalism" saw government regulators working closely with private interests in the regulation of consumer products (Eisner, 2000).

Unlike the experience with a crusader like Wiley several decades earlier, skillful political maneuvering within the policy subsystem was provided by at least three primary figures. Walter Campbell had joined the Bureau of Chemistry in 1907 as one of the agency's first food and drug inspectors. Campbell eventually rose through the ranks to become the bureau's chief inspector and later the acting bureau chief in 1921. Unlike his predecessors Wiley and Alsberg, who were trained as scientists, Campbell was an attorney. During his tenure as an inspector, he was instrumental in developing legal procedures that enabled the bureau to seize violative products (Jannsen, 1981).

On the election of Franklin Roosevelt in 1932, Rexford Tugwell became the assistant secretary of agriculture. Tugwell, previously a Columbia University economist, was part of the "brain trust" assembled by Roosevelt in Washington. Tugwell was universally unpopular with those in the business community, however, largely because of his arrogance and, more important, his preference for the desirability of planned economies.

A chance encounter between Campbell and Tugwell laid the initial groundwork for reforming the 1906 law. As Young (1967), Jackson (1970), and Temin (1980) recount the encounter, Campbell and Tugwell met a few days after Roosevelt's inauguration in 1933 to review Campbell's need for Tugwell's signature on a particular matter. During the course of this encounter, Campbell and Tugwell got around to discussing the inadequacies of existing food and drug legislation. According to Young, "That same afternoon Campbell was again summoned to Tugwell's office. 'Mr. Campbell,' the Assistant Secretary said, 'since I saw you this morning I have talked with the President. I repeated our conversation to him, and he has authorized a revision of the Food and Drugs Act'" (1967: 159).

Shortly following this encounter, a formal proposal was drafted by Department of Agriculture and Bureau of Chemistry staffers and introduced in the Senate by New York Democrat Royal Copeland. The bill presented "radical" changes to existing drug law (Jackson, 1970). Specifically, it increased governmental control over proprietary medicines, included provisions for cosmetics, and gave the agency more authority in the areas of advertising, labeling, and enforcement. "The lines of revision . . . were not theoretical propositions but were dictated by twenty-seven years of experience with the old statute" (Jackson, 1970: 29).

Despite attempts at political maneuvering in the policy subsystem, the bill gained little momentum. Recalling Wiley's use of the "Poison Squad" some thirty years earlier, Campbell created the "Chamber of Horrors" in 1933. Campbell showed senators graphic pictures illustrating the harmful effects of unsafe drugs. Interestingly, though, the Senate bill was referred to as the Tugwell bill. Tugwell's association as the "archenemy of big business" (Silverman and Lee, 1974: 85) meant that the bill would not make significant progress through the legislative process. In linking the 1930s legislative debate with that preceding the passage of the 1906 law, Young notes: "[Harvey] Wiley had been a bureaucratic wild man to opponents of legislation during the first decade of the century. During the thirties, Tugwell was cast in a similar role" (1967: 161). Given the distaste for Tugwell, the strenuous opposition from various industry groups to the bill's proposals, and the timing of the Great Depression, there was little chance for the immediate passage of such a bill. According to Jannsen:

> The "Tugwell bill" was a legislative disaster. The opposition of industry and advertising interests to this New Deal legislation was total and overwhelming. When the smoke cleared away the Senate sponsor, Royal S. Copeland, M.D., of New York, aided by FDA officials, consumer-minded Congressmen, attorneys, and staff members, began the laborious process of fashioning a bill that could be enacted, yet not surrender essential consumer protection. A bitter 5-year legislative battle began. (1981: 37)

In the 1930s, tragedy would again serve as the basis for increased regulation. The Massengill Company marketed a liquid form of the drug, sulfanilamide, in the late 1930s. The drug, previously marketed in a tablet variety, had been remarkably effective in the fight against infections. As sulfanilamide was mixed with the chemical compound diethylene glycol, however, the chemical conversion from tablet to liquid unwittingly created a highly toxic solvent. The solution was examined by its manufacturer for a variety of factors including taste, appearance, and smell, but the potential toxicity of the combination was never checked. As a result, an estimated 107 Americans—mainly children—eventually perished from ingesting the so-called Elixir Sulfanilamide solution (Ballentine, 1981). The episode greatly exposed the weaknesses of the existing drug legislation. Ironically, the FDA did not possess the necessary authority under the 1906 law to prosecute the Massengill Company for the tragic deaths (Temin, 1980). Instead, the company was forced only to pay a fine on the grounds that the product was mislabeled.

Shortly following this disaster, Congress dramatically centralized the drug approval process by enacting the Food, Drug and Cosmetic Act in 1938. The major structural advance of this legislation was the requiring of manufacturers, for the first time, to demonstrate the safety of a drug prior to marketing. Before marketing their products manufacturers had to obtain the stamp of approval from the FDA in the form of a successfully completed new drug application. The NDA was required to satisfactorily demonstrate evidence of safety through successful testing of the compound. In addition to the preapproval safety provisions, the law gave the FDA statutory authority to inspect firms as well as the authority to remove a drug from the market if it was found to be unsafe. The 1938 act also included a labeling provision that made it illegal for drug products to contain false or misleading labels. With this provision, regulation of drug promotion was now divided between the FDA and the FTC. The FTC would continue to regulate drug advertising while the FDA played an important role in regulating drug labeling.

In summary, the 1938 law represented a significant shift in regulatory strategy. First, the New Deal period of the 1930s reflected a time of expansionist state political instruments. In addition to enforcing against false advertising and mislabeling, the 1938 law expanded the regulatory framework to include a preemptive attempt to ensure public safety. Temin notes, "the 1938 law abandoned the market setting for direct commands in specified circumstances" (1980: 45). Thus, beginning in 1938, the federal government asserted itself in seeking to keep harmful drugs out of the hands of the public by creating a centralized regulatory apparatus that placed the responsibility of proving safety into the hands of manufacturers rather than the FDA.

This shift toward centralization naturally invites the question about the extent of the role played by drug-related voluntary organizations in the United States. Perhaps most critically, the 1938 law predates the founding of the leading trade association for pharmaceutical manufacturers. The Pharmaceutical Manufacturers Association (PMA) was not founded until 1958. Thus, while voluntary organizations were significantly influencing drug regulation throughout Europe, similar entities were not yet in place in the United States.

The Food, Drug and Cosmetic Act forms the current statutory basis for new drug regulation in the United States. Following the 1938 act, drug law changed relatively little over the next two and a half decades. The 1951 Durham-Humphrey amendment, which defined which drugs would be made available only by prescription, was one exception. Requiring the use of prescriptions greatly changed the relationship between doctors, pharmacists, and patients.

The food additives amendment, or Delaney clause, was a second exception in 1958. Though the Delaney clause is concerned more with food additives than new drugs and affects the Environmental Protection Agency and the U.S. Department of Agriculture perhaps more than the FDA, in many ways it is emblematic of the controversial nature of food and drug regulations in the United States. With increasing numbers of Americans dying from cancer in the 1940s, the Delaney clause provided an absolute regulatory standard by prohibiting any substance found to cause cancer in food additives. Despite numerous attempts to repeal it, Delaney continues to remain a prominent part of the Food, Drug and Cosmetic Act. An absolute standard of zero tolerance for carcinogens seemed perfectly reasonable in 1958, a time when existing measurement techniques enabled residues to be measured only in parts per thousand. Due to improved measurement techniques, however, in many cases carcinogenic residues can be measured as precisely as parts per quintillion today.[49] Yet the FDA has very little room for regulatory discretion under the statutory provisions of Delaney. Thus, Delaney has generated numerous regulatory debates over the years and, more important, foreshadows some of the many regulatory difficulties routinely encountered by the FDA.

## Conclusion

Building on the discussion of agency theory and structural theories of regulation from the previous chapter, I have developed a framework for understanding regulatory policy change. The early history of U.S. medicines regulation is examined in the context of this framework. This historical experience is important to the varying philosophies toward Type I and II errors and provides a foundation for understanding contemporary regulatory policies and practices. U.S. medicines regulation can be characterized by several distinct periods over the course of the twentieth century. Each period possesses a distinctive regulatory philosophy, as well as a specific set of institutions designed to shape and constrain individual behavior.

Three themes are particularly important for understanding how agency theory can be used to understand U.S. drug regulation. First, interest group politics provide an important dimension for understanding structural theories of regulation. Second, the enacting coalition seeks to make the regulatory institution highly durable so that the actors in the policy subsystem will continue to derive benefits long after the enacting coalition has been dismantled. Finally, because they create a direct linkage between political interests and institutional arrangements, policy monopolies provide an important element of cohesion leading to long-term policy stability.

Pioneering advances in the therapeutic sciences, the birth of the modern pharmaceutical industry, and drug-related tragedies greatly shaped the development of the nation's early drug regulatory framework.

These types of developments, when occurring on a relatively large scale, created opportunities for politicians, regulators, consumers, and public interest groups to mobilize political resources. The mobilizing of these interests around the turn of the twentieth century in conjunction with the skillful political maneuvering of Harvey Wiley at the Bureau of Chemistry led to an enacting coalition that generated the nation's first major piece of drug safety legislation in 1906, the Pure Food and Drugs Act. As the new legislation emerged, the enacting coalition was able to create structures and processes that, while consistent with the broader regulatory approaches of the period, were able to greatly shape and constrain the nature of regulatory behavior.

The regulatory structures and processes created by the 1906 Pure Food and Drugs Act were relatively weak, however. This is perhaps not surprising, given the broader politics of the Progressive era. This was a period dominated by pro-business agendas in the White House and Congress. As Kallet and Schlink suggested, "no officer of the Administration has been able to forget that the Administration is in politics—which to a realist means in business—and that science is, for all administrative purposes, out, so far as it concerns food and drug control operations" (1933: 205–206). Consequently, regulatory institutions featured market-based devices to reflect the personal independence and local autonomy that characterized the period (Eisner, 2000). Moreover, this was not an active time for social regulation in the United States, in general. As Eisner, Jeff Worsham, and Evan Ringquist point out, "Although there were social regulations in the Progressive Era, they were a minor part of the story" (2000: 39).

In the 1906 law, Congress gave the Department of Agriculture and the Bureau of Chemistry regulatory authority over drug substances and food additives. Although congressional appropriations to the Bureau of Chemistry would increase (as the focus on agency structure might suggest), the bureau was not given the legal authority to prevent false advertising, and overall enforcement duties were divided across a number of agencies. In short, the institutional mechanisms afforded to the Bureau of Chemistry were highly limited. Though the 1912 Sherley amendment enhanced the primary principal-agent contract, the contract would remain relatively weak over the next two and a half decades. The Bureau of Chemistry thus persisted with relatively limited regulatory tools at its disposal.

The structures and processes shaping the U.S. approach toward regulating new medicines would take a significant turn with the passage of the 1938 Food, Drug and Cosmetic Act. In the 1938 law, Congress greatly centralized the regulatory process and enabled the FDA to take on a much greater regulatory role. This would begin a long tradition of highly centralized, statutory control. Though the passage of the 1906 Pure Food and Drugs Act represents the nation's first significant piece of drug safety legislation, it had relatively little regulatory teeth. Instead, the FDA's origins in the 1930s as a law enforcement agency have guided the agency's actions in preventing harmful drugs from entering the market. This background becomes highly significant when considering a regulatory agency's propensity to commit or avoid Type I and II errors. This examination of the two early periods of U.S. drug regulation reveals the significance of both exogenous shocks (created by drug-related tragedies) and definable institutional structures (as developed by the enacting coalition).

Examining the first two periods in the history of U.S. drug regulation provides a useful case study for understanding how agency theory can be used to explain the creation and design of institutional structures that govern the regulation of new medicines. In addition, once a particular institutional arrangement is erected, this case study is useful for demonstrating how certain causal mechanisms need to come together in order to modify the initial institutional structure. Agency theory is based on the premise that due to a variety of considerations—typically time, information, or resource-based constraints—political principals delegate authority to agents in order to carry out certain tasks. In addition, a contract formalizes the nature of the exchange or transaction and principals must monitor such exchanges to ensure that the agent will carry out the task in a manner acceptable to the principal. Such contracts typically endure until they no longer serve the interests of principals, agents, or both.

That regulatory policy is characterized by long periods of stability suggests the relative acceptance by principals and agents of the terms of their primary agreement. After time, however, the terms of the contract become less acceptable and the contract is occasionally interrupted by an exogenous shock leading to a policy punctuation. As the following chapter illustrates, the third period of drug regulation centralized U.S. drug review even further. External shocks led to a new, definable institutional structure that clearly moved the FDA to seek to avoid Type II errors. In this case, the timing of particular events (e.g., drug-related tragedies and advances in pharmaceutical science) and the varying levels of influence exerted by actors in the policy subsystem once again precipitated the punctuation. These experiences in the early and mid-twentieth century would greatly condition the nation's evolving regulatory approach.

# 4

## THE DRUG LAG DEBATE AND DEMANDS FOR REFORM

N o politician ever lost votes by denouncing the
bureaucracy.
*—James Q. Wilson, political scientist*

The third period of U.S. drug review was precipitated by a major drug
tragedy primarily occurring in Europe. The revelation of thalidomide's
side effects exposed the inherent weaknesses in many European regulatory authorities. This tragedy, which fueled a lingering sense of vulner-
ability in the United States, coupled with several gradual changes in the
U.S. policy subsystem, eventually led to the creation of yet another
definable institutional structure. The resulting structure further centralized the U.S. regulatory approach and made the avoidance of Type II
errors the FDA's foremost objective. The result of this institutional
structure (i.e., the 1962 Kefauver amendments to the Food, Drug and
Cosmetic Act) was to profoundly shape FDA behavior. Immediately
after the Kefauver amendments went into effect, the agency's cautious
approach to drug approvals was widely embraced by most actors in the
policy subsystem. Safety was regarded as the sole concern, even at the
risk of potentially committing Type I errors.

However, over time, the strength of the principal-agent contract,
which enabled the agency to focus on avoiding Type II errors, waned.
This weakening was largely the result of increasing criticism of the
FDA's regulatory performance in the 1970s and 1980s from a variety of
sources. Critics from academia and industry charged that the highly
centralized regulatory framework stifled drug innovation and impeded
pharmaceutical industry competitiveness. By this time, the relative success of European regulatory review agencies—especially in Great

Britain—led to the so-called drug lag debate. In this chapter, I examine the primary institutional structure and regulatory philosophy of this period, as well as the agency's overwhelming concern with avoiding Type II errors. I also consider the nature of the drug lag debate and its significance in leading to eventual policy change.

## The Thalidomide Tragedy
## and the 1962 Kefauver Amendments

While drug laws were changed relatively little during the 1940s and 1950s, the pharmaceutical industry continued to grow dramatically (Liebenau, 1987). The "therapeutic revolution" and the "Golden Age" of drug discovery were under way following World War II. Industry profits grew as well. Such growth captured the attention of Tennessee senator Estes Kefauver who initiated a series of congressional inquiries during the late 1950s. Kefauver's original concern over drug safety and efficacy was minimal, as his chief interest centered on drug pricing and the immense profits accumulating to pharmaceutical firms. Kefauver's drug reform bill, which sought to shorten the life of drug patents, received little support.[50]

A short time later, however, the shocking news of the thalidomide tragedy spread rapidly and the drug safety issue resurfaced. Between 1959 and 1962, the German manufacturer, Chemie Grünenthal, marketed thalidomide, a tranquilizing drug, throughout Europe. Thousands of pregnant women were among those taking the drug, and it was soon discovered that thalidomide was linked with several extremely harmful side effects, including neural disorders causing birth defects in newborn babies.[51] Tragically, as many as 10,000 babies were born throughout Europe with a condition known as phocomelia (from the Greek for "seal limbs"). The thalidomide disaster occurred largely because of the lack of testing for safety or potential side effects resulting from its usage. The negative effects of this drug rocked much of western Europe and beyond. The reverberations were also felt in the United States.

Although thalidomide was never officially marketed in the United States, it was used by an unknown number of Americans on an experimental basis.[52] Much of the credit for keeping thalidomide off the U.S. market was given to FDA reviewer Dr. Frances Kelsey (see Fried, 1998). The Merrell Corporation had submitted an application to the FDA to market thalidomide in the early 1960s, but Dr. Kelsey was skeptical of the drug's purported effectiveness and consistently pushed for the Merrell Corporation to provide additional safety data. The drug was not approved during this time, and the news from Europe ultimately sealed the fate of the application.

To reward her regulatory persistence in dealing with the thalidomide application, President John Kennedy bestowed the prestigious Distinguished Presidential Service Award on Dr. Kelsey in 1962. Not only did the award recognize Dr. Kelsey's efforts, it also symbolized the agency's regulatory efforts to ensure public health by protecting consumers from potentially unsafe products. Dr. Kelsey has remained a distinguished employee of the agency well into her eighties. With her continuing presence, one agency official told me, the FDA retains a constant reminder of the devastating effects of thalidomide and an ongoing symbol that the fundamental mission of the agency is to keep harmful drugs off the market.

Nonetheless, the European experience with thalidomide provided a clear illustration of the potentially disastrous effects of unsafe medicines. The thalidomide experience also acted as the catalyst for the passage of the 1962 amendments to the Food, Drug and Cosmetic Act, also known as the Kefauver amendments.[53] Prior to the thalidomide disaster, President Kennedy differed with Kefauver on many aspects of pharmaceutical reform (Harris, 1964). Their differences were particularly apparent over the issue of pharmaceutical pricing. With respect to drug safety and efficacy, however, their positions were quite similar. Kennedy's consumer protection speech of March 15, 1962, articulated his position very clearly:

> New drugs are being placed on the market every day, without any requirement of advance proof that they will be effective in treating the conditions for which they are recommended. Over 20 percent of the new drugs available since 1956 were found to be incapable of bearing out one or more of their sponsors' claims on what their effect would be. This means that people are not only wasting their money but are also suffering needlessly. (*Pharmaceutical Journal*, 1962: 344)

From the pharmaceutical industry's perspective, government regulation generally involved (and continues to this day to involve) three major areas. Each regulatory area has direct implications for industry profitability. These three areas are (1) the protection of *patents* on new compounds, (2) the *licensing* of new products, and (3) *pricing* and reimbursement strategies for marketed products. Given the expensive nature of drug development (both in time and resources), protecting drug patents has long been a priority of the industry and its leading trade associations. Additionally, the United States remains one of the few countries in the world that allows virtually unrestricted pricing of pharmaceutical products.[54] Since Kefauver's inquiries were related to industry profitability, the industry response to governmental reform efforts focused primarily on avoiding pricing and patenting restrictions.

Consequently, the pharmaceutical industry was generally supportive of the president's consumer protection proposals. The president of the Pharmaceutical Manufacturers Association, Dr. Austin Smith, remarked:

> We are pleased to note that the President has not endorsed the proposals of that subcommittee to curb drug research by restricting patentability of new discoveries and by requiring compulsory licenses of all drug patents. We look forward to cooperation with the Congress and the administration in development of sound legislation reflecting substantial proportions of the President's recommendations. (*Pharmaceutical Journal*, 1962: 345)

In seeking to avoid pricing and patenting restrictions, the industry apparently underestimated the extent to which the 1962 amendments restricted the licensing and marketing of new drugs. This misjudgment provides a prime example of the significance of regulatory processes as highlighted by structural theories of regulation. Specifically, the 1962 amendments required drug manufacturers not only to demonstrate evidence of safety in their premarketing testing but also to provide substantial evidence regarding a drug's effectiveness. This "proof of efficacy" requirement called for firms to demonstrate in clinical trials that the drug behaved in accordance with the claims of the manufacturer. This provision would have a tremendous influence on both the pharmaceutical industry and the regulatory politics at the FDA.

A second notable provision of the law called for the introduction of the investigational new drug application (IND). The creation of the IND made it necessary for firms to gain FDA approval prior to beginning the clinical testing process in humans. Thus, the stamp of an FDA approval was now required at two different junctures in the development process: prior to clinical testing on humans (the IND) and prior to marketing to the public (the NDA). These two provisions, "proof of efficacy" and FDA approval prior to clinical testing, greatly centralized the regulatory process and also greatly added to both the length and the costs of drug development (see, for example, Grabowski and Vernon, 1983).

In addition, the amendments led to a more active regulatory role for the FDA. Prior to 1962, an NDA became effective automatically if the application satisfactorily demonstrated proof of safety. Following the

1962 amendments, it was up to the FDA to grant an approval for the NDA. Thus, the balance of the FDA's review activity had shifted in favor of increased regulatory authority and responsibility. This provides a clear example of how the change in regulatory process enabled the agency to become more assertive in seeking to avoid Type II errors.

Finally, the law also asserted that any drugs introduced to the market between 1938 and 1962 would also be required to undergo testing with regard to their effectiveness. (Drugs introduced prior to 1938 were exempted or "grandfathered" from the 1962 amendments.) This provision created a rather large practical problem for the FDA. The agency was not at all prepared to deal with the tremendous backlog that it was about to face in having to review pre-1962 drugs for efficacy. At the time, FDA commissioner James Goddard estimated that approximately 3,000 applications had been filed in the period 1938–1962 and roughly another 1,000 products were marketed without applications (IOM, 1992). In order to handle this backlog, the FDA took an unprecedented step by relying on two of the national academies to conduct drug reviews for efficacy. In what later became known as the Drug Efficacy Study, the FDA enlisted the help of the National Academy of Sciences and the National Research Council (NRC) to assist in reviewing drugs that were introduced between 1938 and 1962.[55] Though the National Academy of Sciences and the NRC officially acted in advisory capacities, their judgments were often the decisive factor in the agency's decision (IOM, 1992). The reviews in the Drug Efficacy Study were eventually completed in 1969.

In summary, with the 1962 Kefauver amendments, the enacting coalition in Congress rewrote the principal-agent contract with the FDA and drug regulation became more codified and more centralized. Perhaps more important, however, the agency's safety and efficacy threshold was raised considerably. In essence, Congress enabled the agency to take on a more active regulatory role. Grabowski and Vernon characterize this approach as "one of steady evolution away from . . . making the market work better . . . toward . . . [the] approach of strong centralized regulatory control over firms' decisions about pharmaceutical marketing and testing" (1983: 8). Since 1962, pharmaceutical manufacturers have been required to get regulatory approval at two major junctures in the drug development process: prior to clinical testing (the testing of the drug in humans) and prior to marketing the drug to the general public. In addition, the burden of proof was placed on the manufacturer to demonstrate that the drug was both safe and effective prior to its marketing. These three criteria reflect the strong congressional and agency concern to avoid Type II errors by keeping potentially harmful drug products out of the hands of consumers. These criteria also provide an excellent opportunity to once again consider the nature of structural theories of regulation and the analytical emphasis on regulatory structure and process.

In order to understand fully the effects of the 1962 amendments and the increased regulatory centralization, it is useful to consider two significant implications of the policy change. The first involves a closer examination of a critical regulatory process—the agency's standard used for determining the efficacy of a drug. The second implication involves the effect the amendments, in general, and the efficacy standard, in particular, had on the FDA's regulatory performance. The 1962 changes led to the resulting slowdown of FDA approvals in the decades to follow and triggered the transnational "drug lag" debate.

## The FDA's Efficacy Standard: A Critical Process

The FDA's standard for determining the efficacy of a new drug remains at the heart of U.S. drug regulation. Efficacy is the measure of whether the drug performs in accordance with the claims of the manufacturer. A drug being considered for FDA approval is determined to be efficacious if its therapeutic effects are consistent with manufacturers' claims and if it performs better than a placebo. Because the efficacy standard emerged as a political compromise between the pharmaceutical industry and the enacting congressional coalition of the 1960s, the standard can be used to carefully examine the agency's fundamental approach toward risk and reward.

As mentioned, the current efficacy standard was established in the 1962 Kefauver amendments. Section 505(d) of the FDCA requires that "substantial evidence" is the necessary criteria for determining the safety and efficacy of a new drug being considered for FDA approval. (See Kulynych (1999) for an excellent legal treatment of the "substantial evidence" standard.) In the same section of the law, "substantial evidence" is defined as "evidence consisting of adequate and well-controlled investigations by experts" by which it could be concluded that the drug will have its purported effect. While "substantial evidence" remains the clearly articulated guiding principle when making determinations on efficacy, the definition of "adequate and well-controlled investigations" has remained relatively ambiguous.

The FDA has been given the regulatory authority to develop its own interpretation of the statutory guidelines, including what is required to establish substantial evidence. The agency subsequently developed its interpretation of "adequate and well-controlled investigations" in 1969 (revised in 1985) through the promulgation of rules now codified in the *Code of Federal Regulations* (*CFR*). Through the *CFR* the FDA has interpreted the "adequate and well-controlled investigations" to mean that at least two well-controlled clinical trials (also known as pivotal studies) plus one confirmatory trial performed either before or after are necessary to establish efficacy (see, for example, OTA, 1982; U.S. House, 1982: 434–447; Kulynych, 1999). Other key components of the agency's statutory interpretation guiding clinical investigations include the use of blinded studies, randomization, and placebo controls.

According to many experts, the standard used by the FDA to establish the effectiveness of a drug represents the highest efficacy standard in the world (U.S. Senate, 1974). As former director of the Bureau of Drugs Richard Crout once testified before Congress: "Many countries have an effectiveness requirement in their drug laws. None other, to my knowledge, has the rigorous standard of adequate and well controlled trials, however, as the basis for judgment on effectiveness" (U.S. House, 1980: 13). Yet it is this standard, which the agency was given the bureaucratic autonomy to develop, that clearly signals the agency's approach toward avoiding Type II errors. In a sense, the agency was simply taking advantage of the autonomy it was granted as part of the prevailing principal-agent contract.

Not surprisingly, the ambiguity in the statutory language created the foundation for significant disagreements between the agency and the pharmaceutical industry over clinical testing requirements. The FDA's interpretation of "adequate and well-controlled investigations" to mean two pivotal trials plus one confirmatory study caused a great deal of consternation among pharmaceutical industry officials and members of Congress sympathetic to the industry. Those opposing this regulatory standard argued that requiring two pivotal studies places an unnecessary burden on industry and reduces the efficiency of the drug development process. These opponents argue that a single pivotal study plus the confirmatory trial should be an adequate measure for demonstrating efficacy. As a member of the industry's trade association suggested, "The second pivotal study represents an unnecessary duplication. One well-rounded study plus one smaller, confirmatory study would do quite well."

According to several industry analysts, a reduction from two to one in the required number of pivotal trials would greatly shorten the overall drug approval process. Some estimates have stated that as much as two years of development time could be eliminated if the second pivotal study were dropped (Peck, 1996). Other critics of the efficacy standard assert that the agency emphasizes safety at the expense of facilitation, discourages efficiency and innovation, and leads to imprecise drug labeling (Peck, 1995). One official, commenting specifically on the agency's universal standard, argued: "The FDA's blanket standard just doesn't make sense. Efficacy should be determined on a case-by-case basis."

Since the 1960s the agency has promulgated a number of regulations regarding clinical testing requirements. As agency rules governing the clinical testing phase have increased, the number of clinical trials per drug application has also increased. The average number of clinical studies per NDA actually doubled from thirty during the period 1977–1980 to sixty in 1989–1992 (Mulcahy, 1995). The increasing number of clinical studies for each new drug compound obviously has added greatly to the total length of drug development.[56] According to estimates by Joseph DiMasi of Tufts University's Center for the Study of Drug Development (CSDD) and his colleagues, the average duration of the clinical testing phase increased from 2.5 years in the 1960s to nearly six years during the early 1990s (DiMasi, Seibring, and Lasagna, 1994). Much of the increase can be attributed to meeting the agency's efficacy standard.

Not surprisingly, differences between industry and the FDA on this matter persist. Over the years, the agency's goal of avoiding Type II errors has frustrated pharmaceutical industry officials in the United States. As one industry executive noted, "The law rewards caution. There is no other way to put it. Industry needs to give FDA incentives for expediting the process while preserving safety."

Yet the FDA defends the "substantial evidence" standard, arguing that two pivotal trials are necessary. As one FDA officer said, "As scientists, we never rely on one trial. Results have to be confirmed and we cannot compromise this." One of the common justifications for the multiple study approach is that "sometimes the more adverse reactions aren't detected until the drug has been marketed or in a smaller niche group under study." Thus, relying on more than a single pivotal trial is consistent with the longstanding scientific practice of replicating empirical results.

The significance of this regulatory standard again points to the inherent usefulness of using structural theories of regulation as an explanatory device. The current standard used to establish efficacy— whether the drug performs in accordance with manufacturer claims— remains a critical mechanism in determining the FDA's performance. The standard is the product of 1960s legislation and has been toughened by the FDA in accordance with the agency's interests over the years. The standard rewards caution and clearly reflects the agency's preference for avoiding Type II errors.

Again, it might be useful to consider this critical regulatory process in a comparative context. This standard is perhaps the single largest difference between the U.S. regulatory approach and those taken by most European drug regulatory authorities. Three factors emerge when contrasting approaches to determining efficacy. First, the efficacy standard for new drugs in the United States is formally codified, whereas no formalized guidelines for determining efficacy exist in many European countries. Second, the evaluative standard used by the FDA is universal in that the same standard applies to virtually all new drugs. Decisions on efficacy made by many other nations' regulatory agencies are made on an individual, drug-by-drug basis. Finally, efficacy decisions typically can be differentiated by their timeliness. As one European industry official suggested, "At an earlier point in the process [the British are] willing to say, 'Okay, we think this drug is effective.' In the U.S., however, the lines have been drawn differently." The presumption is that these lines are drawn differently because of the propensity to avoid Type II errors. Nonetheless, each of these three contrasting approaches in making determinations on efficacy—formal or informal guidelines, universal or individual application of the standard, and the timeliness of such decisions—is highly indicative of the differences inherent in U.S. and European philosophies toward risk and reward.

The primary purpose of illustrating the FDA's efficacy standard has been to show the significance of a regulatory "process" in the context of agency preferences and agency performance. The FDA's strict efficacy standard was a clear reflection of both the preferences of the one-time enacting coalition (i.e., the post-thalidomide preferences of the members of Congress and other interests in the early 1960s) and the increasing agency desire during this time to avoid Type II errors. The thalidomide tragedy in Europe made a powerful impression on both congressional and agency officials. In essence, the 1962 Kefauver amendments and the efficacy standard further entrenched the FDA's role as a consumer protection agency. Through this standard, the agency's mission was to clearly protect the public from the potential hazards of unsafe or ineffective medicines. From a political standpoint, the commission of a Type II error was likely to create highly visible victims, as well as the expectation of intense political scrutiny of the regulatory agency. Consequently, the costs of committing Type II errors continued to remain a salient consideration in the minds of policymakers and regulators.

## The Drug Lag Debate

Naturally, there is a tradeoff associated with the emphasis on increased safety and efficacy standards. These standards would have a significant effect on the agency's performance in the decades following the 1962 amendments. Many agency observers and critics saw the increased safety provisions and the increased centralization of regulatory restrictions in terms of the resulting slowdown in the FDA approval process. This slowdown ultimately contributed to what became known as the international "drug lag," in which it was demonstrated that fewer drugs were made available in the United States relative to several other industrialized countries. Of those that were mutually available, it took longer for Americans to gain access to those medicines than it did patients in other countries. In effect, the drug lag debate highlighted substantial divergences in the performance of the FDA and several of its international counterparts.

The earliest and most influential voice in the drug lag debate has been William Wardell. Wardell has published articles on the drug lag for over thirty years and has often presented congressional testimony on the topic of the drug lag. A brief summary of his key findings is provided in Table 4.1.

In these analyses, Wardell found a sizable disparity in drug availability in the United States and the United Kingdom. He concluded that between 1962 and 1976, Great Britain had nearly 3.5 times as many exclusively available drugs as the United States (119:37). In addition, Wardell noted that for the drugs that were mutually available, those first introduced in Britain typically took longer to make their way into the U.S. market than vice versa. For the 110 drugs mutually available during this time period, nearly two-thirds (72) were first made available in Great Britain. The average lead-time for those 72 drugs was 2.96 years. Alternately, the average lead-time for the 38 drugs first available in the United States was only 2.19 years.

Table 4.1 Summary of Wardell and CSDD Drug Lag Studies

| | Wardell Study 1 (1962–1971) | | Wardell Study 2 (1972–1976)[a] | | CSDD Study (1977–1987) | |
|---|---|---|---|---|---|---|
| | Drug Lag[b] | | Drug Lag | | Drug Lag | |
| | NCEs | Years | NCEs | Years | NCEs | Years |
| Introduced in both countries | | | | | | |
| United Kingdom first | 43 | 2.8 | 29 | 3.2 | 114 | 5.06 |
| United States first | 25 | 2.4 | 13 | 1.8 | 41 | 2.41 |
| Same year | 14 | 0.0 | 0 | 0.0 | | |
| Total | 82 | 0.7 | 42 | 1.7 | 155 | |
| Introduced in one country | | | | | | |
| Only United Kingdom[c] | 77 | | 42 | | 70 | |
| Only United States[d] | 21 | | 16 | | 54 | |
| Total | 98 | | 58 | | 124 | |
| Overall total | 180 | | 100 | | 279 | |

Sources: Andersson (1992); Wardell (1973); Kaitin et al. (1989).
Notes: NCEs = new chemical entities.
a. Column includes eighteen NCEs with first introduction before 1972 and the second during the period 1972–1976. In Study 1 they are included as "Introduced in one country."
b. Wardell used the word "lead."
c. Includes twelve NCEs introduced in the United States during the period 1972–1976.
d. Includes six NCEs introduced in the United Kingdom during the period 1972–1976.

Throughout the 1970s Wardell was active in dueling with various FDA commissioners in the pages of medical journals over contentions about the drug lag.[57] Perhaps the fiercest of these debates took place in the *Journal of the American Medical Association* in the late 1970s. In response to some of Wardell's earlier studies, then FDA commissioner Donald Kennedy published an essay entitled "A Calm Look at 'Drug Lag.'" In the essay, Kennedy refuted many of the drug lag claims made by industry critics. Kennedy's principal suggestion was that the drug lag was "not a condition indigenous to the United States" (1978: 424). He also pointed to the absence of a second wave of "miracle drugs" in the 1960s, thus attributing the absolute lag to "the exhaustion of certain basic knowledge" in the drug industry. The "Calm Look" essay concluded with Kennedy confidently suggesting, "the argument that there is something peculiar to our domestic regulatory process that automatically deprives physicians and patients of beneficial new therapies does not stand up under analysis" (425).

A short time later, Wardell used the pages of *JAMA* to respond to Kennedy's "Calm Look" assertions. In reanalyzing the commissioner's data, Wardell suggested, "Dr. Kennedy's data show that numerically there is indeed a large lag between the United States and all the drug-developing countries of Western Europe" (1978a: 2007). Wardell went on to assert that among drugs mutually available in the United States and Great Britain, 2.5 times as many drugs became available first in the UK. He concluded by noting:

> In recent months, there has been a disquieting increase in pseudo-science and sophistry. It would be difficult to regard the 'calm look' article as a cogent argument from anyone; coming from a respected government agency [FDA] . . . it seriously underestimates the intelligence of Journal [*JAMA*] readers and other taxpayers. (2010–2011)

In the tradition established by Wardell, several subsequent international comparisons emerged. For instance, a 1980 General Accounting Office (GAO) report analyzed the 132 new drug applications submitted in 1975. Based on its analysis, the GAO concluded, "The process for approving NDAs takes a long time and needs to be improved" and that this lengthy process "delays the benefits important drugs can provide to the public" (USGAO, 1980: i, 27). In addition to examining the approval process in the United States, the GAO selected 14 of the 132 drugs analyzed for use in international comparisons. Of the five countries involved, Sweden and the United States had the longest average approval times while the UK and Switzerland had the shortest. Average approval times in Canada fell in between the other four countries.

In addition to Wardell's work, Paul de Haen conducted another series of influential drug lag studies. Through his Drug Information Service publications, de Haen is considered an industry leader in providing data on product approvals and the introduction of new drugs. De Haen analyzed the introduction and availability of 116 drugs in twelve therapeutic areas in England, France, Germany, Italy, and the United States between 1967 and 1973. He found a "lag" in some therapeutic areas in all countries, concluding that the drug lag "must be regarded as a worldwide situation" (1975: 150). In a follow-up analysis, however, de Haen (1976) surveyed twenty international pharmaceutical firms to consider the regulatory review times of the same five countries. In analyzing the reviews of forty-two drugs in thirteen therapeutic areas, his findings revealed a gap between the United States and the four European countries. Germany, for example, approved all sixteen drugs in one year or less. The UK approved eighteen of nineteen drugs (95 percent) in one year or less while the review of the lone remaining drug was complete within two years. In France, twenty-four of twenty-six new drugs (92 percent) were approved in one year or less. In Italy, thirteen of nineteen new drugs (68 percent) were approved in one year or less, and only one drug was approved after a period of three years. In contrast, in the United States the FDA approved just twelve of twenty-three drugs (52 percent) in one year or less. Moreover, eleven drugs were approved by the FDA in two years or longer, including four drugs that were not approved within four years. Thus, when considering regulatory review times, the lag between the United States and Europe was readily apparent in de Haen's view.

A significant, though later occurring, contribution to the drug lag literature was made by Kenneth Kaitin and his collaborators at the CSDD. The CSDD was formed in 1976 and since then has become a leading center for collecting and analyzing data on new drugs. Beginning in 1987, the CSDD began publishing a series of reports examining the drug approval performance of the FDA. In the first of these reports, the CSDD found that 72 percent of the drugs (specifically, new chemical entities or NCEs) approved by the FDA during the years 1985 and 1986 were previously available in foreign markets.[58] In addition, these previously available NCEs carried an average lead time of 5.5 years (Kaitin, Richard, and Lasagna, 1987).

A second important finding was the discovery of little difference among FDA review times for drugs with differing priority classifications. This led the authors to suggest that "agents representing important therapeutic breakthroughs are taking nearly the same amount of time to reach the market as those judged to be less therapeutically important" (1987: 547). Despite acknowledging certain limitations inherent in such studies, the CSDD authors concluded that "the current data suggests a continuation of a trend toward a delay between first foreign marketing and U.S. approval of many new drugs" (548).

The second report in the CSDD series, published in 1991, examined NCEs approved by the FDA between 1987 and 1989. The findings were similar to those detailed in the first report. Of the NCEs under examination, 80 percent were previously available in foreign markets. These drugs carried a mean of 6.5 years of prior marketing (Kaitin, DiCerbo, and Lasagna, 1991). Further, results indicated that this delay was just as prevalent for therapeutically important drugs as it was for drugs with lesser importance. Once again, the CSDD pointed to "small differences" in the review times of drugs with various therapeutic classifications.

While the overall results were consistent with the earlier report, CSDD commended the FDA for taking steps during this period to facilitate the review of new drugs and increase the efficiency of the process. It was during this time that pressure on the agency to approve certain life-saving drugs more expediently had continued to mount. (Such political pressure is the subject of the next chapter.) The CSDD authors singled out two particular improvements. The first was the initiation of "end of Phase II conferences," which encouraged and improved dialogue between the agency and the sponsoring firm. It was suggested that these conferences between the FDA and the sponsoring firm could be used to clarify ambiguities in the drug development process and that the resulting decrease in administrative uncertainty would ultimately speed the regulatory review process.

A second improvement came in 1986 when the FDA added an additional therapeutic category in its review division to acknowledge drugs solely intended to treat AIDS and AIDS-related conditions. This support from the CSDD was reflected by evidence published in another CSDD report that examined NCEs approved between 1978 and 1989 (Kaitin et al., 1991). Over a longer time horizon, mechanisms such as the end of Phase II conference and the new therapeutic classification system were effective in shortening review times, according to the CSDD.[59] David Dranove and David Meltzer (1994) also empirically demonstrated that more important drugs reach the market sooner than drugs of lesser therapeutic importance.

Later, a 1989 CSDD analysis specifically compared drug availability and regulatory review times in the United States and Britain. The results of this latter analysis reconfirmed many of the notions originally raised by Wardell in the early 1970s (Kaitin et al., 1989).[60] The drug lag in the United States was especially apparent in comparisons to the UK. Examining the eleven-year period, 1977 through 1987, CSDD found a substantial British advantage in first introductions (114 for the UK versus 41 for the United States). The average lead time for these introductions was also significantly greater (60.7 months versus 28.9 months). Finally, CSDD noted the UK's lead in the number of exclusively available drugs during the period (70 versus 54). Overall, Kaitin and his collaborators were led to conclude, "The results of this study refute the assertion that the drug lag has disappeared. During the 11 year period (1977–1987), the United States not only lagged behind the United Kingdom in the availability of new medications in each therapeutic category, but it also had only one third the number of first introductions of mutually available drugs and 23 percent fewer exclusively available drugs" (1989: 133). The CSDD findings in this report are presented in Table 4.1 for comparison alongside Wardell's earlier data covering the period 1962–1976.

Top FDA officials responded to the criticism of the CSDD by conducting their own analyses of the data, released in a report titled "Timely Access to New Drugs in the 1990s: An International Comparison"

(USFDA, 1995c; Kessler et al., 1996). Rather than comparing mean assessment times, the focus of the FDA's analysis centered on drug availability and first marketing across four countries: Germany, Japan, the UK, and the United States. The FDA report compared the marketing approval dates of 214 NCEs introduced between January 1990 and December 1994. In terms of the U.S.–UK comparison, this report painted a different picture than earlier drug lag studies. The FDA found that 58 of the 214 NCEs were approved in both the United States and the UK. In terms of exclusively available drugs, twenty-nine drugs were approved in the UK but not in the United States. Alternatively, eighteen NCEs were approved in the United States but not in the United Kingdom. On examining the twenty-nine drugs not approved in the United States, the FDA concluded, "there is currently no drug of major public health interest to U.S. patients among the 29 products approved exclusively in the United Kingdom" (Kessler et al., 1996: 1827). The authors also noted that two of the twenty-nine drugs were initially considered priority drugs by the FDA but were ultimately withdrawn from the market by the agency for safety reasons. The FDA concluded its report with a strong attempt to dispel further thinking about the U.S. drug lag. The report confidently asserted,

> The findings presented herein clearly support the conclusion that the FDA does not delay consumer access to safe and effective drugs, compared with other countries. In many cases, the U.S. system allows priority drugs to reach consumers before they become more widely available. Americans have early access to numerous therapies with significant public health benefits and are missing very few drugs that are novel or medically important. (Kessler et al., 1996: 1829–1831)

The release of the FDA's "Timely Access" report generated a great deal of discussion and debate in the medical, pharmaceutical, and political communities. For instance, Robert Goldberg of George Washington University's Center on Neuroscience, Medical Progress and Society immediately released a follow-up report entitled "Untimely Access: A Review of America's Drug Lag." The Goldberg report was highly critical of the FDA's findings. Goldberg suggested, "The FDA's assertion that there is no drug lag—based as it is on a partial consideration of all available data and concerns—is inaccurate and therefore misleading. The facts paint a far different picture than that put forth by the FDA and Dr. Kessler" (1996: 18).

The important point to consider in this context, however, is that the drug lag debate served to create an impression (real or perceived) that the agency was not performing adequately in terms of reviewing and approving new medicines. Obviously, debates over regulatory performance are a consistent feature of regulatory politics. In making international comparisons of new drug approvals and as part of the drug lag debate, it is important to ask, would we expect drug approvals in a single country such as the United States to compare favorably with *every* other country? If not, then this is perhaps an unfair comparison.

In the early 1970s, a substantial body of evidence was amassed on the introduction of new drugs throughout the world. Not surprisingly, one of the themes inherent in the ongoing drug lag debate was the continual difference of opinion between the FDA and critics of the agency. The difference was just as prevalent in the Wardell-Kennedy debates of the late 1970s as it was with the release of the FDA's "Timely Access" report. This controversy suggests that perhaps the existing principal-agent contract dating back to 1962 was beginning to erode.

## The Changing Political Climate

The drug lag debates of the 1970s and 1980s mark a period of active scrutiny by outside groups over agency affairs and the emergence of an increasing tension between the agency and the pharmaceutical industry. In greatly centralizing the review process, the Kefauver amendments increased the duration of the drug development process. Such bureaucratic delays adversely affect industry profits, causing the pharmaceutical industry to be critical of the FDA.

Such criticism, however, was legitimized by the development of a significant academically based regulatory reform movement in the 1970s. This movement was fueled by studies emanating from organizations like the American Enterprise Institute (AEI) and economics departments, such as that at the University of Chicago, that provided a substantial theoretical and empirical basis for criticizing the FDA. The intellectual basis for this movement was the notion that the Kefauver amendments greatly impeded drug innovation. For instance, empirical studies—primarily economic analyses—measuring the economic impact of the amendments were coordinated by an AEI-sponsored monograph series, AEI Studies on the Impact of Regulation on Drug Innovation.

Table 4.2 lists a few of the key studies in this series and the corresponding year of publication. Prominent scholars such as Henry Grabowski, John Vernon, Louis Lasagna, William Wardell, and Robert Helms led this intellectual charge. Another, Sam Peltzman, authored numerous

Table 4.2 Prominent AEI Studies on the Impact of Regulation on Drug Innovation

| Year | Author(s) | Title |
|------|-----------|-------|
| 1974 | Sam Peltzman | "Regulation of Pharmaceutical Innovation: The 1962 Amendments" |
| 1975 | William Wardell, Louis Lasagna | "Regulation and Drug Development" |
| 1976 | Henry Grabowski | "Drug Regulation and Innovation: Empirical Evidence and Policy Options" |
| 1981 | Robert Helms, ed. | "Drugs and Health" |
| 1983 | Henry Grabowski, John Vernon | "The Regulation of Pharmaceuticals: Balancing the Benefits and Risks" |

economic analyses on the subject and provided a key link to the Chicago economics department (see, for example, Landau, 1973).[61] In effect, this movement provided the intellectual challenge to the policy monopoly (i.e., the combination of political interests supporting cautious FDA behavior and the stringent institutional structure supporting those interests) that was created with the 1962 amendments. Critics of the existing contract repeatedly argued that regulatory delays produced a serious impediment to both pharmaceutical innovation and public health.

Congressional committees were well aware of such criticisms, and Congress called for several major reviews of agency drug review activity during this time.[62] In 1974, in what was known as the Kennedy hearings, eleven current and former agency employees and three agency consultants testified before a Senate committee in reference to repeated claims of excessive industry influence at the agency and the tone of agency internal reactions regarding the approval and disapproval of new drug applications. The information revealed in this testimony led to the formation of the Department of Health, Education, and Welfare's Review Panel on New Drug Regulation. The review panel was established in February 1975 to "study current policies and procedures of the FDA relating to the approval and disapproval of new drugs," as well as the possibility of undue industry influence on the agency.

The congressional reviews greatly affected the tenure of then commissioner Alexander Schmidt who, according to several agency observers, "spent most of his time as commissioner testifying before Congress." During its two-plus years in existence, the review panel issued sixteen interim reports plus a final report in May 1977. The panel articulated three principal conclusions (Review Panel, 1977: 1). First, it concluded that the regulatory system for licensing new drugs requiring premarket clearance based on safety and efficacy was "fundamentally sound." Second, in reference to questions regarding excessive industry influence, it asserted that the "FDA is neither pro- nor anti-industry in its review and approval of new drugs." Finally, "substantial improvements" were needed in the FDA's system of drug review. In effect, the panel reaffirmed the agency preference for avoiding Type II errors, but it opened the door for reform by calling for several "legislative, administrative, and procedural reforms" to address these concerns.

In the decades following the 1962 amendments, political support for the agency from Congress remained mixed and was often highly tenuous. Congressional oversight hearings were routinely called to question the agency's decision to approve a particular drug. A number of Democratic members of Congress holding influential committee positions were critical of the agency for rushing the approval of drugs too fast (Quirk, 1980, 1981). Particularly acute during the 1970s and 1980s, this group included Senators Estes Kefauver, Gaylord Nelson, and Edward Kennedy and Representatives L. H. Fountain, Paul Rogers, Norman Lent, Henry Waxman, and John Dingell. These legislators were driven largely by overriding concerns from the public interest movement to ensure consumer protection against unsafe or ineffective drugs.

Perhaps the statement given by then FDA commissioner Alexander Schmidt testifying before joint Senate committee hearings in 1974 sums up the nature of this criticism best:

> By far the greatest pressure that the Bureau of Drugs or the Food and Drug Administration receives with respect to the new drug approval process is brought to bear through Congressional hearings. In all of our history, we are unable to find one instance where a Congressional hearing investigated the failure of FDA to approve a new drug. The occasions on which hearings have been held to criticize approval of a new drug have been so frequent in the past ten years that we have not even attempted to count them. At both the staff level and the managerial level, the message conveyed by this situation could not be clearer. Whenever a difficult or controversial issue is resolved by approval, the Agency and the individuals involved will be publicly investigated. Whenever it is resolved by disapproval, no inquiry will be made. The Congressional pressure for negative action is therefore intense, and ever increasing. (U.S. Senate, 1974: 207)

Congressional criticism exerting pressure on the agency toward disapprovals and negative action (thus, decreasing the propensity for Type II errors) characterized congressional oversight of the agency for most of the postwar period. Yet the tone of criticism directed at the agency vis-à-vis new drug approvals began to change gradually in the 1980s, and this suggests a breakdown in the existing principal-agent contract. The mid-1980s can be viewed as a clear turning point with respect to congressional oversight and congressional criticism of the drug approval process. Prior to 1980, the primary tone of congressional criticism concerned a perceived lack of safety surrounding the approval of particular drugs. Indeed, Commissioner Schmidt could not recall a time when Congress investigated the agency's failure to approve a new drug. In fact, it was not until 1980 that Congress held an oversight hearing that was critical of the agency for moving too slowly. This criticism reflected an emerging shift in the overall tone of FDA oversight. Congressional criticisms of the agency for failing to approve drugs and moving too slowly are a relatively recent phenomenon that gradually emerged throughout the 1980s and has continued since. These criticisms were originally spearheaded by a number of Republicans but later gained widespread acceptance among a broader coalition of actors in the policy subsystem.

## Conclusion

The thalidomide experience in Europe provided an important exogenous event to punctuate the drug regulatory regime that was initiated in 1938. This event, coupled with the persistence of key actors in the policy subsystem, such as Senator Estes Kefauver, eventually led to the creation of a stronger institutional structure—the 1962 Kefauver amendments. Largely concerned with the dual issues of pricing and patent protection, it appears as if the Pharmaceutical Manufacturers Association greatly underestimated the effects that increased licensing requirements would have on the drug approval process. Thus, the amendments greatly increased the safety threshold for new medicines and reflected the stringent centralized controls that have characterized U.S. medicines regulation.

Over time, however, it was argued that this institutional structure imposed a tremendous cost on the pharmaceutical industry, and perhaps a cost to U.S. consumers, by potentially denying them access to new medicines. The amendments greatly increased the cost of drug development and increased the duration of regulatory review. These arguments were well captured in the ensuing drug lag debate. This debate showed that fewer drugs were made available in the U.S. market than in most European markets. Further, of the drugs that were mutually available in

U.S. and European markets, Europeans were gaining access to these drugs much sooner than U.S. consumers.

The drug lag led to deteriorating relations between the FDA and the pharmaceutical industry. The drug lag debate also gradually began to mobilize a diverse set of societal interests—including pharmaceutical industry officials, academics, and Democratic and Republican members of Congress. As the next chapter argues, this thirty-year regulatory regime would eventually be punctuated by yet another set of events. In this case, the confluence of political and societal interests that eventually emerged proved to be an unlikely (though highly effective) political coalition. The outcome of this policy change would significantly alter the nature of U.S. drug regulation.

# 5

# A GRAND COMPROMISE AND
# THE SHIFT TO A NEW ERA

The task before us is not to lower our standards. Our task is to streamline the process. But in the end, there is the same risk/benefit equa-
tion. It hasn't changed. When the benefits are potentially great, the
risks you can take also can be great. It is that basic risk/benefit equa-
tion that you wrote into the law in 1962.
—*David Kessler, FDA commissioner,*
*testifying before Congress, 1992*

The drug lag debate highlighted the variation in regulatory performance
between the FDA and other national regulatory authorities following the
1962 Kefauver amendments. Generally speaking, given the number and
variety of prescription medicines submitted to the FDA for approval on
an annual basis, we might expect to see certain drugs reviewed and
approved faster than others. In 1987, for example, Alcon Labs, a small
Fort Worth pharmaceutical company, sought approval for its new glau-
coma drug, Iopidine. The FDA reviewed and approved Alcon's new
drug application in less than three months. Conversely, the FDA granted
regulatory approval of Burroughs Wellcome's antihistamine product,
Semprex-D, in 1994. In the case of Semprex-D, however, the FDA
review and approval took nearly 6.5 years to complete. Aside from
individual, anecdotal examples, it is not uncommon for regulatory variation to apply to certain classes of drugs. For example, cardiovascular
drugs and drugs affecting the central nervous system have historically
taken considerably longer to review than anticancer drugs (Rawson et
al., 1998).

Further regulatory variation is evident when examining FDA review
times at the aggregate level. Most notably, the FDA has dramatically
decreased the regulatory review time for new drugs since the early

1990s. For example, the Tufts University Center for the Study of Drug Development conducts triennial analyses of various aspects of new drug approvals in the United States. According to the CSDD, the average FDA review time for approved new chemical entities decreased from 35.6 months in 1984–1986 to 16.8 months in 1996–1998 (Kaitin and Healy, 2000). Thus, in a little more than a decade, the FDA essentially cut its average review time in half. Figure 5.1 illustrates the sharp decline in FDA review times.[63]

In addition to the declining review times, the number of drugs approved by the agency each year also rose considerably in the 1990s.[64] The agency approved a total of 232 NCEs between 1993 and 1999, compared to just 163 approvals during the previous seven-year span—a 42 percent increase (Willman, 2000). Figure 5.2 illustrates the number of drugs approved by the FDA on an annual basis between 1966 and 2001. Thus, over the past decade the FDA has approved more drugs and done so in less time than at any other period in history. According to one study, "The total of 110 NCEs approved between 1996–98 far surpasses any three year period since the passage of the 1962 drug amendments . . . this number exceeds by 49% the second highest three year total" (Kaitin and Healy, 2000:12). This change in regulatory performance—especially the declining review times—has been remarkable.

The change in FDA performance over the past decade represents a drastic change in the agency's mode of operation throughout the twentieth century and especially after the Kefauver amendments. Drugs are now being reviewed (and approved) much faster than in past decades.

Figure 5.1  Median FDA Approval Time, 1986–2002 (months)

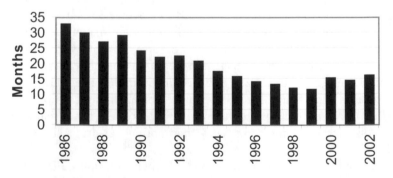

*Source:* FDA Center for Drug Evaluation and Research (various reports).

Figure 5.2 FDA New Drug Approvals, 1966–2001

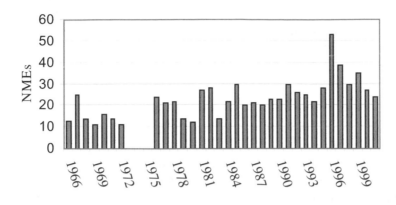

*Source:* FDA Center for Drug Evaluation and Research (various reports).

The dramatic decline in review times seems to run counter to the agency's traditional risk-benefit analysis, which focused on minimizing the risks of prematurely releasing unsafe products into the market. Moreover, the entire nature of regulatory drug review at the Food and Drug Administration has undergone a relative philosophical transformation since the early 1990s. Whereas this regulatory shift has received a great deal of journalistic attention, it has received relatively little systematic treatment in the political science and regulation literature.[65] Although the lack of scholarly treatment may seem surprising, some scholars have noted that understanding policy change "requires the perspective of a decade or more" (Sabatier and Jenkins-Smith, 1999: 118).

## A New Period of Regulatory Governance

In this chapter, I argue that an important policy punctuation occurred in 1992 and that we have now entered a fourth era in FDA drug regulation. The current period reflects an approach to medicines regulation that fundamentally differs from the post-1962 period. Verification of the hypothesized policy punctuation requires the substantiation of at least three factors. First, a new regulatory period requires the presence of a new landmark law (i.e., a regulatory institution) to serve as the legal (and symbolic) cornerstone. Second, such a regulatory change should produce a dramatic difference in regulatory performance. Because FDA performance is typically measured in terms of NDA review times, we would expect to see a dramatic change in agency review times in one direction or the other. Third, one would expect to see change in public perceptions, as well as in the regulatory philosophy guiding FDA decisionmaking. In a sense, we expect to see relative consensus on the powerful idea supporting the new institution. The remainder of this section describes the nature of changes that indicate a fourth regulatory period.

## Institutional Change: Regulatory Policy and Process

The 1980s was a difficult period for the FDA. The agency suffered from a lack of resources and enforcement capability, endured an ideological assault from the Reagan White House and micromanagement from the Office of Management and Budget, and was marred by scandal in the generic drugs division (Burkholz, 1994; Kessler, 2001). During this time, however, the agency began promulgating a series of important administrative changes in the drug review process. Such changes significantly lessened the stringent centralized controls that were characteristic of the previous three decades.[66] For example, the 1988 Subpart E provisions (referring to their location in the *Code of Federal Regulations*) were intended to speed the development of drugs for patients with life-threatening and severely debilitating illnesses, especially in the absence of satisfactory alternative treatments. These procedures, in seeking to weigh a drug's benefits in light of the severity of the disease, enabled the agency and the sponsor of the NDA to work together in developing Phase II clinical trials in support of approval.

In 1992, the accelerated approval mechanism adopted the use of "surrogate endpoints" during clinical investigations as the basis for approval decisions.[67] A surrogate endpoint serves as a proxy measure for a patient's condition when the true endpoint may not be appropriate to use during clinical trials. For example, in the case of early clinical trials for AIDS drugs, "CD4 counts" were adopted as surrogate endpoints.[68] Also in 1992, the FDA simplified its classification scheme by designating each NDA as either standard or priority. Drugs are now given priority status if they have "the potential for providing significant preventative or diagnostic therapeutic advance" when compared to standard applications.[69] Today, approximately 35–40 percent of all applications reviewed by the agency are classified as priority reviews. This is significant because priority drugs are now statutorily targeted for review in six months, while standard drugs have a ten-month target.

The same year, administrative changes creating the fast track and parallel track mechanisms created the possibility for accelerated approval of certain drugs by granting agency approval following Phase II clinical trials. This administrative change was designed for patients whose conditions may not afford the time necessary to wait for standard clinical investigations. "Parallel" track refers to the dual nature of clinical protocols, as the drug under investigation is made available to patients while simultaneously undergoing controlled clinical investigations.

In terms of agency theory, these significant administrative changes can be interpreted in a number of different ways. First, it could be argued that both Congress and the agency sought to retain the status quo contract that had prevailed since the 1962 Kefauver amendments. If so, the administrative changes may have been precipitated by political pressure applied by actors who could potentially influence the electoral fortunes of the principal, including patient groups (seeking more expedient access to potentially life-saving treatments) and industry interests (seeking to protect corporate profitability). In making these administrative changes, Congress and the agency may have been seeking to appease other actors in the policy subsystem and, more important, to retain the existing contract by preempting broader policy change. Second, it could be argued that Congress, acting as the principal, sought to maintain the existing contract whereas the agency preferred to change the terms of the contract. In this scenario, the agency, sensing that Congress was not about to replace the existing contract, used its administrative discretion to alter the existing contract without dramatically overhauling it. Third, one could envision a situation in which Congress sought to change the contract but the agency preferred to keep the status quo contract intact. Since inertial factors often limit agency behavior, one could speculate that the FDA initiated these changes as a way to modify the existing contract. In this scenario, though the agency preferred to retain the status quo, increasing political pressure forced the agency's hand. Consequently, the results of such changes created a gradual weakening of the agency's centralized control. Any one of these scenarios is plausible because all the regulatory changes described above were administrative changes. That is, the changes were made to administrative law by the agency and not by Congress through legislative statute.

In a fourth potential scenario, it could be that both Congress and the agency were ready to replace the existing contract with an entirely new agreement. If so, the ultimate turning point in the post-1962 regulatory period, and policy punctuation, came with the legislative passage of the

1992 Prescription Drug User Fee Act that followed these administrative changes.

In this chapter, I argue that PDUFA is clearly a critical turning point in the regulatory review of new medicines. The influence of PDUFA is difficult to overstate, as the law significantly modified the drug review process in a number of ways. First, in response to agency claims that a lack of resources was impeding agency performance, the law required the FDA to levy a series of user fees on firms sponsoring new drug applications. The intent behind user fees was that funds raised from user fees would enable the agency to hire 600 additional reviewers, thus accelerating the review process. Second, and equally important, PDUFA included a series of agency performance standards mandating the FDA to meet specific annual guidelines during the review process. That is, Congress created a direct linkage between agency performance and future agency appropriations. (Such direct oversight may explain the administrative changes that preceded PDUFA.) Third, PDUFA included an important sunset provision. The law called for an expiration of the user fee program in five years in the absence of congressional reauthorization. It is not atypical for public health service agencies to have time-limited authorizations from Congress, but, politically, this time limit was significant because it gave each of the key actors in the policy subsystem an "out" in the event that user fees were deemed unsatisfactory.

Since its initial passage, the user fee program has been extended twice. In 1997, the FDA Modernization Act (FDAMA) provided additional reforms leading the FDA to further streamline the drug review process by specifically targeting the efficient and expedited review of new products.[70] FDAMA also included, for the first time, an explicit and balanced mission statement for the agency. This mission emphasized both the protection and promotion of public health, increased the agency's public accountability, and, effectively, further institutionalized the policy punctuation. In addition, FDAMA also modified the statutory language to the "substantial evidence" standard for efficacy, long considered the gold standard of the drug approval process.

In 2002, PDUFA III authorized another five years for the user fee program and created additional changes along the same lines as its predecessors, such as enabling the agency to collect over $1.2 billion in user fees and adding another 450 reviewers. In addition, several changes were negotiated as side agreements between the agency and the pharmaceutical industry. For example, the FDA agreed to have an outside consultant available for whenever an NDA sponsor requests one. The

FDA can also now use some of the user fee revenues to fund drug safety–monitoring programs once approved drugs reach the market.

In essence, the institutional effect of PDUFA is analogous to the 1938 Federal Food, Drug and Cosmetic Act and the 1962 Kefauver amendments in that each landmark law triggered a new era in U.S. drug regulation. (See Table 3.1 for a brief overview of the other summary characteristics.)

## Changes in FDA Performance: Declining Review Times

The above-mentioned administrative and legislative changes naturally have had a dramatic effect on the FDA's performance. Figure 5.1 illustrates the decrease in aggregate review times from a median of thirty-two months in the mid-1980s to approximately sixteen months by 2002. Specific statistical aspects of the agency's recent performance have been documented empirically and in much greater detail elsewhere (see, for example, Kaitin and Healy, 2000; Rawson et al., 1998).

To put such performance in the proper context, however, it is useful to refer back to the drug lag debate. The latest evidence indicates that the gap in review times between European regulators and the FDA is virtually nonexistent (CMR, 1996; Rawson et al., 1998; USFDA, 1995b; Kessler et al., 1996). For instance, the UK's Centre for Medicines Research asserted that "regulatory review times are beginning to converge on a mean of around two years in at least five countries," including the United States (CMR, 1996: 1). In comparing review times between the British Medicines Control Agency and the FDA, the U.S. General Accounting Office concluded, "When one examines the total time for both processes, the United Kingdom does not appear to be dramatically faster than the U.S." (1995: 40). Thus, the agency has dramatically decreased review times over the past decade.

## Changes in Regulatory Philosophy: Protecting and Promoting Public Health

The regulatory shift, symbolized by the user fee program, extends beyond policy and performance. The FDA's increasing orientation toward avoiding Type I errors is reflected in the administration and implementation of the new policies. As one high-ranking FDA official summed up this change in philosophy at the agency, "PDUFA produced a profound change, a sea change, in agency attitudes. [With respect to drug approvals] it used to be: do you want the FDA decision to be the right one or do you want it on time? Now, after PDUFA there is no choice." Another senior agency official noted two significant changes in culture at the agency, particularly over the last several years. The first concerns the agency's performance and the resulting timeliness of the review process. He, too, suggested that the old "Do you want it right, or do you want it on time" mentality no longer persists. In the past, proper and expeditious reviews were often thought to be mutually exclusive. However, given the newly emerging regulatory philosophy, this dichotomy may no longer be the case.

This changing sentiment is politically important because PDUFA reflects a significant compromise. The user fee law provided the agency with the additional resources it had long requested, but it tied those resources (and future resources) to regulatory performance. That is, in order for the agency to continue receiving user fee revenues in future years, it pledged to review and take specific action on a previously agreed on percentage of new applications and to report its review performance to Congress (in two separate reports) on an annual basis.[71]

The second change in philosophy centers on the ascribed definition of what it means to protect the public health. A senior agency official acknowledged that public health is now considered to extend beyond solely keeping unsafe drugs off the market. Instead, it should include getting safe drugs approved in a timely manner. This definition was formalized in Section 406(b)(1) of the 1997 FDAMA law. The section now reads, the FDA shall "promote public health by promptly and efficiently reviewing clinical research and taking appropriate action on the marketing of regulated products in a timely manner." These sentiments underpin the regulatory shift in policy and practice. Perhaps just as important, this change in philosophy (and resulting outcomes) is not lost on the minds of U.S. pharmaceutical manufacturers. One industry official suggested, "To the FDA's credit, they are slowly but surely making progress in accelerating the approval of new drugs. However, still more needs to be done." Another offered, "It's important to give credit where credit is due. There appears to be a greater effort at the FDA to communicate with individual firms." Thus, perceptions of such changes are felt both inside the agency and out.

The ascribed changes in policy, performance, and philosophy combine to reflect a fourth distinctive period in regulatory drug review. Whereas elements of centralized regulatory control remain (particularly in a comparative sense), regulatory review policy has shifted from more stringent to less stringent centralized controls. In addition, the agency has expanded its definition of public health not only to include keeping harmful drugs off the market but also to provide needy patients with timely access to new therapies. As a result, the FDA has shifted toward a greater reliance on streamlining the review process. These changes provide a clear contrast to the tradition of strengthened centralized regulatory control typified by the previous two periods. Thus, the 1992 user fee law has replaced the 1962 Kefauver amendments as the defining characteristic of the current regulatory regime. The remainder of this chapter develops an explanation for the latest policy punctuation.

## Explaining the FDA Transformation

The regulation of new medicines illustrates the classic question: To what extent should government regulate? Competing views on drug regulation can be examined across an ideological continuum ranging from individual freedom to societal interests. Proponents of individual choice argue that persons should have access to any medicine that may improve their condition. On the other hand, a broader, societal interest compels governments to protect the well-being of the population as a whole. Based on this societal interest, governments play the role of medical gatekeeper in ensuring that medicines are proven to be safe and effective. The Kefauver amendments entrenched the regulatory philosophy guiding drug review on the side of the societal interest. This philosophy was further institutionalized by consumer protection interests. For example, Ralph Nader and Dr. Sidney Wolfe founded Public Citizen in 1971 as a consumer research and advocacy organization. Since 1971, Public Citizen's Health Research Group, led by Wolfe, has actively lobbied Congress and other federal agencies in promoting consumer health issues.

Given this starting point, an agency theory–based explanation requires an examination of key developments relating to Congress and the agency in the policy subsystem and the shifting of the erstwhile policy monopoly. In examining the dynamics of the policy subsystem, it becomes evident that changes in the three principal explanatory factors—consensus in defining public health, political support for the agency, and the nature of government-industry relations—are instrumental in explaining the broader regulatory shift.

## Policy Subsystem:
### Regulatory Reform and Patient Activism

The 1962 Kefauver amendments and the emergence the societal regulatory philosophy characterized the third period of medicines regulation. Over time, however, a diverse coalition of interests including pharmaceutical industry officials, suffering patients, academics, and members of Congress gradually emerged and mobilized to criticize the existing policy regime.

Consequently, a number of major reviews scrutinized the drug evaluation process in the 1980s.[72] Many such reviews occurred during the Republican presidential administrations of Ronald Reagan and George H. W. Bush. Philosophically, their conservative ideologies reflected an emphasis on freedom and individual choice, and these individualized ideals gradually diminished the societal regulatory philosophy. Politically, each administration was committed to decreasing the size of government, reducing the burden of regulation on industry, and making regulatory policies operate more efficiently. For instance, Reagan's Executive Order 12291 enabled the Office of Management and Budget (OMB) to perform a cost-benefit analysis on (and effectively screen) all major government regulations (Heimann, 1997). One by-product of this order was that the FDA commissioner was required to secure OMB approval of his prepared written remarks when testifying before Congress. According to former commissioner David Kessler, "In practice, the Order gave enormous influence to the advocates of deregulation, sometimes allowing relatively low-level desk officers to thwart regulations proposed by a Cabinet secretary" (2001: 403).

The Council on Competitiveness (also known as the Quayle council) was another institutional manifestation of this approach. Established during the first Bush administration to generate initiatives for reducing regulatory inefficiencies, the council became interested in drug reviews. This interest in reducing regulatory inefficiencies coincided with the creation of an FDA advisory committee chaired by Charles Edwards (the Edwards committee) that is perhaps most important in this context. Edwards was a Nixon-era FDA commissioner generally known to be sympathetic toward industry views. The fifteen-member committee, comprised of academics and representatives from industry, patient groups, and the medical profession, considered the overall direction of the agency and the impact of agency resources on the drug review process. The Edwards committee affirmed that the FDA lacked an official direction with respect to the balance between safety and expediency.

In its 1991 report, the committee asserted, "Until the FDA's fundamental objectives are clearly defined and broadly accepted, its performance always will be measured against a changing and often inconsistent set of expectations. The absence of a comprehensive, unified Statement of Purpose contributes to a sense that the agency is adrift" (USHHS, 1991:10).

The failure by Congress to include a specific set of agency objectives in the original, enacting legislation is highly instructive in this context. Throughout the twentieth century, many of the primary changes in the Food, Drug and Cosmetic Act were preceded by a medical catastrophe (or near catastrophe) involving unsafe or ineffective drugs. This experience led the enacting coalition to construct institutional arrangements that emphasized keeping unsafe drugs off the market above all other concerns. In the absence of explicitly framed agency objectives, the FDA chose to adapt the same approach concerning the avoidance of Type II errors. The Kefauver amendments, whose provisions outlined stringent guidelines for premarket determinations on efficacy, provide a classic example of this prominence. Moreover, discussions of expediting patient access to new medicines were virtually nonexistent in the early legislative debates.

Not coincidentally, one key member of the Edwards committee was Kessler. Kessler had served on the committee until his appointment by President Bush as FDA commissioner in October 1990. Though Kessler's first Washington experience was as a volunteer staffer working on FDA issues for Utah Republican senator Orrin Hatch, Kessler was admittedly not a strong partisan (Kessler, 2001). Yet it was Kessler, trained in both pediatrics and the law, who would ultimately navigate the agency through a series of reforms leading up to the policy punctuation.

Demonstrating a willingness to tackle major issues early in his tenure (e.g., enforcement and product labeling), Kessler proved to be a key link in bridging the concerns of industry and the political right with the similar concerns of a diverse coalition of patient activists. As Kessler would later recall, "I had come to the FDA with one issue about which I cared deeply. As a physician who had worked in the Bronx during the 1980s, I understood what the AIDS epidemic was about, and I wanted to make it one of my top priorities" (2001: 38). In effect, Kessler was at the nexus of an improbable political coalition. The circumstances would require skillful political maneuvering in the policy subsystem in order to create a policy punctuation, and such skillful maneuvering ultimately led to the passage of the Prescription Drug User Fee Act.

Active patient groups added a substantial amount of political pressure on the agency to approve drugs more rapidly during this period.

Intense political pressure by AIDS activists (in various forms) on both government and industry to bring new drugs to the market sooner provided an important exogenous shock, and the FDA's response to such activism provides a critical glimpse into the underlying policy subsystem.

However, perhaps unlike other climates preceding legislative change, political pressure to expedite the drug review process was not limited simply to brute force. Instead, AIDS activists entered deeply into all aspects of the drug review process, including assisting in the development of criteria for approval. Steven Epstein argues that the distinctive feature of AIDS activism was that the movement "was more than just a 'disease constituency' pressuring the government for more funding, but in fact an alternative basis of expertise" (1996: 8). Noting the "complex set of interactions" including the efforts by activists to shift the policy away from clinical endpoints as markers of effectiveness to the reliance on surrogate endpoints (e.g., CD4 counts) as conceptual bases for drug approval, he suggests, "This is indeed the first social movement in the U.S. to accomplish the large-scale conversion of disease 'victims' into activists-experts" (8). As a result, it is difficult to overstate the profound and pathbreaking role played by such activists.

Two groups were primarily at the forefront of the AIDS activism movement. Each group utilized contrasting strategies for inducing the FDA to change its behavior. On the West Coast, San Francisco–based Project Inform was organized in 1985. Founded by prominent AIDS activist and spokesman Martin Delaney, Project Inform began as a forum for increasing awareness of AIDS issues and treatments for AIDS-related conditions in San Francisco's gay community (Clark, 1989; Kwitny, 1992). In the early days of the organization, Delaney was active in obtaining non–FDA approved drugs such as ribavirin in Mexico and delivering them to patients in California and eventually all across the United States. Later in the decade, frustrated by perceived bureaucratic inefficiencies and single-mindedness at the FDA, Project Inform began conducting underground clinical investigations and community-based research. Ultimately, the FDA began to acknowledge Project Inform's activities, and Delaney became an active participant on a National Academy of Science roundtable on AIDS drugs. Through Project Inform, Delaney's efforts led to important changes in FDA policy regarding the importation of drugs, "parallel track" expanded access programs, the use of community trials during the clinical investigation phase of drug development, and eventually the use of surrogate endpoints as markers of effectiveness.

While Project Inform's activities centered on the distribution of potential new treatments and the organization of clinical investigations, the New York–based AIDS Coalition to Unleash Power (ACT UP) relied far more heavily on shock tactics, such as a 1989 invasion of New York's St. Patrick's Cathedral or the 1991 on-air disruption of the *CBS Evening News,* to influence agency behavior and public opinion. Formed in 1987, ACT UP targeted the FDA, the National Institutes of Health, the National Institute of Allergy and Infectious Diseases (NIAID), industry, and other governmental figures for highly visible public demonstrations. The first such protest closed streets and disrupted traffic around New York's Wall Street in March 1987. More Wall Street protests followed in 1988 and 1989. Using the slogan "Drugs into Bodies," ACT UP made the FDA both a literal and figurative target of protest. In perhaps the group's most salient demonstration of AIDS activism, over 1,000 demonstrators gathered outside FDA headquarters in Rockville, Maryland, on October 11, 1988. Attempting to highlight alleged shortcomings at the agency and accelerate the drug approval process, the protest symbolically sought to "shut down" agency operations for a day (Leary, 1988a). Ultimately, 176 people were arrested during the demonstration (Duggan, 1988). Evidently, ACT UP made its point with the demonstration at FDA headquarters as the agency announced new procedures for approving drugs later that same week (Leary, 1988b). As one high-ranking agency official during this time later told me, "This type of politics enabled the agency to bring things forward that would not have been possible otherwise."

ACT UP demonstrations targeted the pharmaceutical industry as well. Upset over perceived delays in drug development, lack of access to new drugs, and the high costs of new treatments, four ACT UP demonstrators used steel plates and rivets to barricade themselves to the Burroughs Wellcome office complex in April 1989. ACT UP members were particularly disturbed by the high costs of available treatments. In 1989, Burroughs Wellcome's Retrovir (AZT) was the only drug approved by the FDA to treat AIDS, and a one-year dosage of AZT cost patients $8,000. Later that year, five demonstrators again targeting Burroughs Wellcome actually halted trading at the New York Stock Exchange as they chained themselves to a banister above the trading floor while unfurling a "Sell Wellcome" banner (Price, 1990). Less than a week later, the company announced a 20 percent reduction in the price of the drug. During an interview, one industry official suggested that both the agency and the industry were "shocked by the tactics of the politically active groups. We'd never seen this type of activity before."

The AIDS experience provided the necessary "focusing event" leading to the change in regulatory policy (Kingdon, 1984; Birkland, 1997). One former high-ranking agency official told me that as AIDS victims became increasingly prominent on the political agenda, Congress and the FDA were forced to respond to their increasing demands: "The pressure from AIDS activists was very, very helpful in getting the agency to move." The intensity of political pressure by AIDS activists and the relentless nature of their activism were unlike any the agency or industry had ever seen before. The agency responded by promulgating regulations that accelerated reviews of potentially new therapies. From a philosophical standpoint, the AIDS experience also served as a catalyst for increasing agency saliency about the balance between safety and expeditiousness in the review process. Thus, by the early 1990s, the erstwhile policy monopoly was under considerable assault by a number of disparate actors including Washington think tanks, industry, congressional leaders, and patient groups. Such a multifaceted assault would require skillful political maneuvering and a grand compromise in order to overturn the existing policy monopoly.

## Convergence in the Policy Subsystem: A Grand Compromise

Another important change in the policy subsystem was the result of a strategic decision by the pharmaceutical industry. Typically, government and industry share similar goals of providing patients with high-quality drugs in a timely manner, yet they generally disagree over how this might be best accomplished. Disputing Charles Lindblom's (1977) contention that business occupies a "privileged position" in the U.S. governing arrangement, David Vogel suggests the adversarial relationship between business and government has been a defining feature of U.S. politics since the Industrial Revolution (1989: 299). Historically, the contentious relationship between the FDA and the pharmaceutical industry was the result of industry perception of an excessively cautious agency. In response, it was no secret that many agency officials grew to become suspicious of industry motives. This contentious relationship became the centerpiece of a drug review regime that relied on centralized controls starting in the 1960s.

The agency's current reliance on user fees provides crucial insight into the nature of the relationship between the FDA and the pharmaceutical industry. Throughout the 1980s, the FDA faced a tremendous backlog of drug applications and routinely argued that additional resources were needed. Congressional Republicans and industry representatives had countered that agency delays stymied product innovation. As a middle ground, user fees to hire additional review staff were thought to have at least a slight appeal to both sides. In 1992, Congress passed the Prescription Drug User Fee Act with these issues in mind. However, this compromise solution was not as obvious as it may appear in retrospect and required skillful maneuvering in the policy subsystem.

The adaptation of user fees for regulatory and other purposes is certainly not new to the federal government, or the FDA. The FDA for several decades has used regulatory fees to certify batches of insulin and color additives for use in food, drugs, and cosmetics. Suggestions by Congress to the FDA to impose regulatory fees on prescription drug manufacturers date back as far as a 1971 General Accounting Office report. Citing the Independent Offices Appropriation Act of 1952, the GAO suggested that the FDA should raise some of its own revenue. Little public discussion of the idea took place, however, until over a decade later. In 1983, President Reagan received a recommendation on federal user charges from the Private Sector Survey on Cost Control, otherwise known as the Grace commission. Reagan had established the Grace commission to "identify opportunities for increased efficiency and reduced costs achievable by executive action or legislation" (PPSSCC, 1983). The commission, a key vehicle in Reagan's budget-slashing crusade, recommended that the FDA could "reasonably charge a fee for new drug and device applications" (275).

In 1985 and 1986 President Reagan included FDA user fees in his annual budget proposals. Reagan's real interest in user fees was their potential contribution to his larger plan of deficit reduction. The critical point in the Reagan plan, however, was that the receipts from FDA user fees were to be funneled into the general fund at the Treasury Department and that they would not be used for specific FDA review purposes. In essence, as constituted by Reagan, FDA user fees would provide no real benefit to the FDA or contribute to expedited drug review. Not surprisingly, Reagan's proposal failed to muster any significant political support and did not lead to congressional action.

At this point, virtually all interested participants were opposed to any user fee plans. The FDA opposed user fees because the plan would provide no additional resources for its review process. Industry rejected the idea on the grounds that fees would serve as an unnecessary tax on it. Key congressional officials such as Senator Edward Kennedy also opposed the idea, arguing that user fees were "ill advised" because they would be of little benefit to the agency (U.S. Senate, 1991: 16). Congressional Republicans felt the fee would create an unnecessary tax on industry and that such a tax would further stifle innovation. Congressional Democrats also opposed the plan, though for different reasons. First, with prescription drug prices already perceived to be high, they argued that fees to drug manufacturers would ultimately mean an increase in drug prices to consumers. Second, leaders of key committees and subcommittees (e.g., Kennedy and Representatives John Dingell and Henry Waxman) overseeing health issues viewed the proposal as a potentially serious threat to future FDA appropriations. They perceived that user fees would become a substitute for future FDA appropriations rather than having the fees be supplemental to annual agency appropriations. As committee and subcommittee chairmen, they were intent on protecting any potential incoming resources destined for the FDA.

Given these political considerations, the turning point in the legislative history of PDUFA came in 1986. A year earlier, the Pharmaceutical Manufacturers Association established an executive committee to focus exclusively on FDA issues.[73] Fearing an adverse effect on profit margins, the committee initially reiterated the PMA's categorical opposition to FDA user fees. In 1986, however, perhaps sensing potentially modest gains, the PMA executive committee advanced a counterproposal. It outlined four specific criteria that had to be met in order for the PMA to back a user fee plan. First, any user fee must be earmarked to the specific product under review and should be used for no other purpose. Second, fee revenues would not be used to substitute for future FDA appropriations. Third, the amount of the fee was to be "reasonable." Finally, the PMA was looking for a long-term commitment from the agency and Congress to improve the drug review process. This counterproposal was significant because it directly earmarked user fees toward product reviews and not, as the Reagan administration had proposed, to be funneled into the general fund. Still, no immediate action followed.

Much later, in mid-1991, Kessler approached one of the agency's top reviewers, Dr. Robert Temple, about the user fee idea.[74] Kessler and Temple concurred that user fees could provide the agency with the additional resources it desired. Kessler then approached PMA president Gerald Mossinghoff with the agency's user fee plan. According to one agency official, Mossinghoff was receptive to the notion that user fees could help expedite the review process and forwarded the issue to Irwin Lerner. Lerner headed the committee of the Pharmaceutical Research and Manufacturers Association charged with handling the user fee issue on behalf of industry interests. Finally, Kessler and other FDA staffers were able to negotiate a mutually acceptable compromise with congressional leaders and PhRMA leaders.

The key to the political compromise was extending the types of drugs under consideration for expedited review beyond AIDS drugs. Instead, drugs intended to treat patients with "serious" and "life-threatening" conditions were targeted. This opened the door for those interested in, for example, the treatment of Alzheimer's disease, cancer, and other illnesses. After late-session hearings in both houses a consensus was reached: if the proposal met the criteria elaborated earlier by the PMA, a user fee plan could benefit all participants involved. A bill that did just this was co-authored in the House of Representatives by Energy and Commerce Committee chairman John Dingell, a Michigan Democrat, and Health Subcommittee chairman Henry Waxman, a California Democrat. A similar bill was offered in the Senate co-authored by Kennedy and Hatch, the chair and ranking Republican, respectively, of the Senate Labor and Human Resources Committee. Less than one month after the bill was introduced in the Senate, President Bush signed into law the Prescription Drug User Fee Act of 1992, P.L. 102-571.

PDUFA contained a sunset provision calling for its expiration at the end of five years if not renewed by Congress. The FDA Modernization Act of 1997 renewed the user fee program. FDAMA did more than extend the user fee program, however. It provided a clear mandate for the agency, upheld specific performance standards in the review of new drugs, modified the efficacy standard, and reflected the new direction of the agency. Thus, it is clear that the relationship between the FDA and the pharmaceutical industry had changed, particularly in light of the negotiations surrounding PDUFA. PhRMA described the reform measures as "common sense improvements to the way the FDA regulates the development of new drugs" (Seachrist, 1997). PhRMA and the FDA have worked together since these negotiations on several other initiatives and seem to view each other in a different light. Such a transformation is consistent with the notion that a new policy monopoly has emerged.

Perhaps surprisingly, until it was amended in 1997, the Food, Drug and Cosmetic Act did not provide an official, formally stated mission for the Food and Drug Administration. Thus, in implementing the relatively broad and ambiguous congressional statutes, the agency was able to capitalize on its bureaucratic discretion and acquire a reputation over the years for acting excessively cautious. This orientation was primarily

based on avoiding medical catastrophes when reviewing new medicines. Symbolic of the policy punctuation, the lack of a formal mission
statement attracted considerable congressional attention following
PDUFA, as two large-scale FDA reform bills received serious consideration during the 104th Congress. Though the legislative session
ended before either bill could be passed, language in the Senate bill
sponsored by Nancy Kassebaum would have amended the 1938 drug
law to read, "the mission of the FDA is to promote and protect the
health of the American public by facilitating the rapid and efficient
development and availability of products, protecting the public from
unsafe or ineffective products, and enforcing the law in a timely, fair,
consistent, and decisive manner" (U.S. Senate, 1996: 66). At the time,
such wording represented a dramatic shift in thinking about the
agency's goals, particularly when compared to the public debates of the
1960s through the 1980s.

Though FDA reform legislation failed in 1996, the topic remained a
priority for the Senate Labor and Human Resources Committee. Senator James Jeffords replaced Kassebaum, who retired as chair of the
Labor and Human Resources Committee.[75] According to one Jeffords
staff member, "If you thought the pendulum had swung to the extreme
of regulation in the past, we hope this legislation stops the pendulum in
the middle rather than to the other extreme" (Seachrist, 1997). In 1997,
the passage of FDAMA provided an official mission statement for
the FDA.

Figure 5.3 illustrates the new FDA mission statement. The new mission redirects the agency's original focus and, in an unprecedented fashion, emphasizes the dual mandate of protecting and promoting public
health. Specifically, promoting public health was meant to include
approving drugs in a timely fashion. Plus, for the first time, the agency
was formally mandated by Congress to work with other countries
toward "reducing the burden of regulation" and "harmonizing regulatory requirements." Indeed, for the first time in the history of the FDA,
Congress provided the agency with a clear and ambitious mandate.

The formal change in mission symbolizes the transformation of the
agency's orientation toward Type I and II errors. On one hand, this orientation remains focused on keeping harmful drugs out of the hands of
consumers. On the other hand, the notion of safeguarding public health
has now been broadened to include the promotion of new and effective
treatments through the expeditious review of new drugs. Thus, the new
mission for the first time mandates "prompt" and "efficient" reviews

Figure 5.3  Congressionally Mandated FDA Mission Statement

Section 903 (21 U.S.C. 393) is amended—(1) by redesignating subsections (b) and (c) as subsections (c) and (d), respectively; and (2) by adding after subsection (a) the following:

"(b) Mission.—
      "The Food and Drug Administration shall promote the public health by promptly and efficiently reviewing clinical research and taking appropriate action on the marketing of regulated products in a timely manner, and with respect to such products shall protect the public health by ensuring that—
            "(1) foods are safe, wholesome, sanitary, and properly labeled;
            "(2) human and veterinary drugs are safe and effective;
            "(3) there is reasonable assurance of safety and effectiveness of devices intended for human use;
            "(4) cosmetics are safe and properly labeled; and
            "(5) public health and safety are protected from electronic product radiation.

      "The Food and Drug Administration shall participate with other countries to reduce the burden of regulation, harmonize regulatory requirements, and achieve appropriate reciprocal arrangements."

      *Source:* U.S. House (1997: 29).

and directs the agency to participate with other countries in "reducing the burden of regulation."

To realize fully the significance of this change in agency mission, one must consider the new mission in relation to the agency's previous mission. In the absence of a congressionally defined mission statement, the earlier mission was developed internally by the agency. The previous mission statement is included as Figure 5.4. It clearly reflects the agency's efforts to avoid Type II errors as the sole priority, which was characteristic of the agency during the previous regulatory period. It also reflects the agency's law enforcement origins.

The primary mission of the agency until FDAMA was "to protect, promote, and enhance the health of the American people." Specifically, the agency was to ensure that "human and veterinary drugs, biological products, and medical devices are safe and effective." Significantly, though not coincidentally, the FDA's self-imposed mission statement failed to mention any guidelines regarding the expedient review of new drugs. Above all other factors, as reflected by the intentions of the enacting coalition during the 1960s and clearly demonstrated through its internally devised mission statement, the agency viewed itself as a law

---

### Figure 5.4 Internally Devised FDA Mission Statement

The Food and Drug Administration is a team of dedicated professionals working to protect, promote and enhance the health of the American people. FDA is responsible for ensuring that:

- Foods are safe, wholesome and sanitary; human and veterinary drugs, biological products, and medical devices are safe and effective; cosmetics are safe; and electronic products that emit radiation are safe.
- Regulated products are honestly, accurately and informatively represented.
- These products are in compliance with the law and FDA regulations; noncompliance is identified and corrected; and any unsafe or unlawful products are removed from the marketplace.

We strive to:

- Enforce FDA laws and regulations, using all appropriate legal means.
- Base regulatory decisions on a strong scientific and analytical base and the law; and understand, conduct and apply excellent science and research.
- Be a positive force in making safe and effective products available to the consumer, and focus special attention on rare and life-threatening diseases.
- Provide clear standards of compliance to regulated industry, and advise industry on how to meet those standards.
- Identify and effectively address critical public health problems arising from use of FDA-regulated products.
- Increase FDA's effectiveness through collaboration and cooperation with state and local governments; domestic, foreign and international agencies; industry; and academia.
- Assist the media, consumer groups, and health professionals in providing accurate, current information about regulated products to the public.
- Work consistently toward effective and efficient application of resources to our responsibilities.
- Provide superior public service by developing, maintaining and supporting a high-quality, diverse work force.
- Be honest, fair and accountable in all of our actions and decisions.

*Source:* Adapted from FDA website, www.fda.gov, March 1996.

---

enforcement agency. In accord with this focus on consumer protection, the agency is still continually engaged in law enforcement activity. This position has engendered a great deal of controversy, particularly by those arguing for a more expedient regulatory process.

Another highly significant aspect of FDAMA is that the legislation addressed the controversy over the "substantial evidence" standard (described in Chapter 4), which long symbolized the "gold standard" for new drug approval but was the target of agency critics seeking to lessen overall drug approval times. FDAMA amended Section 505(d) of the Food, Drug and Cosmetic Act to make clear that the agency *may* consider "data from one adequate and well-controlled clinical investigation and confirmatory evidence" to meet the substantial evidence clause if the FDA determines that such data and evidence are appropriate to demonstrate effectiveness (see Kulynych, 1999). A subsequent FDA guidance outlined the specific situations in which one pivotal trial may be adequate (USFDA, 1998). Such scenarios include situations where information from supporting studies may be used or evidence may be extrapolated from existing studies. These legislative and administrative provisions emerging in the latest regulatory era, made easier because of significant advances in drug development, represent a substantial shift in the regulatory review process and an equally large symbolic shift in regulatory philosophy.

Pressures for FDA reform altered the balance within the policy subsystem. Beginning in the late 1980s, the agency began responding to intense pressure for change from Congress, the pharmaceutical industry, and consumer interest groups. An examination of the skillful political maneuvering that altered the nature of business-government relations and forged an unlikely policy coalition helps illuminate this policy punctuation. Moreover, such changes in the policy subsystem helped create a new policy monopoly and provide clear evidence of a fourth distinctive period in regulatory governance. It should be noted, however, that Sidney Wolfe's Health Research Group (HRG) has strongly opposed the current policy monopoly. HRG releases occasional surveys that criticize the new regulatory regime and point to the large number of drug withdrawals over the past few years as evidence that the current regime provides inadequate safeguards for consumers.

## Consequences of the Regulatory Shift

The true significance of the regulatory shift is perhaps best understood in the context of the four-way schema depicted in Figure 1.1. The regulatory shift and the gradually evolving change in regulatory philosophy have had several effects. First, the regulatory shift has made U.S. decisionmakers (policymakers and regulatory officials) more aware of the negative aspects associated with Type I errors (i.e., not approving or delaying the approval of safe and effective medicines). For years the dominant motivations of drug reviewers, and the agency in general, were to ensure that consumers not be exposed to harmful drugs. This thinking still prevails. Increasingly, however, a second realization of near equal importance has emerged: public health can also be considered at risk when consumers do not have access to important drugs. Hence, regulatory officials have now become much more aware of the critical nature of expeditious reviews and approvals, and this philosophy is now institutionalized. Regulatory thinking at the FDA has become similar to the thinking that is pervasive in Europe. The Europeans have followed a more balanced strategy of protecting public health while simultaneously taking steps to promote it as well.

The longstanding paradigm of highly centralized regulatory controls governing the review of new medicines is gradually weakening. While the regulatory controls are still highly centralized, they are clearly less stringent. The key link in the regulatory transformation has been the change in focus toward making new drugs available to the public sooner and the corresponding streamlining of the review process. This philosophical shift is significant for three reasons. First, following the strengthening of centralized controls emanating from the 1960s, this fourth regulatory period, punctuated by PDUFA, largely typifies the spirit of the new regulatory era. The new policy monopoly favors the weakening of stringent, centralized controls. Second, the regulatory transformation yields several important distributional consequences. Primarily, regulatory officials at the FDA have developed a broader definition of what it takes to protect public health. In addition to the protection of public health, this broadening encompasses the promotion of public health and the realization that public health is also at risk when consumers do not have access to new and effective therapies. Therefore, expediency has emerged as an important criterion as U.S. regulators have become more aware of the perils associated with delays in the approval of new drugs. Finally, as I have attempted to illustrate in this chapter, skillful political maneuvering is indeed a critical component for inducing changes in institutional structure and, ultimately, a policy punctuation.

## Conclusion

The 1992 Prescription Drug User Fee Act provides a meaningful starting point for the latest regulatory period. PDUFA provides the institutional foundations and an updated regulatory arrangement between Congress as the principal and the FDA as agent. In conjunction with PDUFA as a landmark law governing agency structure and process, the law largely typifies the spirit of the new regulatory era (often dubbed the user fee era). The spirit of the new era is reflected both in the agency's regulatory behavior and its revised mission of protecting public health. Clearly, the fourth regulatory period has witnessed a significant change in the FDA's regulatory performance. The key link in the regulatory transformation has been the generation of industry user fees to supplement agency revenues and the increased reliance on streamlining the approval process. Collectively, these changes reflect the powerful supporting idea that expands the agency's traditional mission of protecting public health. The FDA's mission no longer solely mandates the agency to protect public health by keeping harmful medicines out of the hands of consumers. Instead, that mission has been enlarged to include the additional responsibility of promoting public health by making new medicines available to the public on a timely basis.

This regulatory transformation yields several important distributional consequences. First, regulatory officials at the agency have seemingly developed a broader—or what might be better termed, a more republican—definition of public health. That is, in addition to its longstanding (and perhaps paternalistic) view that protecting public health was done by keeping harmful drugs out of the hands of consumers, the agency has clearly acknowledged that public health is also at risk when consumers do not have access to new and effective therapies. As such, expeditiousness has emerged as an important criterion, as U.S. regulators have become more aware of the perils associated with delays in the approval of new drugs. It is in this sense that the agency has seemingly shifted toward a more republican view of public health. In a world where all medical products are associated with some level of risk, the implicit acknowledgment by the agency in the new regulatory era is that drug safety must be considered relative to both the benefits provided by a given drug and to the needs of the patients the drug is ultimately intended to serve.

A second consequence of this transformation lies in the apparent changing nature of the interactions between the agency and other actors in the policy subsystem. In one sense, the FDA has taken on a more active role in working with the pharmaceutical industry in the drug development process. As noted in Chapter 1, Representative Bilirakis pointed out that some in Congress now view the FDA as a "partner" of the industry. Such sentiment would have been unimaginable in the previous period characterized by the 1962 Kefauver amendments. In a related notion, agency officials have increasingly used the term *stakeholder* to refer to other primary actors in the policy subsystem who have an interest in agency activity—including the pharmaceutical industry, patients, consumers, and other public and private organized constituencies. In this republican sense, the agency is gradually altering its interactions with those it is charged to regulate.

Third, FDA behavior during this period also points toward a broader convergence with European and Japanese regulatory agencies in designing regulatory standards. In effect, Congress mandated the FDA to work with foreign regulatory agencies to develop a set of harmonized standards that may someday be globally consistent. Given the differences in regulatory styles occurring across national boundaries, this type of convergence may have significant implications for commission of Type I and II errors.

In the context of agency theory, the regulatory changes stemming from PDUFA, the subsequent changes in regulatory performance by the agency, and the gradually evolving changes in attitudes by Congress and other public health officials regarding the promotion of public health collectively indicate that a new era in U.S. medicines regulation has emerged. The promotion of public health by making new medicines available to consumers in an expedient fashion has now become entrenched as one of the core ideas at the basis of this contract.

# 6

# WHITHER THE FDA?

President Clinton explained the guiding philosophy in our examination of how we are performing: "protect people, not bureaucracy; promote results, not rules; get action, not rhetoric." That is what we have been trying to do. We are working hard to make FDA more efficient and to maintain the high quality of work.

—*Michael Friedman,*
*former deputy FDA commissioner*

Drug regulation in the United States is now at an important juncture. It has been a decade since the establishment of the latest regulatory period, marked by the 1992 Prescription Drug User Fee Act and the redefinition of the FDA's mission. Since that time, the agency has attempted to increase patient access to new medicines, and the balance in the overall risk-benefit calculation has shifted in favor of benefits. In light of these considerations, PDUFA has created a number of important regulatory challenges and opportunities for the FDA. In this chapter, I examine several of these challenges and opportunities facing the agency in the user fee era.

First, the nature of agency leadership remains one of the most important issues facing the FDA in the latest regulatory period. As I have demonstrated in earlier chapters, top agency officials have navigated the agency through important transitions in each of the preceding regulatory regimes. Issues related to agency leadership became especially apparent during the tenure of Commissioner David Kessler (1990–1997). Yet, in the years since Kessler's departure, it has been the *absence* of high-level leadership that has been a defining characteristic of the FDA. This relative leadership vacuum not only creates a number of challenges to the agency, it also makes it more difficult for the FDA to fulfill its mission of protecting and promoting public health.

In addition to agency leadership, I also look at two important external sources of influence on the agency—the pharmaceutical industry and foreign regulatory agencies. The FDA's new congressionally mandated mission magnifies the importance of relations between FDA and the pharmaceutical industry. As Representative Bilirakis's comments noted in Chapter 1 indicate, some see the pharmaceutical industry as a partner of the FDA. Others see this relationship quite differently, however. Critics have repeatedly warned that the agency, as the primary regulator of pharmaceutical industry activities, is not and should not be a partner of industry.

Foreign regulatory agencies also figure more prominently in the new regulatory arena. Considerable regulatory dialogue has taken place across the Atlantic and Pacific since 1992. In conjunction with the agency's new mission, increasing dialogue with foreign regulatory agencies has led the FDA to modify a number of policies. In some cases, it can be argued that a harmonization of worldwide regulatory standards is gradually emerging. If so, such harmonization will undoubtedly have significant implications for the future of U.S. public health.

In the remainder of this chapter I identify perhaps the single greatest challenge to drug regulators in the new era—drug safety. Making new medicines available to consumers in a timely fashion (i.e., avoiding Type I errors) remains a fundamental component of the fourth regulatory period. Yet one direct consequence of this strategy is the potential for heightened concerns over drug safety and the widespread occurrence of adverse drug reactions. Since all pharmaceutical products contain some element of risk, drug safety remains a relative rather than an absolute concept. Adverse drug reactions occur for a variety of reasons, ranging from a drug's negative side effects to improper usage by either doctors or patients. Consequently, the risks associated with new pharmaceutical products are increasingly evaluated relative to the benefits that such substances provide.

## Agency Leadership

The title of this chapter expresses an important question facing the FDA in the fourth regulatory period. "Whither the FDA?" is especially prominent in the context of agency theory. PDUFA provides the FDA with an important set of institutional structures and processes, and, given these parameters, we should expect the agency to carry out its regulatory mission. Yet significant issues pertaining to agency leadership have arguably hindered the agency from effectively performing such duties. The previous chapter demonstrated the significance of agency leadership and the skillful political maneuvering of former commissioner David Kessler during the transition into the current regulatory period. Kessler navigated the agency through the first five years of the current regulatory era before stepping down to become dean of the Yale University School of Medicine in 1997. Since Kessler's departure from the agency, the position of FDA commissioner has remained *unfilled* for longer than it has been occupied. The vacancy of such a high-level governmental position is not conducive to protecting and promoting public health. Agency leadership requires a commissioner who can articulate a broad vision for the agency and represent the agency during difficult moments. "The primary job of a commissioner," as industry observer Ira Loss put it, "is to be a lightning rod to protect the agency, to absorb and deflect criticisms from the agency" (Schwab and Todd, 2002).

The following discussion provides an illustration of the agency's leadership difficulties since Kessler's departure. Kessler's successor was Jane Henney, an oncologist, and the first woman to be FDA commissioner. However, Henney was nominated for the position seventeen months *after* Kessler's departure. After an additional four months to conclude the confirmation process, Henney finally took over as commissioner. Thus, it took nearly two years to replace Kessler. During the interim, the lead deputy commissioner, Michael Friedman, led the agency quite capably. In holding the post for an interim period, however, Friedman lacked the legitimacy of a Senate-confirmed commissioner.

Henney's tenure as FDA commissioner was relatively brief. Henney was confirmed in October 1998 and remained in the position until President George W. Bush accepted her resignation in January 2001. The post continued to remain vacant following Henney's resignation and was the highest-ranking government position to remain unfilled until nearly two years into the Bush presidency. In essence, apart from Henney's brief tenure, the agency has lacked the necessary type of "lightning rod" since Kessler's departure in 1997.

Technically speaking, the FDA commissioner is appointed by the secretary of health and human services and is not a presidential appointee. In practice, however, the president clearly maintains a dominant role in selecting the agency's commissioner. Historically, Senate confirmation of the nominee was not required for the appointment. This would later change, however, in an effort to increase congressional control over the

FDA. Following Kessler's tenure, the appointment of FDA commissioner is now subject to Senate confirmation. Generally, in order to be confirmed, the prospective candidate must have the approval of the Senate Health, Education, Labor and Pensions Committee and at least tacit approval from both the pharmaceutical industry and core consumer advocacy groups.

In addition to the appointing of agency heads, the *removal* of top agency officials is also a critical element of political control. Horn (1995) argues that the employment conditions of key decisionmakers and their degree of independence from the political process are important considerations for the potential removal of agency heads. Specifically, he suggests that agency heads that serve on multiple member "commissions" such as the Securities and Exchange Commission, the Federal Trade Commission, and the Federal Communications Commission are more likely to be insulated from such political wrangling. By contrast, individual heads of executive branch agencies such as the Environmental Protection Agency and FDA are more susceptible to removal for political reasons. The scenario described by Horn fits the FDA quite well during the latest regulatory period.

Commissioner Henney submitted her resignation upon the arrival of the new presidential administration in early 2001. This practice of resigning is customary for high-level bureaucratic appointees across the entire federal government. Agency heads and high-ranking appointed officials offer their resignation so that incoming presidential administrations can fill these posts with replacements of their choosing. For example, Kessler, who was appointed by George H. W. Bush, quickly submitted his resignation to President Bill Clinton in 1993. In somewhat of a departure, however, Clinton did not accept Kessler's resignation (despite the fact that Kessler was a Republican appointee).

During the course of the 2000 presidential campaign, the FDA approved the controversial abortion pill, Mifeprex (RU-486). The approval was a high-profile decision, and each presidential candidate publicly remarked on the agency decision. Thus, despite the fact that Henney had enjoyed broad support from the pharmaceutical industry during her tenure as commissioner, her resignation was immediately accepted by the incoming Bush administration.[76] Most news accounts suggested that the agency's approval of Mifeprex was the primary reason Bush accepted Henney's resignation. The issue was a prominent theme during the confirmation hearings for former Wisconsin governor Tommy Thompson, who at the time had been nominated to head the Department of Health and Human Services. In referring to Bush's acceptance of Henney's resignation during the Thompson confirmation hearings, Senator Barbara Mikulski suggested to Thompson, "Let's not politicize FDA. . . . I ask you to look into this matter" (Weiss, 2001).

Dr. Lester Crawford was named deputy commissioner in February 2002, just over one year after Henney's departure. Crawford was considered for the position of FDA commissioner, but several consumer advocacy groups (including Public Citizen's Health Research Group) strongly opposed his nomination. The opposition to Crawford's potential nomination was largely due to his past connections to the food industry. Core consumer advocacy groups and the pharmaceutical industry subsequently deemed several other prospective candidates unsuitable as well.

Finally, President Bush nominated Mark McClellan for the position of FDA commissioner in September 2002. McClellan received Senate confirmation a short time later. McClellan took over the agency nearly two full years since the departure of the previous full-time commissioner. If for no other reason, merely filling the post of FDA commissioner was an important and positive step for the agency. More important, though little is known about how McClellan will lead the FDA, his confirmation has brought a sense of optimism for the agency's future. Perhaps part of this optimism is based on the remarkable similarities that McClellan shares with Kessler. At the time of his nomination, McClellan was a member of Bush's Council of Economic Advisers. McClellan, like Kessler, was very young at the time of the appointment (age thirty-nine), and each possessed both a medical degree and an advanced degree in another field. (McClellan has a doctorate in economics, Kessler in law.) Thus, now that McClellan has taken over the agency, it remains clear that agency leadership will be critical in this new era of regulatory activity.

In conjunction with agency leadership, two other factors are critical to the FDA's expanded mission in the new regulatory era: agency relations with the pharmaceutical industry and with foreign regulatory agencies. These two relationships are the subject of the following sections.

## The FDA and the Pharmaceutical Industry

Whereas government and industry share similar goals of providing patients with high-quality drugs in a timely manner, they generally disagree over how this might best be accomplished. Yet, as the PDUFA legislative debates in the early 1990s demonstrated, despite these fundamental differences, the pharmaceutical industry played an important role in negotiating and ultimately shaping the current regulatory structures and processes.

On the surface we might expect the pharmaceutical industry's view of the FDA to be a two-sided coin. On one side, because agency delays in approving new medicines can impede industry profitability (as was seen through the regulatory regime dominated by the 1962 Kefauver amendments), it would not be uncharacteristic of pharmaceutical industry officials to be critical of the agency's performance. On the other side, in terms of appropriation requests and the annual agency budget, the pharmaceutical industry is likely to be supportive of the FDA (Quirk, 1981). While the pharmaceutical industry relies on the FDA to approve its products, the relationship between the two has not been close, historically. At times this relationship has been characterized as formal, distant, and lacking mutual trust. Consequently, conflicting relations, breakdowns in communication, and acrimony have characterized the nature of the relations over the years. This relationship provides an important backdrop when considering the politics of drug risk and effectiveness.

## The Domestic Pharmaceutical Market

A first general consideration is the interest of the government in the financial well-being of the domestic industry. For example, in countries with nationalized health systems such as Britain and Canada, the national-level governments have an acute interest in the commercial success of the domestic pharmaceutical industry. In the case of countries with centralized health systems, the state-run national health service provides "cradle to grave" medical coverage for citizens and pays for the prescription medicines of consumers. Given this arrangement, these governments act as a monopsony purchaser in the domestic pharmaceutical market. Consequently, individual retail and wholesale pharmacy outlets play a much smaller role in the domestic market. Further, the close proximity of the government to the well-being of the industry in a country like Britain or Canada suggests that the regulatory apparatus may not be onerous and excessively burdensome on the pharmaceutical industry. Due to the repeated nature of the interactions and because of the financial incentives associated with being the dominant pharmaceutical purchaser, national-level governments in such countries are likely to have a better overall working relationship with the domestic pharmaceutical industry.

From a purely regulatory standpoint, a similar connection has not traditionally existed in the United States. Over the years the federal government has had arguably little connection to the financial well-being of the domestic pharmaceutical industry. Milton Roemer's (1991) typology of worldwide health systems classifies the U.S. health care system as one that is entrepreneurial and permissive in nature. Because the private health system leads to a domestic market without the presence of a monopsonist, the FDA has little or no attachment to competitive marketplace outcomes. Despite proposals during the Clinton administration to implement a plan of national and universal coverage and despite recent legislative debate over a prescription drug plan for Medicare, the U.S. health care system remains oriented toward the private market and heavily dependent on payments by third-party insurers.[77]

Medicare and Medicaid remain the two largest governmental health programs in the United States. Medicare, which insures Americans aged sixty-five and older and covers roughly 13 percent of the population, is funded through a combination of payroll taxes and general revenues. However, recipients are expected to pay deductibles and obtain co-insurance. Medicare provides hospital and physician care for the elderly, but it does not cover the cost of outpatient prescription drugs. The latter issue has figured prominently on the domestic health agenda in recent years. The other large governmental health program, Medicaid, was developed in the early 1960s and remains the nation's primary health care program for the poor. The Medicaid program insures roughly 10 percent of the U.S. population. Funding is jointly provided and administered by individual state governments and the federal government.

Given the private-market orientation of its system, the United States spends a far greater share of its gross domestic product (GDP) on health care than any other member of the Organization for Economic Cooperation and Development (OECD). Table 6.1 illustrates the three major health expenditure categories for OECD nations in 1998. Relatively speaking, the United States spends considerably more on health than other OECD countries, especially those with centralized systems. In 1998, health expenditures as a percentage of GDP in the United States (13.1 percent) was nearly twice as high as the OECD average (7.9 percent). Moreover, health expenditures per capita in the United States amounted to $4,177 compared to an OECD average of $1,707.

The amount of expenditures by public sources is another important measure. In the United States, funding for health from government sources provides less than half of total health expenditures (45.4 percent). Meanwhile, the average share of public expenditures on health

Table 6.1  Primary Health Expenditure Indicators, OECD Countries, 1998

| Country | Health Expenditure (% of GDP) | Per Capita Health Expenditure ($) | Public Share of Health Expenditure[a] (% of total) |
|---|---|---|---|
| Australia | 8.6 | 2,085 | 68.2 |
| Austria | 8.0 | 1,894 | 70.9 |
| Belgium | 8.6 | 2,050 | 89.3 |
| Canada | 9.3 | 2,360 | 69.4 |
| Czech Republic | 7.1 | 937 | 91.7 |
| Denmark | 8.3 | 2,132 | 82.4 |
| Finland | 6.9 | 1,510 | 76.1 |
| France | 9.4 | 2,043 | 76.4 |
| Germany | 10.3 | 2,361 | 76.9 |
| Greece | 8.4 | 1,198 | 57.7 |
| Hungary | 6.8 | 717 | 75.3 |
| Iceland | 8.4 | 2,113 | 83.9 |
| Ireland | 6.8 | 1,534 | 75.0 |
| Italy | 8.2 | 1,824 | 67.5 |
| Japan | 7.4 | 1,795 | 79.5 |
| Korea | 5.1 | 740 | 40.6 |
| Luxembourg | 6.0 | 2,246 | 92.5 |
| Mexico | 5.3 | 419 | 60.0 |
| Netherlands | 8.7 | 2,150 | 69.6 |
| New Zealand | 8.1 | 1,440 | 77.3 |
| Norway | 9.4 | 2,452 | 83.0 |
| Poland | 6.4 | 524 | 72.0 |
| Portugal | 7.7 | 1,203 | 67.1 |
| Spain | 7.0 | 1,194 | 76.5 |
| Sweden | 7.9 | 1,732 | 84.3 |
| Switzerland | 10.4 | 2,853 | 73.2 |
| Turkey | 4.8 | 316 | 72.8 |
| United Kingdom | 6.8 | 1,510 | 83.7 |
| United States | 13.1 | 4,177 | 45.4 |
| OECD average | 7.90 | 1,707 | 73.7 |

Source: OECD, OECD Health Data, 2000: A Comparative Analysis of 20 Countries. CD-ROM (Paris: OECD).
    Note: a. Data are for 1997.

among the OECD countries was approximately 50 percent higher (73.7 percent). Thus, as Table 6.1 illustrates, the high cost of health care in the United States remains evident when compared to other industrialized democracies. These broad-based national comparisons of health expenditures are important to consider because an emerging body of economic literature seeks to establish a relationship between aggregate-level pharmaceutical consumption and an aggregate national health profile (Frech and Miller, 1999). Establishing a clear empirical linkage between these areas may have a significant effect on the way polities perceive the contribution of pharmaceutical products to their overall health profile.

The public/private balance in a nation's health system structures the domestic pharmaceutical market in profound ways. For instance, due to the comprehensive nature of the Canadian and British health systems, those systems serve as virtual monopsonistic purchasers of pharmaceuticals (Reekie, 1988). These systems provide drugs at virtually no out-of-pocket cost to patients. As a result, government expenditures in those countries account for nearly 50 percent of the domestic pharmaceutical market. Meanwhile, given the system's private-market orientation, the government represents a far smaller share of the domestic U.S. market.[78]

Undoubtedly, the differing approaches to national health coverage profoundly influence the nature of government–pharmaceutical industry relations. There is no equivalent in the United States to the centralized health service acting as a monopsonist player in the Canadian and European domestic markets. This monopsony relationship closely links government-run health systems with the domestic pharmaceutical industry. Alternatively, since wholesale and retail pharmacies are the primary purchasers of pharmaceuticals in the U.S. market, the U.S. Department of Health and Human Services lacks an equivalent connection with the domestic pharmaceutical industry.

## Anecdotal Accounts of Industry-Agency Relations

In the absence of the centralized health connection, the drug lag history, and the occasionally conflicting interests of both PhRMA and the FDA, one might also expect a relatively contentious working relationship between the agency and the domestic industry. Stemming from long-standing industry concerns that the agency was impeding drug development (and ultimately profitability) in the decades following the 1962 amendments, agency relations with the pharmaceutical industry were strained and often contentious. Though the nature of this relationship is difficult to measure systematically, the anecdotal and conventional wisdom suggests this discord to be a natural outcome of the system. One industry representative asserted the industry's chronic concern with the FDA saying, "There is a fundamental degree of trust missing between FDA and the industry." Several examples of this lack of trust in the regulatory process (e.g., the bottom-up review approach, raw data requirements, etc.) were discussed in previous chapters. General explanations behind this perceived lack of trust range from instances of simple bureaucratic politics to industry suspicion of agency motives (and vice versa) to fundamental differences in economic perspectives.

At an extreme level, several stereotypical industry fears of the FDA reviewer extend to mythical levels. For example, some industry officials spoke of the great concern and uneasiness conjured up by the image of the "robed reviewer" operating in a "blind alley" when reviewing the sponsor's new drug application. Drug sponsors often fear that the role of the reviewer is simply to "look for trouble" in the application. In doing so, the reviewer is likely to become bogged down in the minutiae of the application. A similar fear is that the agency drags its heels on some applications and not others. The absolute worst practice, according to one industry official, is to have your application put "on the bottom of the pile" by an FDA reviewer. Perhaps summing up these stereotypical perceptions, as one industry official pointed out, "The FDA exhibits such capricious behavior when it comes to deciding what it takes to approve a new drug. It can be frustrating."

At the other end of the continuum, it could be argued that relations between the agency and the pharmaceutical industry have improved during the user fee era. If for no other reason, the agency's improved review performance (as measured in terms of shortened review times) has significant implications for industry profitability. A central part of the political compromise brokered by then commissioner David Kessler was that performance standards would be set by the agency in exchange for user fees. Future streams of user fee revenue were then tied to the agency's ability to meet the designated performance goals. In this case, it could be argued that industry-agency relations could be (and should be) improved because each is working to meet specific performance goals.

It is in this spirit that some industry officials adopt a more utilitarian view of the FDA's role. As one industry official pointed out, "My firm's view of FDA regulation is based on a pure financial interest, especially in a patented product. We only make money when a product is under patent." Another, referring specifically to approval decisions, commented, "Industry, to be quite honest, is a friend of the FDA. We have a government seal of approval on every product. Our difference, we've argued, is that sometimes we don't like how they're doing their job." As the user fee era continues and FDA review times continue to hover around an average of twelve months per new drug, industry concerns about lost profitability should be greatly lessened (at least compared to previous regulatory periods).

## Industry Influence in Congress

Beyond industry-agency relations, the pharmaceutical industry has long enjoyed a close relationship with the agency's primary principal—Congress. PhRMA, the industry's leading trade association in the United States, has long maintained a powerful influence in Washington. The association, which currently has thirty-four full members, dozens of associate members, and at least a half dozen international affiliates, represents the interests of "the country's leading research-based pharmaceutical and biotechnology companies."[79] In 2001, PhRMA ranked twenty-fourth on the list of *Fortune's* "Power 25"—the magazine's annual list of Washington's most powerful lobbying groups.[80] The primary regulatory-related interests of PhRMA generally center around issues of patent protection, pricing, and licensing.

The pharmaceutical industry is routinely one of the leading contributors to presidential and congressional election campaigns. According to the Center for Responsive Politics (CRP), the industry contributed over $26.4 million to House and Senate members during the 2000 election cycle.[81] Examining the distribution of these funds yields insights into the political nature of FDA regulation. Historically speaking, pharmaceutical contributions are not evenly distributed to Democratic and Republican members of Congress. CRP reports that 68 percent of these contributions went to Republicans whereas 31 percent went to Democratic candidates.

The contributions to leading legislators are not insignificant. CRP reports that three members of Congress received over $100,000 in contributions from pharmaceutical interests. The top three congressional recipients for the 2002 electoral cycle were Republican representative Nancy Johnson ($190,317), Democratic senator Robert Torricelli ($149,453), and Democratic senator Max Baucus ($105,372).[82] Also among the top twenty recipients was Florida representative Michael Bilirakis, who suggested that the FDA and the pharmaceutical industry are "partners" during a 2002 congressional hearing. Bilirakis received $73,242 during the 2002 election cycle.

Given such financial contributions, the industry has been relatively successful in protecting its interests on Capitol Hill. This success is illustrated by the extension of patent protection for brand medicines and the longstanding inertia against the implementation of pricing controls. In the former case, the 1984 Drug Price Competition and Patent Term Restoration Act reflected a compromise between brand-name pharmaceutical manufacturers and their generic competitors. U.S. patents generally apply for a period of seventeen years following their issuance. Essentially, the 1984 law enabled drug makers to add up to five years of patent protection for brand-name medicines (thus increasing the duration of market exclusivity). In exchange, brand-name drug makers agreed to have the FDA speed the approval process of generic drug products, thus promoting price competition.

Despite repeated attempts to enact legislation aimed at implementing pricing restrictions or a prescription drug plan for Medicare, such efforts have failed consistently over the years. Consequently, people in the United States pay more for prescription medicines than anywhere else in the world, and the pharmaceutical industry has remained incredibly successful from a commercial standpoint.

## Common Criticisms of the Pharmaceutical Industry

The commercial success of the pharmaceutical industry comes with a fairly sizable political price, however. The industry's market successes make it the target of frequent criticisms from consumer advocates, patient groups, and some members of Congress. Typically, criticism stems from the standard "business case" argument made by industry officials. In defending its profitability, the argument goes something like this. Pharmaceutical firms are forced to charge high prices for prescription drugs because large revenue streams are necessary in order to maintain a high level of research and development. Since drug development is both risky and costly, industry officials maintain that a substantial research and development budget is needed to ensure that innovative new drugs are continually pushed through the development pipeline.

Given its insistence on this standard argument, the pharmaceutical industry continually suffers from image problems in the eyes of some consumers, media organizations, and political officials. These image problems (whether real or perceived) are a clear indication that the pharmaceutical industry is not a partner of the FDA. Consider the following industry criticisms:

*1. The pharmaceutical industry is just too profitable.* According to *Fortune* magazine, the pharmaceutical industry ranked first in 2001 among all industries in each of the three profitability categories: return on revenues, return on assets, and return on shareholders' equity.[83] The fourteen *Fortune* 500 drug companies garnered a total of $37.7 billion in profits in 2001. In that same year, profits earned by drug companies as a percentage of revenues was an incredible 18.5 percent. This remarkable performance, especially during a time when many other industries in corporate America were experiencing widespread losses, led Congress Watch, the government watchdog arm of the consumer advocacy group Public Citizen, to coin the phrase "Druggernaut" in referring to the nation's largest drug companies (Public Citizen, 2002). In reviewing pharmaceutical industry profitability over the past three decades, Congress Watch noted that the *Fortune* 500 drug companies were twice as profitable as the median company for all industries during the 1970s and 1980s, and almost four times as profitable (as the median company) during the 1990s.

2. *Pharmaceutical industry executives are excessively compensated.* "Profiting from Pain," a July 2002 report from Families USA, a Washington, D.C.–based consumer health advocacy organization, analyzed executive compensation from nine leading pharmaceutical companies (Families USA, 2002). The report compiled a list of the top five highest-paid executives from each company for 2001. During that year, the average compensation for the single highest-paid executive of each company was nearly $21 million. Among the nine companies analyzed, Bristol Myers Squibb's former chairman and CEO, C. A. Heimbold Jr., received the highest compensation package. In 2001, Heimbold earned $74.89 million (excluding unexercised stock options). John Stafford, chairman of Wyeth, was second on the list with a total compensation package of $40.5 million. Though executive compensation has become an issue of interest across all industries, the compensation of pharmaceutical industry executives, coupled with the high levels of industry profitability, especially has attracted the attention of industry critics.

Pharmaceutical industry defenders argue that such profits and compensation are warranted, given the costly and risky nature of drug development. This too, however, has become an increasingly sensitive point of contention.

3. *The pharmaceutical industry exaggerates the costs of drug development.* It is difficult to estimate precisely the cost of developing a new drug from the time of its discovery until it is made available to consumers. Perhaps the toughest aspect of the task is utilizing an appropriate accounting methodology. In 1991, Joseph DiMasi and colleagues produced one of the earlier and more frequently cited figures. Using data from 1987, DiMasi and colleagues estimated that the cost to bring a new drug (in this case, a new chemical entity) to market was $231 million (DiMasi, Hansen, and Grabowski, 1991). Shortly later, the Office of

Technology Assessment (OTA), a research arm of the U.S. Congress, conducted an extensive review of earlier estimates. Though the OTA concluded that the costs of drug development "cannot be measured with great accuracy," the OTA study estimated that the cost to bring an NCE to market was "somewhere between $140 million and $190 million (in 1990 dollars)."[84]

Given the difficulty of the enterprise, these figures were largely accepted until nearly a decade later when the pharmaceutical industry asserted that the cost of drug development was approximately $500 million. PhRMA arrived at this figure by extrapolating the original estimates derived by DiMasi and colleagues, and it published the figure as a part of its annual pharmaceutical industry profile in 2001. To support this figure, PhRMA cited two studies emanating from private consulting organizations.[85] First, a Lehman Healthcare study placed the figure at $675 million. Subsequently, a Boston Consulting Group study estimated the figure to fall somewhere within the range of $590 million and $880 million. The range of the latter estimates, PhRMA argued, lent support to PhRMA's extrapolation. The $500 million figure was quickly challenged on several fronts, however. Perhaps most notably, the consumer group Public Citizen referred to the $500 million figure as "highly misleading." In response, Public Citizen published its own report, which both scrutinized the figures presented by PhRMA and attempted to recalculate the estimated drug development figure by using a simpler and slightly different accounting procedure (Public Citizen, 2001). According to Public Citizen, the actual figure was closer to $110 million. Later, DiMasi and colleagues at the Tufts University Center for the Study of Drug Development published an update from DiMasi's earlier work. Using proprietary data made available by ten pharmaceutical companies, the CSDD study found that the cost of drug development was approximately $802 million (DiMasi, Hansen, and Grabowski, 2003).

It remains evident that a definitive figure for the cost of drug development has yet to emerge. What remains clear, however, is the tremendous gap as suggested by the estimates of PhRMA, CSDD, and Public Citizen. Disparities in official estimates, which arise due to the lack of agreement on which drugs should be considered, how tax figures are calculated, and how potential opportunity costs are evaluated, will likely continue to persist. The aforementioned estimates all make differing assumptions when considering factors such as risk, time, and money. Nonetheless, PhRMA and the pharmaceutical industry have been criticized for allegedly exaggerating the costs of drug development.

4. *Despite industry claims about the significance of research and development expenditures, the pharmaceutical industry actually spends more money on marketing and promotion than it does on research and development.* To this end, Families USA evaluated the annual Securities and Exchange Commission (SEC) financial reports of nine leading pharmaceutical companies. In its report, "Profiting from Pain," the authors found that each of the nine companies in the analysis spent more on marketing, advertising, and administration (MAA) than on research and development.[86] This result is noteworthy because it essentially contradicts the industry's longstanding defense of the need for unrestrained pricing and shortened regulatory review times.

Moreover, the study found that eight of the nine companies in the study spent more than *twice* as much on MAA than on research and development. Collectively, the average percentage of revenues devoted to MAA for the nine firms was 27 percent, compared to just 11 percent for research and development. In dollar terms, these nine firms spent just over $45.4 billion on MAA compared to $19.1 billion on research.

In addition, independent of its analysis of promotional spending, the Families USA report also cited a 2001 Boston University School of Public Health study that noted that U.S. brand-name drug companies employed nearly twice as many people in marketing (87,810) as in research (48,527) (Sager and Socolar, 2001). Pfizer, for example, employs more than 8,000 drug reps in the United States alone. Merck recently pledged to increase its force of 5,000 reps by more than a third by 2003 (Michaels, 2001). Thus, despite its claims that large research and development budgets are necessary to ensure the continued flow of drug development, many leading pharmaceutical firms now spend a much healthier sum on the marketing and promotion of their products.

5. *The pharmaceutical industry cares more about profits than patients.* Collectively known as "Big Pharma," the world's leading pharmaceutical manufacturers clearly have a vested interest in protecting corporate profits. One recurring threat to corporate profitability occurs when industry patents are not protected. The highest-profile case of alleged patent infringement and perhaps the most salient example of the allegation that the industry cares more about profits than patients involved the HIV/AIDS pandemic.

Short of finding a cure, the United States has arguably turned the corner on the deadly disease since the mid-1980s. Infection rates have decreased, and infected individuals are living longer as the result of innovative drug therapies. Yet, in contrast to the successes in the United

States regarding the treatment of AIDS patients, the level of access to innovative drug therapy is certainly not uniform around the world. Specifically, much has been made about the fact that though effective treatments are available from a technological standpoint, the allocation and distribution of HIV/AIDS therapies has been sharply divided (as well as controversial). A 2002 United Nations report estimated that of the approximately 40 million adults living with HIV/AIDS in 2001, approximately 28 million infected persons resided in sub-Saharan Africa (UNAIDS, 2002).

In 1997, the government of South Africa enacted what became known as the Medicines and Related Substances Control Amendment Act. Under the leadership of Nelson Mandela, this law made it legal for the South African government to purchase pharmaceutical products through a method known as parallel importing. Rather than the government purchasing brand-name pharmaceuticals directly from the drug manufacturer, parallel importing involves the purchase of virtually identical products from third-party sources at a fraction of the costs. Such practices, however, violate the patent protection afforded to brand-name drugs.

In response to parallel importing, approximately thirty-nine pharmaceutical companies joined together in filing a lawsuit against the government of South Africa, claiming that the 1997 law violated South Africa's obligations to the World Trade Organization's patent agreements. The lawsuit, however, created a tremendous row and eventual backlash against the pharmaceutical industry. Newspapers and consumer advocacy groups around the globe took the industry to task for seemingly placing profits ahead of patient welfare. Finally, amidst intense public scrutiny, the pharmaceutical companies decided to drop the lawsuit in the spring of 2001. Even so, the damage had already been done in terms of negative publicity and the targeting of the industry's image. Collectively, these types of issues coupled with the pharmaceutical industry's immense profitability at times create an image problem for the industry.

In summary, given the institutional mechanisms (i.e., structures and processes) created by Congress in ushering in the user fee era, it is important to understand the nature of FDA relations with the pharmaceutical industry in this fourth regulatory period. The nature of the domestic pharmaceutical market, anecdotal accounts of industry-agency relations, industry influence in Congress, and common criticisms of the pharmaceutical industry each provide an important layer or context in which to examine the FDA's role of protecting the public from unsafe medicines while also promoting access to innovative therapies.

## New Drug Regulation in Europe and Japan

Given changes in the FDA's statutory mission that direct the agency to engage in a dialogue with foreign regulatory agencies, it is also instructive to examine the impact of foreign regulatory agencies on FDA behavior in the fourth regulatory period. The variation in regulatory performance across national regulatory authorities (such as between the U.S. Food and Drug Administration, the European Medicines Evaluation Agency [EMEA], or the Japanese Ministry of Health, Labor, and Welfare) reflects the tradeoff between politics and markets as a means of allocative decisionmaking (Okun, 1975; Schultze, 1977; Hirschman, 1982). Consequently, the politics of regulatory drug licensing demonstrates a powerful example of the competing tensions inherent in virtually every political and economic system. Such tradeoffs include the ongoing tension and ultimate balance between regulation and competition; cost and benefit; and risk and reward. It is for this reason that regulatory authorities in the United States, Europe, and Japan attract the greatest attention (and regulatory workload).

In comparing the relative performance of drug regulators in the world's leading pharmaceutical markets of the United States, Japan, and Europe, it is also apparent that the behavior of regulatory agencies changes over time. The United States was on the short end of an international drug lag during the 1970s and 1980s. The FDA was criticized for being slow to respond to licensing applications and for being overly cautious in approving new medicines. In recent years, however, the FDA has been among the world leaders in the rapid approval of new medicines and the quantity of drugs approved in any given year. Ironically, there is considerable debate currently taking place in both Japanese and European political circles concerning how these regions may revise their regulatory structures and processes in order to increase the rate at which new drugs are approved and decrease average approval times.

Many of the drug regulatory authorities in the world's leading pharmaceutical markets are currently in the process of transition. This transitory phase is largely the product of globalization and the changing nature of the pharmaceutical market. In Japan, for example, lawmakers are in the process of revising the Pharmaceutical Affairs Law (PAL). Such changes, which began in 1997, are expected to "drastically reform" the Japanese regulatory system, thereby modifying regulatory structures, organizations, and requirements across the board. These regulatory changes, induced largely by the changing nature of the pharmaceutical market, are expected to culminate with the creation of an entirely new regulatory agency in 2005.[87] As the new Japanese institutional structure emerges, issues such as agency design and regulatory structure and process remain critical.

In Europe, prior to 1995 drug regulatory agencies of individual European Union (EU) member states (e.g., the Irish Medicines Board, the German BfArM, the Dutch Medicines Evaluation Board, or the Swedish Medical Products Agency) conducted drug reviews independently of one another. So, at that time if one of the world's leading pharmaceutical manufacturers wanted to market a product in Europe, it had to gain the regulatory approval of each national regulatory authority. In addition, under the pre-1995 European regulatory arrangement, the Committee on the Propriety of Medicinal Products (CPMP), acting as a scientific advisory body to the commission, would evaluate a company's dossier (new drug application) and render its decision. The problem with this prior arrangement was that the decisions of the CPMP, and ultimately of the commission itself, were not binding on the member states. If one state did not agree with the decision of the CPMP, it was not legally required to accept its decision. Naturally, such a regulatory system became quite burdensome on manufacturers. So, after years of lobbying by pharmaceutical manufacturers and endless negotiations at the European Commission (EC) level, a new regulatory system—the European Medicines Evaluation Agency—was implemented in 1995.[88] Once again, we can point to the significance of agency design and institutional structure.[89]

The EMEA coordinates the drug approval procedures among the fifteen member states of the European Union, as well as with Norway and Iceland. This can be quite a task given the many cultural and political differences of the member states. For instance, there are eleven different languages spoken among member states. Even a seemingly subtle barrier such as differences in national languages can make the review and analysis of the highly technical information contained in drug dossiers extremely problematic.

Under the current European arrangement, a company can undertake one of two routes to get a new product approved. A centralized procedure enables a company to submit a dossier directly to the CPMP, which comprises two representatives from each member state. With input from the sponsoring firm, the CPMP then selects two of its members to become *rapporteurs,* or evaluators, of the application. Once the rapporteurs evaluate the dossier on the basis of safety, quality, and efficacy, the CPMP then issues its decision. The European Commission must then approve the CPMP's decision. If approved, a marketing authorization for the new drug is granted and the approval decision is legally binding across all member states.

Under the decentralized (or mutual recognition) procedure, a company can submit its dossier to the regulatory authority of an individual member state. The said authority then must make a formal decision within a designated time limit. If the decision is favorable, the company can then begin to market its product in that particular country. Also, on the rendering of a favorable decision, the sponsoring company is then free to approach the regulatory authorities of other member states requesting approval based on the acceptance of the initial member state.

In 2002 and 2003, the European Commission, the European Parliament, and the EU Health Council reviewed and revised current proceedings in which all new active substances (NAS) may go through either the centralized procedure or the decentralized procedure. Originally, the EC considered having all NAS go through the centralized procedure, although the pharmaceutical industry prefers the status quo in which companies can decide which route they prefer. In the final revision, a compromise was reached where the EU member states will now require medicines for cancer, AIDS, diabetes, and neuro-degenerative diseases to go through the centralized marketing authorization procedure. For all other new medicines, the sponsoring firm will have the option of choosing either the centralized or decentralized procedure.

The creation of a European-wide regulatory body has not diminished the significance of national regulatory authorities.[90] In fact, it could be argued that some agencies have become even more important in the new regulatory structure. In the first five years of the EMEA's operation, between 1995 and December 2000, a small number of EU regulatory agencies were conducting the majority of assessments for applications submitted through the centralized procedure. British, French, Swedish, German, and Dutch assessors conducted 59 percent of the NCE and biotech reviews on behalf of the CPMP during this time period.[91] The British Medicines Control Agency conducted more reviews than any other European national regulatory authority.[92] This popularity is a reflection of the generally high regard held for the MCA among member states.

## Increased International Collaboration

Regulatory change has been a common thread in the United States, Japan, and Europe over the past decade. These domestic transitions also provided important opportunities for cross-national regulatory discussions. Such discussions were initiated in the early 1990s in an attempt to coordinate or harmonize the technical requirements needed for the approval of new medicines in the world's three largest pharmaceutical markets. The ultimate goal of such discussions has been to promote an international collaboration that may ultimately harmonize regulatory standards for new drug products. Industry actors, in conjunction with the major trade associations operating in each market, were largely responsible for getting harmonization efforts off the ground during the early stages. In an era of increasing competition over drug development, and ultimately profitability, pharmaceutical firms viewed harmonization as a potential opportunity to shorten the drug development cycle. Since that time, the regulatory actors in each of the three major markets have been generally supportive of the efforts to harmonize. The result of these transnational discussions is the International Conference on Harmonization of Technical Requirements for the Registration of Pharmaceuticals for Human Use (ICH).

Established in 1989, the ICH is comprised of representatives from regulatory agencies in North America, Europe, and Japan. It provides a forum for regulatory authorities and pharmaceutical industry experts to discuss the scientific and technical aspects of product registration.[93] The FDA has been actively engaged in ICH discussions with other worldwide regulatory authorities. Harmonizing international safety, efficacy, and quality standards remains an important item on the agenda for several of world's leading regulatory authorities.

While ICH members remain divided over certain issues related to standards, the Common Technical Document (or CTD) is one of the most important developments to emerge from the ICH initiative. In principle, the CTD would make it easier for firms to submit drug applications and easier for agencies to review. The CTD is also highly desirable from an industry perspective because it would make the application dossier uniform for all member countries. However, as one FDA official suggested, "We are a long way from international reviews." This statement clearly reflects the notion that regulatory tradeoffs between risk and reward are not uniform among the countries of the three largest pharmaceutical markets. Thus, it is likely that complete harmonization remains a distant possibility. Complete harmonization would require bridging the gap between several political, cultural, and other regulatory differences.

PDUFA is a landmark law that effectively created a new contract between Congress and the FDA, but it also created several new opportunities and challenges for the agency. Thus, in the user fee era, agency leadership and FDA relationships with both the pharmaceutical industry and foreign regulatory agencies remain critical. With these factors providing an important backdrop, it is clear that the central topics of regulatory concern during the new period are drug safety and risk management. The following section considers these prominent issues in a little more detail.

## Drug Safety, Product Withdrawals, and Risk Management

The issue of drug safety requires us to return once again to the framework laid out in Chapter 1. For most of the twentieth century, FDA regulatory activity was centered on avoiding Type II errors—or avoiding the approval of potentially unsafe or ineffective drugs. During the drug lag years, a by-product of this regulatory strategy was an increased occurrence of Type I errors. That is, during the 1970s and 1980s, it was argued that the FDA was acting too cautiously, and empirical evidence demonstrated that many important drugs were not reaching the market in a timely fashion. Thus, in response to changes in the policy subsystem, Congress expanded the FDA's mission to include not only the protection of public health (by seeking to avoid Type II errors) but also the promotion of public health (with an emphasis on avoiding Type I errors). This new mission remains a vital characteristic of this fourth regulatory period.

In the context of Type I and II errors, we must return to the inherent tradeoffs associated with each approach. In 1990, for example, the percentage of new drug applications approved by the FDA in one year or less was below 20 percent. By 1999, the percentage of new drug applications approved in one year or less exceeded 60 percent (Rhein, 2001). According to Kenneth Kaitin and Elaine Healy, "The reduction in the mean approval phase for 1996 to 1998 NCEs continues the dramatic decline that began with the passage of PDUFA. . . . [These drugs] were approved in less than half the time of 10 years ago" (2000: 12). The disparities in review times for the pre- and post-1992 period are quite convincing.

Because the drug lag debates of the 1970s and 1980s also became an important forum for considering the tradeoffs between Type I and Type II errors, it is instructive to mention the FDA's review and approval behavior in the post-1992 period relative to other national drug regulatory authorities. In the same study, Kaitin and Healy found that

"The percentage of products first marketed in the United States has increased dramatically over the past 10 years—from 20 percent in 1987–1989 to 49 percent in 1996–1998" (2000: 12–13). This result led the authors to conclude, "The large increase . . . in the percentage of new products first marketed in the United States (49 percent) supports former FDA commissioner David Kessler's contention that this country has become the worldwide leader in the introduction of important new drugs" (12). These findings and related assertions provide clear evidence that over the course of the 1990s, the drug lag has become an artifact of the past.

Yet, perhaps as a result of the reduction in the FDA's average review time for new drugs and the increased number of worldwide drugs appearing first in the U.S. market, a number of drugs have been withdrawn from the U.S. market for safety reasons. Twelve drugs were removed from the U.S. market between 1997 and 2001 due to safety concerns.[94] Many of the withdrawn drugs were popularly prescribed products. These drugs—which included the leading-selling antihistamine Seldane, both elements of the popular "Fen-phen" diet drug combination (Redux and Pondimin), and the popular diabetes drug Rezulin—are listed in Table 6.2.

These withdrawals are especially worth noting when considering two other relative factors. First, a total of only six drugs were withdrawn for safety reasons during the eight-year period preceding PDUFA (USGAO, 2002). Perhaps more to the point, of the twelve drugs withdrawn from the U.S. market since 1997, the FDA approved nine of the drugs during the current regulatory regime (i.e., after 1992). In addition to the drug names and their indications, Table 6.2 illustrates the year in which each drug was approved and subsequently withdrawn, as well as the average approval time (in months) used by the agency.

Examining the individual safety concerns of each of the withdrawn drugs is beyond the scope of this book. Such analyses, especially extensive scholarly and medical analyses, are only now emerging.[95] However, in 2001 the Senate Committee on Health, Education, Labor and Pensions commissioned the General Accounting Office to evaluate the prescription drug user fee program with respect to approval times, drug withdrawals, and other agency activities. The GAO examined drug withdrawals for the eight-year period immediately prior to PDUFA (1985–1992) and the eight-year period immediately following PDUFA (1993–2000). Due to the relatively short nature of the time frame involved, it is difficult to draw accurate inferences regarding patterns of drug approvals and withdrawals. Yet, during the pre-PDUFA period, the

Table 6.2 Drugs Withdrawn for Safety-Related Reasons, 1997–2002

| Brand Name | Generic Name | Manufacturer | Approved | Withdrawn | Approval Time (months) | Indication | Health Risk |
|---|---|---|---|---|---|---|---|
| Baycol | Cerivastatin | Bayer AG | 1997 | Aug. 2001 | 12.0 | Lowers cholesterol | Organ failure |
| Duract | Bromfenac | Wyeth-Ayerst | 1997 | June 1998 | 27.7 | Pain killer | Liver failure |
| Hismanal | Astemizole | Janssen | 1988 | June 1999 | 46.1 | Antihistamine | Irregular heartbeat |
| Lotronex[a] | Alosetron | GlaxoSmithKline | 2000 | Nov. 2000 | 7.4 | Irritable bowel syndrome | Inadequate blood flow |
| Pondimin | Fenfluramine | American Home Products | 1973 | Sept. 1997 | 75.5 | Diet drug | Heart valve defects |
| Posicor | Mibefradil | Roche | 1997 | June 1998 | 15.3 | Blood pressure drug | Fatal heart problems |
| Propulsid | Cisapride | Janssen | 1993 | Mar. 2000 | 23.0 | Heartburn | Irregular heartbeat |
| Raplon | Rapacuronium Bromide | Organon; J&J | 1999 | Mar. 2001 | 13.8 | Injectable anesthesia | Broncho-spasm |
| Raxar | Grepafloxin | GlaxoWellcome | 1997 | Oct. 1999 | 11.9 | Bronchitis, pneumonia | Irregular heartbeat |
| Redux[b] | Dexfenfluramine | American Home Products | 1996 | Sept. 1997 | 35.2 | Diet drug | Heart valve defects |
| Rezulin | Troglitazone | Warner Lambert | 1997 | Mar. 2000 | 6.0 | Diabetes | Liver failure |
| Seldane | Terfenadine | IVAX | 1985 | Feb. 1998 | 26.2 | Antihistamine | Irregular heartbeat |

Sources: USGAO (2002); Willman (2000).
Notes: a. Approved by the FDA for use in a limited population in June 2002.
b. Redux is not an NME, but is included here since the combination of Pondimin and Redux (known as "Fen-phen") resulted in both drugs being withdrawn from the market.

GAO calculated that 3.1 percent (6 of 193 NMEs) of new drugs were withdrawn for safety reasons. The comparable figure for the post-PDUFA period was 3.47 percent (9 of 259 NMEs). The GAO's overall conclusion was "a higher percentage of drugs has been withdrawn from the market for safety-related reasons since PDUFA's enactment than prior to the law's enactment" (USGAO, 2002: 24).

Given the relatively short time frame and the relatively limited amount of information, it is relatively difficult to measure accurately and precisely both the magnitude and nature of harm caused by prescription drugs in the current regulatory regime. Even the GAO acknowledged, "An examination of drug withdrawals, by itself, may not provide a complete picture of drug safety" (USGAO, 2002: 27). The GAO offered a number of reasons for this difficulty. First, as was mentioned earlier, drug safety is a relative rather than an absolute concept. In this new regulatory regime, judgments about the safety of a drug are made in the broader context of the purported benefits of the drug and the alternative therapies available to the patient. Second, drug withdrawals may occur because doctors or patients incorrectly use some drugs by improperly combining them with other drugs. Third, some patients may use prescription medicines for purposes other than the manner in which they were tested and approved.

In addition to the GAO's multiple explanations, there are several other reasons why it is difficult to measure drug safety accurately. First, adverse drug reactions may result in any number of outcomes, including injury, hospitalization, or even death. Oftentimes, adverse reactions are only reported when they lead to fatalities. Second, since it is difficult to obtain a nationwide accounting of medication errors, many studies of adverse drug reactions are conducted at the state or regional level or in hospital settings. When conducted at the level of these subnational units, study results must be extrapolated to get a nationwide total. Third, it is often difficult to ascertain what may have triggered an adverse drug reaction. For instance, an adverse drug reaction may arise as the result of the interaction of more than one drug in the human body. In some cases, taking a medicine with a particular food or drink can also trigger an adverse reaction. Also common are drug-disease interactions in which a given medicine creates a negative side effect as the result of an additional, preexisting medical condition.[96] Finally, the reporting of adverse drug reactions remains voluntary. Consequently, many such reactions potentially are never even reported to federal regulatory authorities.

## Risk Management Concerns
## in the New Regulatory Period

The time-honored debate over the performance of the FDA and the approval of new medicines has continued into the new regulatory era. Perhaps ironically, the most recent criticisms of the agency are the polar opposite to what the FDA experienced between the 1960s and 1980s. The wave of recent withdrawals has sparked a considerable debate on whether or not the FDA now approves drugs too quickly (see, for example, Friedman et al., 1999; Rubin, 1998). Many of these withdrawals were occurring just around the time the *Journal of the American Medical Association* published a research article estimating that adverse drug reactions were the sixth leading killer of Americans—ahead of pneumonia and diabetes—for the calendar year 1994 (Lazarou, Pomeranz, and Corey, 1998).

In addition to the relatively limited quantitative assessments of drug safety in the current regulatory regime, it is also important to consider some of the safety concerns raised by other actors in the policy subsystem. For example, Dr. Sidney Wolfe of Public Citizen's Health Research Group has been one of the agency's most persistent critics over the years. In the context of the current regulatory period, Wolfe has vigorously questioned the agency's safety and efficacy standards in the drug approval process. Following the nine-month period between September 1997 and June 1998 in which five drugs were withdrawn from the market, the HRG surveyed 172 FDA medical officers, asking whether there was now pressure to approve drugs more rapidly, and whether drugs had been approved inappropriately. The survey results led HRG to the following two main conclusions:

> (1) Changes in FDA review and approval policies codified in FDAMA in the past several years appear to have led to a significant decline in the safety and efficacy standards for new drugs. Many drugs that have come on the market in the past three years have done so despite the opinion of the Medical Officer reviewing the drug that the drug should not have been approved. . . .
> (2) Inappropriate pressure from Congress, the drug companies and senior FDA employees create an atmosphere in which the likelihood of drug approval is maximized. The pressure takes the form of inappropriate phone calls, pressure to withhold data or personal opinions unfavorable to a drug from FDA Advisory Committees, and pressure from supervisors to change their opinion in the direction of approving the drug. (Public Citizen, 1998)

The allegations made by Wolfe and the HRG are serious and should not be taken lightly by those associated with Congress or the agency. In addition to these general concerns about the nature of the principal-agent contract in the user fee era, criticisms of the current regulatory regime also arise each time a drug is withdrawn from the market for safety considerations. The controversy generated over the approval, withdrawal, and subsequent reintroduction of GlaxoWellcome's Lotronex provides a useful illustration of the safety concerns arising in the current regulatory regime. The FDA originally approved Lotronex in February 2000 to treat irritable bowel syndrome (IBS) in women. The company withdrew the product from the market in November of that year after evidence of serious adverse effects appeared. Yet, after "100 reports of hospitalization, 50 cases of surgery and at least seven deaths" the FDA reapproved Lotronex in June 2002 (Griffin, 2002: 19). The agency contended that the drug was reintroduced on the basis of the benefits provided by Lotronex to IBS patients. In describing the FDA's handling of Lotronex, Richard Horton delivered a sharp criticism of the FDA in the commentary pages of *The Lancet,* a leading medical journal in the United Kingdom. Horton wrote, "The Lotronex episode may show in microcosm a serious erosion of integrity within the FDA, and in particular CDER, whose operating budget now depends greatly on industry money" (2001a: 1545). Horton also pointed out, "This story reveals not only dangerous failings in a single drug's approval and review process but also the extent to which the FDA, its Center for Drug Evaluation and Research (CDER) in particular, has become the servant of industry" (1544). In a subsequent exchange in the pages of *The Lancet,* several agency officials responded to many of the allegations made by Horton and provided justifications for the agency's decisions about Lotronex (Horton, 2001b).[97]

In response to these drug safety concerns and the wave of drug withdrawals, a 1999 report by the Institute of Medicine, *To Err Is Human: Building a Safer Health System,* addressed the issue of patient safety (Kohn, Corrigan, and Donaldson, 1999). The IOM's primary objective in producing the report, one of several in IOM's Quality of Health Care in America project, is to create a "national agenda for reducing errors in health care and improving patient safety." Among the report's recommendations was the establishment by Congress of a federal Center for Patient Safety. Patient safety and risk management have clearly become highly salient issues at the agency during the latest regulatory period.

To this end, the FDA's Center for Drug Evaluation and Research conducted its own analysis of drug withdrawals in 1999 (Friedman et al., 1999). At that time, the agency concluded that "there has been no increase in the rate of drug withdrawals in the United States since PDUFA was enacted" (USFDA, 1999: 34). Later, the agency also raised concerns over the GAO's accounting methods in the 2002 GAO study (USGAO, 2002).

In addition to the obvious concerns over drug withdrawal rates, Jane Henney established a task force shortly after becoming FDA commissioner to consider and evaluate the agency's system for managing the risks of FDA-approved products. The Task Force on Risk Management issued its final report in May 1999 (USFDA, 1999). The report reaffirmed the agency's contention on the drug safety issue. Specifically, it noted:

> The Task Force has found that available evidence does not support the charge that unanticipated serious adverse events are occurring at a higher rate since the implementation of PDUFA. We found that under PDUFA, there has been a lower rate of serious adverse events identified during the postapproval phase (30.3 percent of products) than during the 1976 to 1985 baseline years (51.5 percent of products). (1999: 35–36)

Given the relatively recent transition into the new regulatory period, the FDA's figures remain encouraging. Yet it remains premature to come to any definitive conclusions concerning this very serious risk management issue. Nonetheless, as was the case during the drug lag debate, it seems as if the new regulatory era has ushered in a variety of drug safety studies providing empirical evidence that may be used to support each side of the argument.

To add to the above discussion, and despite the inherent measurement difficulties, there have been increasing attempts in the medical literature to quantify the costs of medication errors and adverse drug reactions in terms of the number of deaths and injuries, as well as the financial cost imposed on society. The following two sections identify recent studies that attempted to analyze drug withdrawals on a global level and to estimate the costs associated with adverse drug reactions.

## Analyzing Worldwide Drug Withdrawals

Studies of drug withdrawal rates are rare. As a result, it is difficult to get an entirely clear picture of drug safety. One exception is an analysis of worldwide drug withdrawals between January 1960 and December 2000 (Fung et al., 2001). The authors identified a total of 121 pharmaceutical products withdrawn from worldwide pharmaceutical markets for safety reasons during this time.[98] They report that the distribution of withdrawal rates for each decade were 12.4 percent in the 1960s, 16.5 percent in the 1970s, 39.7 percent in the 1980s, and 31.4 percent in the 1990s. Thus, in terms of the absolute number of withdrawals, one can argue that the percentage of drugs withdrawn in the 1990s was roughly 2.5 times greater than the percentage withdrawn in the 1960s.

One needs to interpret such data with caution, however. The study by M. Fung and colleagues is somewhat limited in that the authors were unable to collect or calculate the total number of drug approvals each year. Therefore, it is difficult to compare the withdrawal percentages across decades as there is not a relative sense of how many different drugs were available during the particular time period.

Finally, the authors identify the geographic locations for where the various drugs were withdrawn. Overall, nearly half of the withdrawn drugs (49.6 percent) were withdrawn in more than one market. For comparative purposes, the authors also provide data on "single market" withdrawals (where the drug was withdrawn only by one country). Interestingly, just 6 of the 121 drugs withdrawn (5 percent) globally between 1960 and 1999 were withdrawn only in the United States. By contrast, the withdrawal figure was much greater in the major European pharmaceutical markets such as France (13.2 percent), Germany (13.2), and the United Kingdom (10.7 percent). The rate of single market withdrawals in Japan was much less than in North America and Europe (0.8 percent).[99]

Drug safety analyses are much more involved than simply examining the mortality rates or the resulting negative side effects (such as hepatotoxicity) associated with a given drug. Instead, drug safety requires an examination of the much broader therapeutic milieu involving the drug's benefit-risk ratio, including considerations for the availability of alternative treatments and the impact of removing a particular drug from the market on patients currently benefiting from the drug. As Fung and colleagues point out, a good example of this was the FDA's rapid decision to withdraw Posicor and Duract but to keep Rezulin on the market longer because at the time it was considered "an important therapeutic modality for diabetic patients" (2001: 310). Thus, at times, despite the seemingly obvious safety concerns that a drug may pose to the general public, decisions on drug withdrawals and drug safety ultimately involve considerations of the much larger benefit-risk profile.

## Estimating the Costs Associated with Adverse Drug Reactions

As is the case with drug withdrawals, it is also relatively difficult to estimate the costs of adverse drug reactions to U.S. society. Jeffrey Johnson and Lyle Bootman (1995) calculated the estimated costs to society resulting from the misuse of prescription medicines. They estimated that the annual cost to society associated with drug-related morbidity and mortality was $76.6 billion. Based on their estimates, drug-related hospitalizations accounted for the largest component of the total cost. For 1992, an estimated 8.76 million hospital admissions due to "drug-related problems" came at a cost of $47.4 billion. Moreover, again for 1992, they estimated that "28.2 percent of all hospital admissions were a result of drug-related morbidity and mortality" (1995: 1952).

Generally speaking, complications resulting from the use of medicines in hospitals have been found to be the largest single cause of all adverse events occurring during hospitalization (Leape et al., 1991). Investigators of the Harvard Medical Practice Study found that nearly one-fifth (19 percent) of all adverse events during hospitalization could be attributed to medicine use (Leape et al., 1991). Other studies appearing in leading medical journals also estimate the *costs* associated with adverse drug events by examining factors such as length of hospitalization, additional costs of medical treatment, and mortality. For example, in a study of medical records of more than 91,000 patients admitted to Salt Lake City's LDS Hospital between 1990 and 1993, over 2,200 patients (2.43 percent) experienced an adverse drug event. In terms of costs arising from adverse drug events, the authors of the Utah study concluded that, on average, adverse drug events increased the length of the hospital stay by almost two days, increased the average cost of hospitalization by over $2,000 per patient, and nearly doubled the risk of death during hospitalization.

In a similar study, medical records were examined of all patients admitted to two Boston hospitals—Brigham and Women's Hospital and Massachusetts General Hospital—between February and July 1993 (Bates et al., 1997). Similar to the findings of the Utah study, the Boston study estimated that adverse drug events increased the average hospital stay by 2.2 days and increased the cost by an average of nearly $2,600. Using an extrapolation of these figures, the authors of the study calculated that the annual nationwide hospital costs resulting from adverse drug events would be $4 billion.

In one of the few studies of medication errors at the national level, David Phillips, Nicholas Christenfield, and Laura Glynn (1998) examined all U.S. death certificates between 1983 and 1993. These authors found that medication errors accounted for a total of 7,391 deaths in 1993. Using this accounting scheme, deaths resulting from medication errors increased 257 percent from the total of 2,876 deaths in 1983.

Cumulatively, these studies suggest that adverse drug events remain a significant problem in the United States (see, for example, Lasser et al., 2002; Temple and Himmel, 2002). Not only do they lead to increased mortality rates, but such reactions also contribute additional costs to an already rapidly increasing expenditure total in the health care sector. In summary, it is terribly difficult to gauge accurately both the cause and the number of adverse drug reactions occurring in the United States on an annual basis. The relatively limited time frames and multitude of other potential causes also makes it extremely difficult to directly connect the drug safety and withdrawal issues with the current regulatory regime. Given that the current regulatory period suggests a shift in the risk-benefit calculation in favor of benefits and increased patient access, the FDA's approach to risk-management and the nature of drug safety will likely remain highly salient issues under Commissioner McClellan's leadership. Overall, drug safety and risk management issues will remain two of the defining issues in the current regulatory regime.

## Conclusion

U.S. drug regulation in the latest regulatory period remains at a very important juncture. Questions of agency leadership have plagued the FDA since the departure of David Kessler in 1997. In addition, given the FDA's statutorily defined mission, external actors such as the pharmaceutical industry and foreign regulatory agencies will likely continue to play a significant role in shaping current and future regulatory structures and processes. These actors play prominent roles in the policy subsystem and exert an important influence on agency behavior.

The current regulatory period is a critical one from a drug safety standpoint. Several risk management issues currently facing the FDA will ultimately define the latest regulatory period. At a fundamental level, agency leadership will play an increasingly prominent role in shaping both current and future regulatory performance. Regulatory outcomes often hinge on the fundamental balance between risk and reward. Finding and maintaining this balance will likely be the function of the agency's top officials, operating within the parameters of the institutional framework constructed by Congress.

# 7

## PROTECTING AND PROMOTING PUBLIC HEALTH IN THE UNITED STATES

I am disappointed in the continued emphasis on review times as the name of the game. Public health is the name of the game.
—*Pharmaceutical industry official*

The policy shift to a fourth regulatory period has critical implications for both the *protection* and *promotion* of public health in the United States. One of the themes developed in the previous two chapters was that the traditional emphasis on protecting public health produced a relatively cautious regulatory approach over the years. Yet both Congress and the FDA now recognize the significance of promoting public health by enabling consumers to access new and effective therapies in a timely manner. In effect, the pendulum of public health and safety has swung in the other direction. The current principal-agent contract has created a more republican approach to drug safety. Drug safety is a relative concept and the risk-management paradigm suggests that the risks of a particular drug must be weighed in relation to its benefits. This transformation makes it increasingly imperative for consumers to play an active role in promoting their own individual health and well-being.

In this chapter, I continue the discussion begun in the previous chapter concerning a number of critical FDA regulatory issues that have direct implications for public health. Such issues are characteristic of the new era of FDA regulation in which the agency is increasingly cognizant of promoting public health in addition to simply protecting public health. Two specific issues discussed in this chapter—direct-to-consumer (DTC) advertising and the debate between off-label prescribing and off-label promotion—have important implications for consumers.

Since 1997, for instance, the agency has broken a long tradition of prohibiting pharmaceutical manufacturers from advertising their products directly to consumers. This change in practice has greatly changed the nature of patient-doctor relations and is arguably having a significant impact on public health in the United States. Also, FDA regulations now allow pharmaceutical firms to promote (and doctors to prescribe) approved medicines for unapproved indications. This change reflects some modification in agency process and also likely has significant implications on public health. Each of these processes is consistent with the new era of FDA drug regulation. Each also differentiates the FDA from its worldwide regulatory counterparts. Finally, each issue represents the importance of framing our analytical focus on procedural aspects and structural theories of regulation.

## The Promotion of Public Health in the United States

Prescription drug products have become an increasingly valuable weapon in the nation's public health armamentarium. Table 7.1 lists the leading causes of death in the United States, including many of the usual suspects (heart disease, cancer, stroke, diabetes and lower respiratory disease) notoriously known for threatening the long-term health of Americans.

Given that heart disease is the leading killer of Americans, it should come as no surprise that Americans now spend more on cardiovascular drugs than on drugs in any other therapeutic category. In addition to the

Table 7.1 Ten Leading Causes of Death in the United States, 2000

| Cause | Cases |
| --- | --- |
| 1. Heart disease | 709,894 |
| 2. Cancer | 551,833 |
| 3. Stroke | 166,028 |
| 4. Chronic lower respiratory disease | 123,550 |
| 5. Accidents | 93,592 |
| 6. Diabetes | 68,662 |
| 7. Pneumonia/influenza | 67,024 |
| 8. Alzheimer's disease | 49,044 |
| 9. Nephritis, nephrotic syndrome, nephrosis | 37,672 |
| 10. Septicemia | 31,613 |

*Source:* National Center for Health Statistics (2001).

direct effects associated with the leading causes of death, there are also several secondary or late effects associated with such conditions. Thus, some drugs like Pfizer's Lipitor are designed to lower cholesterol. According to IMS Health—a leading provider of health information— over 47.7 million prescriptions were written for Lipitor alone in the United States in 2000, making it the country's leading prescribed drug.[100] The other most highly prescribed drugs also directly relate to the nation's core health concerns. Rounding out the top five are drugs such as Wyeth-Ayerst's Premarin (for the treatment of osteoporosis— 46.7 million prescriptions), Knoll Pharmaceutical's Synthroid (a hormone replacement—43.5 million), AstraZeneca's Prilosec (for heartburn and acid reflux treatment—32.8 million), and Pfizer's Norvasc (a long-acting calcium channel blocker—30.7 million). These heavily prescribed products enable a substantially large segment of the U.S. population to lead happier, healthier lives.

As one of the primary actors in the U.S. Public Health Service, the FDA has as its new statutory mission to promote public health by reviewing new medicines in a timely and efficient manner. If the fourth regulatory period provides a more republican approach to drug regulation, at the same time we are now seeing large numbers of Americans seeking to obtain health information. This suggests that a large segment of the population desires to play a more proactive role at influencing their personal health profile. In recent years, the Internet has become an important medium in which individuals seek information about their individual health (Klotz and Ceccoli, 2002). A report from the Pew Internet Research Group found that over 55 million Americans currently use the Internet to obtain health-related information (Pew Internet, 2002). In this sense, the Internet is revolutionizing the way patients obtain health information. Not surprisingly, many individuals using the Internet for health information seek information about prescription drugs. According to the Pew study, nearly two-thirds of those seeking health information (64 percent) have looked for information about prescription drugs (Pew Internet, 2002).

Two important aspects of the FDA's regulatory process have significant implications for the promotion of public health. First is the FDA's 1997 decision to allow pharmaceutical manufacturers to advertise drug products directly to consumers. A second, stemming from the 1997 FDAMA law, makes it legal for pharmaceutical manufacturers to promote approved medicines for unapproved indications. Each of these regulatory processes has significant implications for this interaction between individual behavior and promoting public health.

## Direct-to-Consumer Promotion

Given the competitive nature of the brand-name pharmaceutical industry and the constant competition provided by generic versions of brand-name drugs, pharmaceutical companies are forced to spend considerable sums promoting their products. According to one estimate, the pharmaceutical industry spent $13.8 billion marketing its products in 1999 (Brichachek and Sellers, 2000). Of this total spent on promotional spending, by far the largest amount (approximately $12 billion) was spent on traditional physician-directed programs. Such promotional tactics have long been a hallmark practice of the pharmaceutical industry. Physician-directed programs enable pharmaceutical company representatives to interact personally with doctors and educate physicians about the latest products available. Yet, the competitive nature of the pharmaceutical industry has forced firms to explore other avenues for promoting their products.

In August 1997, the FDA issued a draft guidance easing restrictions governing the promotion of pharmaceutical products in the mass media. In the practice known as DTC promotion or advertising, pharmaceutical manufacturers are now able to market their products to mass audiences through various media outlets, such as television, radio, and print. Prior to the FDA's 1997 guidance, pharmaceutical manufacturers faced highly restrictive guidelines when seeking to advertise their products via broadcast airwaves. Primarily, manufacturers were formerly required to depict product labeling information in the advertisement. Given the expensive nature of broadcast advertising and the condensed time frame of television commercials, advertising such products on television prior to 1997 was virtually untenable. In essence, in the act of advertising a product, the manufacturer was forced to provide a full statement of the highly detailed information that accompanies prescription medicines. In response to this onerous requirement, quipped one former agency official, "Imagine what percentage of an audience would be left after watching a 'dead see' scroll" on the television screen (Morris, 1999: 14).

The FDA followed its original 1997 draft guidance with a final set of guidelines two years later. The FDA's strategy in allowing DTC promotion is that pharmaceutical manufacturers must now make *provisions* in the ads to disseminate product labeling information. In liberalizing DTC ads, the FDA maintains the following standards as specified in Section 202.1 of the *Code of Federal Regulations*. First, the ads cannot provide false or misleading statements. Second, the ads must provide a "fair balance" of benefit and risk information. That is, they must provide the bad information as well as the product benefits. Third, the ads must contain a "major statement" conveying the product's risk information. Additionally, certain drugs such as those containing "black box" warning labels are prohibited from DTC promotion.

Under the new regulatory framework, manufacturers must provide several sources where consumers can obtain such information. These sources typically include toll-free phone numbers, an Internet web page address, referral to an existing print advertisement or product brochure, or referral to a health care provider. Today, the FDA's Division of Drug Marketing, Advertising and Communications (DDMAC) is charged with reviewing promotional materials. DDMAC (known at the agency as "Dee-Dee Mac") reviews advertisements on a case-by-case basis.

Since the liberalization of advertising restrictions in 1997, promotional spending on DTC advertising has grown tremendously. According to the National Institute for Health Care Management Research and Educational Foundation (NIHCM), pharmaceutical companies spent approximately $2.5 billion on DTC advertising in 2000 (NIHCM, 2001). This figure, according to NIHCM, has more than doubled since the liberalization of FDA regulations in 1997 when the industry spent a total of $1.1 billion on DTC ads. Given the importance placed on demographics by television and radio producers, well-placed DTC ads can target a specific population of consumers.

In addition, the pharmaceutical industry has been largely successful in recruiting well-known political personalities, Hollywood celebrities, and prominent sports figures (e.g., former presidential candidate Bob Dole, legendary golfer Jack Nicklaus, and television personality Joan Lunden to name a few) to market its products (see Petersen, 2002). In recent years, many personalities have become advocates to raise awareness for particular medical conditions that may impact their personal lives in one way or another.

Generally speaking, pharmaceutical manufacturers run three types of DTC ads. First, "help-seeking" ads mention an ailment but do not mention the drug by name. Such ads encourage consumers to consult with their physicians about their condition. Second, "reminder" ads mention the drug by name but do not mention what the drug is used for. Such ads cannot make "suggestions or representations" about the product being advertised. Finally, "product claim" ads are the most common types of DTC ads. Such ads specifically mention the name of the product and the condition the product is intended to treat. Product claim ads prompt viewers to "ask your physician" about the benefits of the advertised product.

The new DTC requirements have had a stunning impact. Consequently, perhaps few Americans realize that more money ($160.8 million) was spent on DTC advertising to promote a single drug—Merck's anti-arthritis drug, Vioxx—in 2000 than was spent on many other familiar products (NIHCM, 2001). For instance, during the same time period, PepsiCo spent $125 million to promote Pepsi and Anheuser Busch spent $146 million to promote Budweiser (NIHCM, 2001). The proliferation of DTC advertising since 1997 has essentially transformed the U.S. lexicon when it comes to drug therapy. As a result of DTC advertising, many Americans can recognize prescription drugs based on simple catch phrases or word associations. For instance, consumers have now been conditioned to know AstraZeneca's heartburn drug, Nexium, as the "purple pill" or Pfizer's Viagra as "the little blue pill."

DTC promotion is an interesting issue in that it demonstrates the balance at the FDA between protecting public health and promoting public health. Based on its 1997 regulation, FDA officials believe that the benefits of DTC outweigh the costs. In ensuring this balance, two important questions must be answered. First, how has DTC promotion generally affected public health? Second, how can risk messages best be incorporated into mass media advertising of prescription drugs?

Given the evidence that Americans have demonstrated an increasing interest in learning more about their own health and are taking more proactive steps to remain healthy, DTC ads can play a vitally important role in promoting public health. Advocates of DTC advertising are quick to cite the many benefits of DTC ads. By far, the leading argument in favor of DTC advertising is that such ads benefit consumers by educating them about particular conditions and the drugs available to treat such conditions. Along with DTC ads, pharmaceutical companies let consumers know about additional information available to them (for example through toll-free phone numbers and web addresses).

On the other hand, the proliferation of DTC ads pose significant costs, according to critics. Criticisms of DTC ads focus on issues ranging from escalating costs to the nature of doctor-patient interactions. First, a common argument made by opponents is that DTC ads are expensive to produce and that the proliferation of ads contributes to the rising costs of pharmaceuticals in particular and health care in general.

Perhaps more important, increasing evidence is pointing to a serious change involving clinical interactions between doctors and patients. In the relatively short period of time that a patient spends with his or her doctor, DTC ads undoubtedly lead patients to spend far more time telling doctors about what they saw about a particular drug on television or in a magazine. Generally speaking, if patients do discuss a particular drug with a doctor as a result of exposure to a DTC ad, they may take the conversation in one of two directions. First, they might ask their doctor *about* an advertised medicine. Second, they may ask their doctor *for* an advertised medicine.

One downfall of such questions is that it potentially distracts the physician from taking care of other, perhaps more important, clinical matters. The FDA is also concerned about a number of other health and safety issues pertaining to how DTC ads influence this relationship. For example, the DTC laws may encourage the potential for the overprescribing of particular medicines or even creating an overemphasis on the newer, more expensive drugs (which are more heavily advertised). Such newer medicines would be overprescribed at the expense of cheaper, older drugs that perform equally effectively. Finally, there is an ongoing concern in the medical community that DTC advertising likely contributes to the "medicalization" of otherwise trivial conditions. DTC promotion likely influences consumers about the possibility of using so-called lifestyle drugs for treating male pattern baldness or improving sexual performance.

In many ways, DTC promotion reflects both the pros and cons of promoting public health. On the one hand, it has enabled consumers to play a more proactive role in seeking to maintain their health. On the other hand, the practice is fundamentally changing the nature of patient-physician relations, and the full consequences of this transformation have yet to be realized. Regardless, DTC promotion remains very controversial. Regulatory problems particularly arise in areas where the form of the promotion is difficult to regulate. The FDA, for example, remains concerned about the propensity for DTC ads to overstate the efficacy claims of new drugs. Or, in many instances, there is a fine line between promotional material and educational material. Generally speaking, if an advertisement does not mention a particular drug product by name, the FDA considers the advertisement to be educational. Educational advertising is largely outside of the realm of federal advertising regulations. Mentioning a particular product by name, however, makes an advertisement promotional and therefore subject to federal advertising regulations.

## "Off-Label" Prescribing and Promotion

Another prominent public health promotion issue involving the FDA concerns the distinction between what is known as "off-label prescribing" (or off-label use) and "off-label promotion." The Food, Drug and Cosmetic Act clearly states that FDA approval of a drug product, based on the clinical evidence reviewed during the approval process, is for specific indications in specific circumstances. The law also states that all intended usages must be printed on the label of the product.[101] (Product labels accompanying approved drug products provide physicians with information about appropriate uses as well as any product warnings.) Therefore, in approving specific dosages of a medicine for specific indications, the FDA maintains that effective labeling by the manufacturer and adherence to labeling information by physicians can reduce the occurrences of adverse drug reactions.

The broader issue becomes murky, however, because the FDA does not regulate the practice of medicine (for a brief discussion, see English, 2002). In the practice of medicine in the United States, physicians have the authority to prescribe medicines in any way they see fit. Therefore, once the FDA approves a drug, doctors are able to prescribe the drug for any condition (regardless of whether or not that condition appears on the drug label). Off-label prescribing technically occurs when physicians write prescriptions that differ from product labeling information. Specifically, off-label prescribing has been defined in the following way: "Using an approved drug to treat a disease that is not indicated on its label, but is closely related to an indicated disease, treating unrelated, unindicated diseases, and treating the indicated disease by varying from the indicated dosage, regimen, or patient population may all be considered off-label use" (Christopher, 1993).

What makes off-label prescribing such a delicate issue is the potential connection between off-label prescribing and the occurrence of adverse drug reactions. On the one hand, such prescribing may offer the patient a clinical benefit that regulators may have been previously unaware of. For example, Lilly's leading-selling antidepressant drug, Prozac, was initially marketed as an appetite suppressant. Pfizer's anti-impotency drug, Viagra, was originally developed as a drug used in the treatment of hair loss. Additionally, the immunosuppressant drug, cyclosporin, which made the transplant of organs other than the kidney feasible in the early 1980s, was originally developed as a fungal antibiotic. In this sense, off-label prescribing has the potential to uncover all sorts of important (and unanticipated) therapeutic remedies.

On the other hand, off-label prescribing on the surface runs against all that goes into the approval of a medicine. In some cases, fairly safe drugs have been removed from the market because of adverse reactions that occurred, perhaps, as a result of the drug not being used in accordance with labeling instructions. One of the more high-profile recent cases of off-label prescribing gone bad involved the prescribing of two popular weight-loss drugs, fenfluramine and phentermine, in combination with one another. Though the FDA approved both fenfluramine and phentermine, the agency did not approve the two-drug combination. Over time, numerous occurrences of adverse drug reactions emerged among consumers taking the two drugs in combination. Adverse drug reaction reports revealed potential damage to heart valves associated with the use of the drug combination. Eventually, both drugs were removed from the market.

Unlike off-label prescribing, which remains an entirely legal practice, it is illegal for pharmaceutical firms to engage in off-label promotion. Off-label promotion occurs when representatives of pharmaceutical firms make claims about specific drugs that are not substantiated by medical evidence. In many instances, however, it is difficult for the FDA to police off-label promotion.[102]

The FDA prohibits pharmaceutical manufacturers from disseminating information about an approved drug or medical device for unapproved uses. The longstanding logic behind this prohibition (again pointing to 21 CFR 201.5 and 201.128) was that FDA-approved products are approved not for general dispensation but for specific purposes with specific indications.

Challenging this authority on legal grounds, the Washington Legal Foundation (WLF) filed a citizen petition with the FDA in 1993, claiming that the FDA lacked the proper authority to prohibit the dissemination of such information. The WLF is a nonprofit advocacy organization dedicated to protecting "the economic and civil liberties of individuals and businesses." When the FDA rejected the WLF's petition, the WLF filed suit against the FDA in 1994 to overturn the agency's position.

In 1997, in conjunction with the agency's efforts (and the efforts of agency supporters) to increase its role in promoting public health, the FDA Modernization Act contained a provision for disseminating off-label information. The provision allows pharmaceutical manufacturers to disseminate study findings contained in articles found in peer-reviewed scientific journals. Thus, pharmaceutical firms are now able to disseminate peer-reviewed journal articles about an off-label indication of its product. Such dissemination is possible with the caveat that the manufacturer files a supplemental application demonstrating the safety and efficacy of the unapproved use. Companies are required to file such applications within a specified time frame.

In July 1998, U.S. District Court for the District of Columbia judge Royce Lamberth ruled that FDA regulation of off-label promotions was an unconstitutional violation of free speech (Rhein, 2001). Lamberth's ruling effectively determined that FDA restrictions on such information violated the First Amendment. Judge Lamberth thus stopped the FDA from "restricting the dissemination of peer reviewed articles or reference texts that cite unapproved uses" (Rhein, 2000).

Consequently, the FDA appealed the ruling. In addition, and despite this ruling, the FDA outlined its position in March 2000 as to why the agency has the authority to regulate off-label promotion.[103] For now, the regulatory debate on this issue seems far from over.

The issues of off-label prescribing and off-label promotion have important implications for individuals and for public health in the United States. On the surface, though perfectly legal, off-label prescribing runs against all that goes into the approval of a medicine (namely the clinical testing for approved usages). On the other hand, off-label prescribing might provide clinical advantages of certain drug products that regulators or drug developers may have been previously unaware of. The off-label promotion issue is one in which the FDA is seeking to retain a measure of regulatory influence over pharmaceutical firms. The legality of this issue remains tied up in the courts, and the final ruling has yet to be determined.

## The Confluence of Pills and Politics

Prescription drugs affect nearly every citizen in the United States in one way or another. Billions of prescriptions are dispensed annually. Such medicines enable individuals to lead happier, healthier, and ultimately longer lives. In a perfect world, all new drugs would be safe, free of side effects, and would work as intended. Unfortunately, given the complexities of science, the human body, and numerous other uncertainties, we do not live in a perfect world. As a consequence, the regulation of new medicines is an important governmental task, and government regulatory agencies are forced to make critical decisions.

Given the presence of incomplete information and other complexities, decisions on new drug approvals inherently contain a degree of risk and uncertainty. For example, approval decisions are based on information compiled from a series of clinical trials typically involving as few as 3,000 to 5,000 people. Once approved, such drugs may be consumed by millions of Americans. Thus, as regulatory decisions are often made with a degree of uncertainty, they typically involve unforeseen risks.

As the guarantor of public goods, government holds the ultimate responsibility for ensuring a general safety threshold. Regulatory policy involves assessing and managing risk and reward. Science, medicine, and the interaction of pharmaceutical products in the human body each involve some degree of uncertainty. Whereas doctors and patients are free to make individual choices, government regulators are responsible for managing risk on behalf of society.

This risk component creates a fundamental dilemma for government actors. Regulators are forced to make decisions, decisions that are often constrained by limited quantities of time and information. In accelerating the approval of new medicines, governments risk the possibility of committing Type II errors. In addition to a potentially devastating social impact, Type II errors pose serious political hazards as well. No government wants to be responsible for approving unsafe medicines. Alternately, regulators also face risks in failing to approve drugs that should be made available for public consumption. In the case of such Type I errors, there is a high cost in preventing good drugs from entering the market. This cost has historically often been overlooked, though, as it is largely unobservable. Yet the transition into the latest regulatory period suggests that regulators are increasingly concerned about the perils associated with Type I errors.

Regulatory agencies act as agents in an ongoing principal-agent relationship with Congress. In this relationship, the mission of the agency is to approve and reject various medicines. Institutional structures are designed by Congress to constrain the behavior of regulators and encourage agents to live up to their end of the political transaction. Regulators do not operate in a vacuum, however. Instead, they operate within a much broader political context. Consequently, competing interests exert various degrees of pressure on agencies to achieve favorable outcomes.

Drug laws in the United States emerged in response to drug-related tragedies. Over the course of the first three regulatory periods, FDA regulations became increasingly centralized. Subsequently, the FDA was criticized throughout the 1970s and 1980s for being too slow to approve new medicines. The agency's harshest critics charged that the FDA's lengthy approval process was actually obstructing U.S. public health. The politics associated with AIDS in the late 1980s and early 1990s created an opportunity to punctuate the erstwhile regulatory period. This punctuation led to the acknowledgment by both Congress and the agency that the FDA's mission extended beyond the mere protection of public health. The latest regulatory period is predicated on both protecting public health (by keeping unsafe drugs off the market) and promoting public health (by making new medicines available to patients at an earlier stage in the process).

Research into the changing nature of regulatory drug review involves the core aspects of agency design, institutional structure, and regulatory process. Differences in review styles and regulatory standards, for example, greatly affect regulatory outcomes. In this book, I have argued that structure and process matter a great deal. Structure and process generally result from the bargaining and compromise among the primary actors in the policy subsystem. Consequently, political factors remain the most important of determinants in considering regulatory behavior both across time and across nations.

Regulation is a distinctly political process. The various constituencies involved in the regulation of new medicines provide perhaps another reason behind the importance of political factors in influencing regulatory outcomes. Specifically, one might consider the various patient groups that rely on new medicines. The general patient constituency can be thought of as two distinct groups. These groups are consistent with the drug approval model discussed in Figure 1.1. The first group of patients involves those affected by Type I errors. That is, this group of individuals potentially stands to benefit from a particular drug that either does not have regulatory approval or has yet to gain such approval. This group includes a range of patients suffering from various life-threatening illnesses such as cancer, HIV/AIDS, and heart disease to those afflicted with other non-life-threatening maladies such as the flu, chicken pox, and the common cold. People suffer and even die of these conditions on a daily basis. In sum, many individuals in this group potentially stand to benefit from new treatments but are unable to receive them due to regulatory restrictions.

Of course, patients suffering from HIV/AIDS present a glaring exception to this general rule. Working through politically active organizations such as New York–based ACT UP and San Francisco–based Project Inform, sufferers of HIV/AIDS have mobilized successfully, forming an incredibly effective force in challenging government policy and influencing public opinion. Outside of victims of HIV/AIDS, however, individuals suffering from other afflictions are relatively difficult to mobilize from a political standpoint. While these conditions affect millions of citizens, patient sufferers of Type I errors generally do not present a unified and significant political voice. This is largely because in the realm of the policy subsystem, these patient groups are unable to mobilize effectively. In effect, they are unable to generate enough political leverage to instigate a policy punctuation that would alter the prevailing regulatory status quo.

Victims of Type II errors, however, are relatively far more salient and easy to identify. These victims generally fall into two categories. First, some people ultimately die as the result of consuming unsafe or ineffective medicines. From a political standpoint, these victims are highly salient in the eyes of the public. Survivors of Type II errors are also relatively easy to mobilize.

Perhaps one of the clearest examples is the Thalidomide Victims Association of Canada (TVAC). TVAC is a well-organized and politically active victim group. The group, which largely functions as a member support group, also maintains its own web page and is active in policy issues. In short, patients that consume unsafe or ineffective drugs are relatively easy to identify, easy to mobilize, and present a far louder voice in society. Such groups have a highly salient political presence and are likely to be heard from. The availability of numerous legal options in the United States through tort liability laws also gives this group a vehicle for mobilization.

In addition to patient mobilization, one must return to the issue of risk faced by governments and government agencies. In terms of public relations, government agencies have a far easier time defending why they failed to approve a particular drug than explaining why a drug approved by the agency turns out to have negative or dangerous consequences. Thus, for government agencies, it is easier to commit and defend an act of omission rather than one of commission.

It remains fairly evident that the current ethos in drug regulation is that faster is somehow better. However, this could change with time. Is there an ideal length of time in which regulatory actors could review and approve new medicines? Probably not. Given the nature of scientific uncertainty, predetermining and effectively utilizing a prescribed review period would appear to be a remote possibility. Is there a danger in moving too fast? Possibly. Many senior regulatory officials have recently started wondering whether regulatory agencies are concentrating too much effort in seeking to rapidly approve new drugs. As one senior FDA official lamented, "There is a danger in going too fast. It is worrisome that timeliness has been made the main concern of interest." Another former senior official at the agency echoed this sentiment: "The FDA worries that [pending] FDA reform legislation puts speed ahead of all other factors. The agency worries for good reason." The possibility of regulatory bodies moving too fast also remains a concern across the Atlantic. One European regulatory official shared a similar sentiment regarding the possibility of moving drug approvals along too rapidly: "We cannot reduce evaluation time and time again. The two [U.S. and European] systems should probably set one year as a goal. Six months for all drugs is just too fast."

Given the sustained emphasis on reducing review times, perhaps equilibrium levels of review time lie ahead. Some industry observers have already hinted at the notion of prescribed lengths for drug approvals. Such predefined limits could be made on a drug-by-drug basis in seeking to avoid the possibility of Type II errors. The results of such a strategy remain to be seen. Thus, the debate over FDA performance and the approval of new medicines continues. Ironically, the most recent type of criticism is the polar opposite to what the agency experienced during the 1960s–1980s. The emerging criticism is that the FDA now approves drugs too quickly.

Finally, beyond the pure public policy dimension, it is vital to consider institutional design. Government regulatory authorities often exhibit large degrees of variation both in terms of process and performance. As social scientists, we are interested in asking and answering questions as to why similar regulatory structures yield highly variable outcomes. Such differences in process are influenced by a number of factors, including regulatory attitudes, historical experience, political pressure, and the nature of the policy subsystem. Differences in structure and process lead the Food and Drug Administration to evaluate new medicines in a specific fashion. Regulatory outcomes such as these often hinge on the fundamental balance between risk and reward. Finding and maintaining this balance remains a significant issue in the United States and with virtually every regulatory agency across the globe.

# APPENDIX

## DRUG DEVELOPMENT AND THE FDA'S APPROVAL PROCESS

Drug development in the United States and around the world is an expensive, time-consuming, and highly complicated process. Estimates suggest that the average duration of the drug development process—that is, from the time a given compound is first synthesized in the laboratory until it reaches the stage of marketing approval—is approximately fifteen years.[104] This duration has nearly doubled from the average of approximately eight years during the 1960s.[105] Given the increasing complexities of pharmaceutical sciences, the process is also highly risky. Generally speaking, of any 5,000 compounds experimented on, only five will enter clinical trials and just one will be granted FDA approval (Wierenga and Beary, 1995). It is no surprise, then, that as the risks remain high, the length of the drug development process continues to increase.

Given the risky nature of drug development and the increasing duration, drug development is also quite costly. Precise estimates of the costs of drug development are relatively difficult to ascertain and existing estimates tend to vary tremendously. On the high end, economist Joseph DiMasi of the Tufts University Center for the Study of Drug Development estimated the figure to be in the neighborhood of $800 million (DiMasi et al., 2003). On the lower end, Public Citizen's Health Research Group estimated the total to be closer to $110 million (see Chapter 6).

One of the most significant aspects of the drug development process involves meeting the federal government's standards for safety and efficacy. The FDA plays an active role in the drug development process. Specifically, FDA approval is required at two distinct stages of the drug development process. In addition to the two major junctions at which FDA decisions are required by federal drug law, the agency also acts an active partner by meeting with the sponsoring firm at several junctions during the development process. Such meetings, which have become much more prominent (and more routine) in recent decades, allow the agency to provide advice to the sponsoring firm.

In the earliest phases of development, a pharmaceutical laboratory conducts in vitro experiments with a specified compound to determine its reaction to a particular disease. At this stage, the scientists are primarily evaluating a compound on the basis of safety, potential toxicity, and biological activity. In these trials, however, the investigations are limited to animal and laboratory studies in what is referred to as the preclinical-testing period. Preclinical testing for a given compound generally averages three to four years. On completion of preclinical testing, a company can file an investigational new drug application with the FDA. If the FDA does not reject the application within a thirty-day period, the company can begin clinical testing on humans. The drug development and approval process is sketched out in Table A.1.

Clinical testing on humans can begin on the successful completion of an IND. At this point, the agency and the sponsoring firm convene for a "pre-NDA submission" meeting where they discuss details about the nature of clinical investigations. Clinical testing of the compound entails a long and detailed series of investigations that take place in three stages. These clinical testing stages are known as Phase I, II, and III. Phase I typically involves trials on a group of twenty to eighty healthy volunteers. The primary task of the researchers in Phase I is to once again determine the safety and toxicity of the compound and also monitor the drug's in vivo behavior. In addition, preliminary dosage requirements or indications are established during this phase. Phase I typically takes one year.[106]

In Phase II, controlled studies are conducted on approximately 100–300 volunteers. A major difference, however, is that these volunteers are typically afflicted with the disease under consideration. In this phase, which lasts roughly two years, experimenters seek to evaluate the effectiveness of the compound and determine any of its potential side effects. In 1978, the agency established a mechanism to increase dialogue between the agency and the sponsor, known as end of Phase II conferences, to be held at this point in the investigation process. The end of Phase II conferences enable the sponsoring firm to confer with the agency in preparation for establishing the parameters of the large Phase III study to follow.

In Phase III the drug is given to roughly 1,000–3,000 patient volunteers who are monitored closely by physicians. The primary emphasis of

Table A.1 The Drug Development and Approval Process

| | Preclinical Testing | Clinical Trials | | | FDA Review | Phase IV |
| --- | --- | --- | --- | --- | --- | --- |
| | | Phase I | Phase II | Phase III | | |
| Years | 3.5 | 1 | 2 | 3 | 2.5 | |
| Test population | Laboratory and animal studies | 20–80 healthy volunteers | 100–300 patient volunteers | 1,000–3,000 patient volunteers | | |
| Purpose | Assess safety and biological activity | Determine safety and dosage | Evaluate effectiveness; side effects | Verify effectiveness; monitor effects of long-term use | Review and approval process | Post-market testing |
| Success rate | 5,000 compounds evaluated | | 5 enter trials | | 1 approved | |

Source: Wierenga and Beary (1995).

this phase is to reestablish the efficacy of the compound and, given its long time frame, to evaluate the in vivo effects of long-term use. Also in this phase, dosage requirements are refined and any adverse reactions or long-term side effects can be monitored. Phase III typically lasts about three years. The experimental design of these clinical investigations remains critical, and the studies must be controlled. Uncontrolled clinical trials are generally found to be unacceptable to the FDA.

Studies also characteristically include a placebo control. The form of investigation generally encouraged by the FDA is the randomized double-blind, placebo-controlled clinical investigation in which neither the investigator nor the patient is aware of where the placebo lies. The double-blind, placebo-controlled study is generally considered to be the "gold standard" in clinical investigations. In addition, the total amount of safety data in humans required to approve each drug varies widely, depending on the drug and the indication. Generally speaking, however, the minimum size of a clinical safety trial is 1,500 patients or volunteers.[107]

On completion of these three phases, the company can then submit a new drug application with the FDA. In the NDA, the company must submit its data and subsequent analyses regarding the safety and efficacy of the compound collected during the Phase I–III trials. Much of the content of this data comes from individual case report forms from patients. Investigators are required by the FDA to submit the individual case report forms of patients who either die or suffer an adverse event during the clinical investigation. Since clinical investigations typically involve only 3,000–8,000 patients, company scientists and statisticians and FDA reviewers must carefully scrutinize the data on a drug that may be taken by millions of consumers within the first year of its approval. Therefore, important review decisions are routinely made on a relatively limited amount of clinical safety and efficacy information. According to one industry analyst, "Clinical trial data is not true life; it must be interpreted with caution." In a sense, the analyst said, "we are all struggling to find a mechanism to identify signals and reduce noise" while evaluating clinical data.

Three of the FDA's six centers are responsible for the evaluation and review of new therapeutic products. These are the Center for Drug Evaluation and Research for prescription drugs, the Center for Biologics Evaluation and Research for biological products, and the Center for Devices and Radiological Health for medical devices. CDER review teams are typically made up of physicians, pharmacologists, chemists, microbiologists, and statisticians. Reviewing this data is no small task given the amount of information involved. Reports of clinical studies, including individual case report forms from patients, can run into the thousands of pages. Typically, the report itself may be only 100–200 pages, but the appendices usually run into thousands of pages. Generally speaking, complete NDAs can range anywhere from 50 to 1,500 volumes with each volume consisting of 250 pages. The average NDA runs well in excess of 200,000 pages.

In order to facilitate the handling and processing of such large dossiers, the FDA began accepting clinical data in electronic form in 1997. Since 1999, the agency has accepted entire NDA submissions in electronic format. Though agency reviewers were originally skeptical of reviewing electronic submissions and some reviewers still prefer to read paper NDA submissions, agency officials now concede that electronic NDA submissions, otherwise known as computer-assisted new drug applications (CANDAs) offer several advantages. Namely, CANDAs allow for keywords to be searched much faster and easier. In addition, keywords can also be hyperlinked to provide the reviewer with supplemental information instantly. Electronic submissions were largely made possible once case report forms could be scanned into a computer and read electronically. According to the FDA's associate director for information management, Randy Levin, one-third of all NDA submissions are now completely electronic (Law, 2001). With CANDAs, the new reality is that drug sponsors increasingly have to manage both paper and electronic submissions. The result is that the traditional notion of the "volume" associated with the NDA is becoming increasingly irrelevant.

FDA reviewers are not the only ones making important decisions during the review process. Advisory committees, comprised of independent scientific experts, provide the agency with technical assistance in the drug review process.[108] Advisory committee meetings take place on a regularly scheduled basis and are usually held in a suburban Washington, D.C., hotel. The meetings are open to the general public, and the minutes of the meetings are made available for public consumption afterward. (The transparency of advisory committee meetings is not uniform around the world. In many European countries, for example, such meetings and the subsequently produced minutes are closed to the public.)

The exact number of CDER advisory committees generally varies between fifteen and twenty, as these committees are organized on the basis of therapeutic classification. In order to meet the changing needs of drug review, two additional advisory committees were recently formed. In order to consider the effects of drugs taken by children, a Pediatric Advisory Committee was formed in 1999. In 2002, the Drug Safety and Risk Management Advisory Committee was formed to advise the agency with respect to specific risk-management issues. Generally speaking, the FDA is not legally bound to adhere to the decisions of its advisory committees, but in practice the agency usually follows an advisory committee decision.

The enactment of the Prescription Drug User Fee Act in 1992, and the subsequent reauthorizations of the law in 1997 and 2002, set specific performance standards that the agency must meet in reviewing NDAs. For instance, the FDA must now review and act on 90 percent of a standard NDA submission within ten months of receiving the original NDA. For drugs given a "priority" review status by the agency, 90 percent of the NDA must be reviewed or acted on within six months of the receipt. In reviewing the NDA, the review team carefully examines all of the data while paying particularly close attention to the Phase III study results. Following the review, the agency can respond to an NDA in several different ways. The decision of the agency on how to proceed with an NDA submission typically comes in one of four forms: approved, approvable, not approvable, and refused to file.[109] Also, the sponsor of the application may withdraw the application at any time during the NDA phase.

Once the FDA approves a drug, there are no time limits placed on the validity of the approval. In several European countries the equivalents of INDs and NDAs are subject to recertification after periods ranging from two to five years. In Britian, for example, clinical trial certificates (equivalent to approved INDs) are effective for a period of two years and product licenses (equivalent to approved NDAs) are good for five years. Both the clinical trial certificates and product licenses are eligible for renewal following the expiration of their initial time period. In the United States, however, once a drug is approved, the product remains on the market as long as the drug is useful, barring any safety difficulties.

Another interesting aspect of agency approval is that drugs being considered for approval are not considered on a relative or comparative basis. That is, the FDA does not require the sponsor of a new drug application to show that the particular product is superior to products already available for use in treating the same condition. The FDA, however, encourages pharmaceutical firms to sponsor comparative studies and make the evidence available during the review process.

Finally, one of the most critical, though difficult to manage, aspects of the approval process occurs after a particular drug has been approved by the agency. Often referred to as Phase IV, the agency has a systematic pharmacovigilance program to monitor the safety of approved drugs. The nation's pharmacovigilance program was originally sponsored by the American Medical Association. The FDA took responsibility for postmarketing surveillance (PMS) in 1962 (Henkel, 1998). Pharmacovigilance is a difficult endeavor, and it continues to present manufacturers, doctors, patients, and regulators with dilemmas for how best to monitor drug safety. Even industry officials agree that current PMS is not as good as it could be.

CDER currently maintains a computer database known as the Adverse Event Reporting System (AERS), which contains information on adverse events that may be associated with approved drug products. With this information on hand, agency PMS activities may involve a variety of forms. Perhaps most common, the agency relies on the voluntary reporting of serious adverse reactions by physicians, hospitals, patients, and drug manufacturers to the agency. The agency may also require the manufacturer to conduct follow-up clinical studies on smaller niche groups of patients.

In 1993, under the leadership of Commissioner David Kessler, the FDA implemented the MedWatch program to make it easier for doctors and hospitals to report adverse events. Participation in the MedWatch program is voluntary, as the FDA seeks to increase the number of "serious adverse events" reported to the agency. Officially, the MedWatch program has four stated goals: (1) to clarify what should and should not be reported to the FDA, (2) to increase awareness of serious reactions caused by drugs or medical devices, (3) to make the reporting process easy, and (4) to give the health community regular feedback about product safety issues (Henkel, 1998). The FDA received reports of 279,305 adverse events in 1999, approximately two-thirds of which came from health professionals (McDonald, 2002).

In practice, the FDA may rely on a number of different techniques to educate physicians, pharmacists, and patients when safety concerns arise (McDonald, 2002). One of the more common agency reactions to particular safety concerns includes the issuance a safety alert, often in the form of a "Dear Healthcare Professional" letter. Such letters provide important product safety information to doctors, pharmacists, and other health professionals. Second, the agency may request the company to produce and disseminate informational brochures that alert consumers about potential negative side effects associated with the drug. Third, the agency may take more dramatic steps by requiring the manufacturer to change the labeling on the product or to include "package inserts" that tighten the restrictions on the use of the drug. Finally, the agency may request that the manufacturer withdraw the product from the market. Legally speaking, the FDA must meet a relatively high standard before it can order the company to remove a drug from the market.

# Abbreviations

| | |
|---|---|
| ACF | Advocacy Coalition Framework |
| ACT UP | AIDS Coalition to Unleash Power |
| AEI | American Enterprise Institute |
| AIDS | Acquired Immune Deficiency Syndrome |
| AMA | American Medical Association |
| CANDA | computer-assisted new drug application |
| CBER | Center for Biological Evaluation and Research (FDA) |
| CDER | Center for Drug Evaluation and Research (FDA) |
| CFR | Code of Federal Regulations |
| CMR | Centre for Medicines Research (UK) |
| CPMP | Committee on the Propriety of Medicinal Products (EU) |
| CRP | Center for Responsive Politics |
| CSDD | Center for the Study of Drug Development (Tufts University) |
| CTD | Common Technical Document |
| DDMAC | Division of Drug Marketing, Advertising, and Communications (FDA) |
| DTC | direct-to-consumer |
| EMEA | European Medicines Evaluation Agency |
| EPA | Environmental Protection Agency |
| FACA | Federal Advisory Committee Act |
| FCC | Federal Communications Commission |
| FDA | Food and Drug Administration |
| FDAMA | FDA Modernization Act (1997) |
| FDCA | Food, Drug and Cosmetic Act (1938) |
| FTC | Federal Trade Commission |

173

| | |
|---|---|
| FTE | full-time equivalents |
| *FR* | *Federal Register* |
| GAO | General Accounting Office |
| GDP | gross domestic product |
| HHS | Department of Health and Human Services |
| HRG | Health Research Group (Public Citizen) |
| ICH | International Conference on Harmonization |
| IND | investigational new drug |
| IOM | Institute of Medicine |
| *JAMA* | *Journal of the American Medical Association* |
| MAA | marketing, advertising, and administration |
| MCA | Medicines Control Agency |
| NAS | new active substances |
| NCE | new chemical entity |
| NDA | new drug application |
| NIAID | National Institute of Allergy and Infectious Diseases |
| NIHCM | National Institute for Health Care Management |
| NME | new molecular entity |
| NRC | National Research Council |
| OECD | Organization for Economic Cooperation and Development |
| OMB | Office of Management and Budget |
| OTA | Office of Technology Assessment |
| OTC | over-the-counter |
| PAL | Pharmaceutical Affairs Law (Japan) |
| PDUFA | Prescription Drug User Fee Act (1992) |
| PFDA | Pure Food and Drugs Act |
| PhRMA | Pharmaceutical Research and Manufacturers Association |
| P.L. | Public Law |
| PMA | Pharmaceutical Manufacturers Association |
| PPSSCC | President's Private Sector Survey on Cost Control (the Grace commission) |
| SEC | Security and Exchange Commission |
| TVAC | Thalidomide Victims Association of Canada |
| USC | United States Code |
| *USP* | *United States Pharmacopeia* |
| WTO | World Trade Organization |

# NOTES

Chapters 3, 4, and 5 draw on material previously published from Stephen Ceccoli, "Divergent Paths to Drug Regulation in the U.S. and the UK," *Journal of Policy History* 14, no. 2 (2002): 135–169. Copyright 2002 by Pennsylvania State University; and Stephen Ceccoli, "Policy Punctuations and Regulatory Drug Review," *Journal of Policy History* 15, no. 2 (2003): 157–191. Copyright 2003 by Pennsylvania State Universtiy. The material is reproduced by permission of Pennsylvania State University.

1. See "2002 Community Pharmacy Year-End Results," National Association of Chain Drug Stores, 2003.

2. As Garrett (2001: 572) points out, "by the late 1990s the biggest selling drugs [in the United States] were those that promised the individual a cheery personality (e.g., Prozac), plenty of hair on their head (e.g., Propecia), and staying power during sexual intercourse (Viagara)."

3. See National Center for Health Statistics (2002), Table 116.

4. "Pfizer Holds Largest Share of U.S. Market," *Scrip*, no. 2620 (February 2001): 16–17.

5. To put its sheer size in relative terms, the U.S. pharmaceutical market is roughly ten times the size of the Canadian ($5.6 billion) and Mexican ($5.0 billion) markets combined.

6. Among Europe's five largest pharmaceutical markets, Germany ($14.4 billion) is the largest, followed by France ($13.2 billion), Italy ($8.9 billion), the UK ($8.9 billion), and Spain ($5.3 billion). See, for example, "World Pharma Sales Up by 10%" *Scrip,* no. 2652 (June 2001): 17.

7. The FDA has undergone several administrative reorganizations (and name changes) since its inception and today remains a part of the nation's Public Health Service (PHS). Administered through the Department of Health and Human Services, the PHS also includes federal health agencies such as the Centers for Disease Control and Prevention, the National Institutes of Health, and the Health Resources and Services Administration.

8. *Drug review* and *drug approval* are broad terms, and their usage, in the absence of a precise definition, may be applied to a variety of FDA activities. As used in this book, the terms refer specifically to the agency's handling of a

certain type of drug known as a new molecular entity (NME). NME refers to any drug whose active ingredient has never been approved for use in the United States. It should be noted, though, that in addition to NMEs, the agency handles applications for a variety of other drug-specific purposes such as new or expanded uses of already approved products (i.e., efficacy supplements), applications to alter manufacturing procedures (i.e., manufacturing supplements), and applications to test new drugs in humans for the first time (i.e., investigational new drug applications) among others. For the purposes of this book, the terms NME and NCE (new chemical entity) are used interchangeably.

9. The figure listed is the agency's budget for fiscal year 2002. The federal government's fiscal year begins on October 1.

10. An August 2001 Gallup poll demonstrated the relative parity between Americans who consider themselves "pro-choice" (46 percent) and "pro-life" (46 percent). See Lydia Saad, "Public Opinion About Abortion—An In-Depth Review," at www.gallup.com (September 14, 2002).

11. See "Regulations Restricting the Sale and Distribution of Cigarettes and Smokeless Tobacco Products to Protect Children and Adolescents," 61 *Federal Register* (*FR*) 44395 (August 28, 1996). For a legal treatment of the agency's decision, see Rienzo (1998).

12. In what may amount to the final blow to the FDA's regulatory authority on this matter, the U.S. Supreme Court ruled in March 2000 that the agency could no longer regulate tobacco (as a drug) and cigarettes (as medical devices). Despite the High Court's ruling, Congress has continued to consider legislation that would give the FDA legal authority to regulate tobacco. See "Bills to Allow FDA to Regulate Tobacco," *Scrip,* no. 2629 (March 2001): 15.

13. "The Power 25," *Fortune,* May 28, 2001, at www.fortune.com/fortune/power25 (June 18, 2003).

14. Dr. Michael Friedman, FDA lead deputy commissioner, statement before the Subcommittee on Health and the Environment, Committee on Commerce, U.S. House of Representatives, April 23, 1997.

15. See, for example Herring (1936); Huntington (1952); Bernstein (1955); Noll (1971); and Wilson (1980).

16. Grabowski and Vernon (1983) and Heimann (1997) also use this illustration.

17. Technically speaking, this is not always a binary decision situation. In some cases, the agency may take a middle position by deciding that a particular drug is "approvable" if further studies support the drug's safety and efficacy.

18. See, for example, Ceccoli (2002). In the United Kingdom, a major overhaul of British medicines regulation did not occur until the passage of the Medicines Act in 1968.

19. See Ceccoli (2002) for a discussion of one particular example.

20. See, for example, Moe (1984); North (1981, 1990); Eggertsson (1990); Rothenberg (1994); Knight and Sened (1998).

21. In every instance, open-ended questions were used and the author conducted focused interviews. That is, the author approached each interview with a prepared list of topics and questions. In some cases, interviewees preferred to receive a list of questions and topics in advance. Given the variety of interviewees, a standard list of questions was not used for every interview. The majority of interviews were conducted face to face, and the remainder of interviews

were conducted over the telephone. The interviewees provided invaluable insights and clarified policy details in a number of specific areas.

22. There are essentially two different views when considering the political economy of the pharmaceutical industry and the domestic origin of firms. One view refers to the increasing global integration of the pharmaceutical industry, in which firms headquartered in one country maintain research and development and/or manufacturing operations in another country (e.g., the presence of the UK's GlaxoWellcome in North Carolina). An alternative view considers what would essentially be separate nationally based pharmaceutical industries (e.g., the U.S. pharmaceutical industry, the British pharmaceutical industry, the Japanese pharmaceutical industry). Firm membership in a "U.S.," "British," or "Japanese" pharmaceutical industry would be defined in this case by membership in the leading trade associations of each region.

23. Epstein and O'Halloran (1999) characterize the issue of whether or not to delegate responsibility to the bureaucracy as the "make or buy" decision confronting the legislature.

24. The administrative discretion inherent in such transactions also imposes costs on the various actors. Legislators, for example, must determine whether administrative agents are likely to carry out delegated responsibilities. Legislators must also consider the inherent opportunity costs in determining how much time to spend crafting the specific details of legislation (e.g., time spent on the phrasing of a precise regulatory standard or developing provisions that ensure the legislative durability). Alternately, administrative agents must balance the objectives of the legislature with their own objectives. This type of balance naturally invites the possibility of moral hazard problems insofar as regulators may tailor their behavior to conform solely to the regulatory standard at the expense of other regulatory duties. Finally, third-party actors face transaction costs in relation to the time and resources they dedicate toward attempting to influence policy in their favor.

25. Ronald Coase (1937) provided the seminal work on the significance of transaction costs and his work was gradually extended through the insights of scholars such as Armen Alchian, Harold Demsetz, and Herbert Simon.

26. See, for example, Hammond and Knott (1996).

27. See Worsham, Eisner, and Ringquist (1997) for a discussion and useful critique of five assumptions of agency theory; and Eggertsson (1990).

28. Furthermore, regulation on behalf of the public interest cannot account for the inherent difficulty in identifying a single public interest. The difficulty of aggregating the preferences of numerous individuals into a single collective choice has been proven to be a vexing and irresolvable problem in the social choice literature (Arrow, 1951).

29. For a broader discussion of the relationship between organized interests and executive agencies, see Schlozman and Tierney (1986: chap. 13). Schlozman and Tierney also provide a concise discussion of the organizational "capture" of executive agencies as well as critiques of capture theory. For a useful theoretical perspective and a typology describing the relationship between interest groups and the bureaucracy, see Chubb (1983: chap. 2).

30. For a useful review of the claims about industry using regulators for protection from competition, see Skowronek (1982: chap. 5). Skowronek

acknowledges that Kolko "must be credited with illuminating the changing relationship between business and government in the evolution of the private economy" (129).

31. Carpenter's formal work builds on the empirical findings of Olson (1995, 1996, and 1997).

32. For more thorough critiques of regulatory capture theories, see Wilson (1980); Quirk (1981); Breyer (1982); Derthick and Quirk (1985); Schlozman and Tierney (1986); and Meier (1988).

33. Horn's analysis also applies to tax-financed bureaus and state-owned enterprises.

34. This figure is an estimate by the author. The estimate was derived by combining a figure of eighty-four appearances between 1985 and 1990 as cited in USHHS (1991) with a manual count by the author using the *Annual Abstracts* of the Congressional Information Service (CIS).

35. Remarks of Rep. Thomas Bliley at the 1995 annual meeting of the Food and Drug Law Institute (FDLI), Washington, D.C.

36. For a long time, the "full reports of investigations" clause was interpreted by the agency to include *all* case report forms and case report tabulations, among other things. The agency modified its interpretation in 1985 to ease this interpretation slightly.

37. The Medicines Control Agency (MCA) is the British counterpart to the FDA.

38. See the discussion in Chapter 5 for an example of varying performance in the FDA's case.

39. In doing so, they emphasize the importance of both positive and negative feedback systems. See, for example, Arthur (1994) for a discussion of positive feedback and increasing returns and Wlezian (1995) for a substantive discussion of negative feedback. Subsequent work by Jones, Baumgartner, and True (1998) refers to this phenomenon as a "policy punctuation."

40. For a more detailed and comprehensive discussion of the early period, see Blake (1968); Jackson (1970); Jannsen (1981); Temin (1980); and Young (1961, 1967).

41. See Rothstein (1995) for a brief review of early pharmacological developments. For additional historical accounts, see Sneader (1985) and Burger (1986).

42. See Fried (1998), for an illuminating account of the early years of U.S. drug regulation from an interview with the FDA's Frances Kelsey.

43. See Temin (1980) for a discussion of the legal challenge and the ramifications of the legal opinion proffered by Justice Oliver Wendell Holmes.

44. See Fried (1998) for a discussion.

45. For a discussion of this debate, see Numbers (1978) and Duffy (1979).

46. The British experience provides a useful comparison here. The British government has generally enjoyed a close and amicable working relationship with the pharmaceutical industry. This is significant because firms that are either headquartered in the UK or have a substantial industry presence there produce 90 percent of the pharmaceutical products purchased by the British National Health Service. In practice, this close relationship enables much of the policy detail to be developed informally. The outcome of such policies, then,

reflects a political compromise between the primary government and industry-related interests.

47. Quoted in Young (1967: 60).

48. Consider the following excerpts from Kallet and Schlink: "The *Pebeco Toothpaste* with which you brush your teeth twice every day—do you know that a tube of it contains enough poison, if eaten, to kill three people; that, in fact, a German army officer committed suicide by eating a tubeful of this particular tooth paste?" (1933: 4). "But the roughage in that box of Kellogg's [*All-Bran*] which Mrs. Jones is going to feed her family is a powerful intestinal irritant to many persons; its continued use may be harmful to most persons; to some it will be dangerous" (20). "If you do not want *Marmola* [a thyroid preparation] the druggist can give you any of a dozen 'obesity cures' of the cathartic type, comparatively less harmless in themselves if known and used occasionally as cathartics, but capable of doing serious damage if used according to the directions—every day" (70–71).

49. Perhaps the most succinct criticism of Delaney is offered by science writer Michael Fumento (1995: A19): "Let's say you detect a part per quadrillion in a plum product. That's the equivalent of one plum in 73,511,000 tons."

50. For an illuminating account of the Kefauver drug hearings and a legislative history of the 1962 amendments, see Harris (1964).

51. There are a number of well-written (firsthand and otherwise) accounts of the impact and aftermath of thalidomide. See, for example, Insight Team (1979); Teff and Munro (1976); and, more recently, Stephens and Brynner (2001).

52. See McFayden (1976) for a discussion of the use of thalidomide in the United States during this time.

53. Despite Kefauver's original intent to pursue drug pricing and industry profits, the 1962 amendments lacked such provisions. Though drug pricing has surfaced many times in subsequent congressional hearings and national debates, it has continued to elude federal drug legislation.

54. Unlike in the United States, for instance, governments in several other large pharmaceutical markets place restrictions on either the price of a particular drug product (e.g., France and Germany) or impose a ceiling on the amount of profits a company can earn from any one particular drug (e.g., the United Kingdom). Consequently, Americans pay higher prices for prescription drugs than virtually anywhere else in the world. The drug pricing systems in each country are largely tied to the nature of health care delivery and health insurance. Essentially, the nature of the relationship between the domestic government and the pharmaceutical industry largely structures the pharmaceutical pricing/profit arrangement.

55. The National Academy of Sciences (NAS) was created by Congress in 1863 to "investigate, examine, experiment, and report upon any subject of science or art." Today, the NAS and the National Research Council (NRC) comprise two of the four national academies. The others are the National Academy of Engineering and the Institute of Medicine. Each of these academies is a nonprofit organization that relies on experts from around the country to provide independent analyses and assessments of scientific and technical matters of public policy.

56. To put the number of clinical studies in perspective, a survey of 1,000 clinical trials, conducted by nine firms, found the average length of a single clinical investigation to be about 200 weeks (3 years, 10 months). Moreover, despite conventional wisdom to the contrary, very little difference has been found in cycle times between Phase I, II, and III studies (Barnett and James, 1995).

57. For a comprehensive review of the early drug lag studies, see Schifrin and Tayan (1977).

58. For each FDA approval, the authors identified the initial market and year of introduction.

59. The third report in the CSDD series, examining FDA approvals between 1990 and 1992, found that 58 percent of the seventy-four NCEs included in the study were previously available in foreign markets for at least a year prior to U.S. approval (Kaitin et al., 1994). The report also noted similar results to those found in the late 1980s.

60. See Andersson (1992) for a more recent review of the drug lag literature. The Andersson review includes a greater level of empirical detail than earlier reviews.

61. Though Peltzman wrote many of his important studies while a faculty member at UCLA, he was a graduate student at the University of Chicago and was later on the faculty of the Chicago business school.

62. See Shulman, Hewitt, and Manocchia (1995) for a more thorough overview of the various FDA reviews.

63. While Figure 5.1 may give the impression of incremental change, the change in agency performance has been dramatic. The 53 percent reduction in review times over this period is remarkable.

64. The measure of annual approvals is only one measure of agency workload and is used for illustrative purposes in this case. Workload is generally better measured by the number of submissions to the agency—INDs and NDAs for drugs, INDs and Biologics License Applications for biologics, and Investigational Device Exemptions, PMAs, and 510(k)s for medical devices, than by approvals.

65. Exceptions include, for example, the work of Daniel Carpenter (1999, 2000) and Mary Olson (1995, 1996, 1997).

66. Discussion of legislative and administrative changes is largely based on reviews contained in USFDA (1995a) and 57 *FR* 13234 (April 15, 1992).

67. See 57 *FR* 58942 (December 11, 1992).

68. CD4 cells are white blood cells that play an important role in the immune system and are a major target for HIV. The National AIDS Treatment Information Project (www.natip.org) provides an accessible discussion and useful educational material on HIV, AIDS, CD4 counts, and related topics.

69. Specific guidelines are provided in the FDA's Center for Drug Evaluation Manual of Policies and Procedures (MaPP 6020.3).

70. See USFDA (2000) for the agency's statutory compliance report.

71. PDUFA Performance Reports to Congress and PDUFA Financial Reports to Congress can be viewed on the FDA website at www.fda.gov/oc/pdufa/reports.html.

72. For instance, the McMahon committee (1982) considered IND requirements and the efficacy standard in the attempt to accelerate clinical testing and

the Lasagna committee (1990) examined procedures for reviewing AIDS and cancer drugs.

73. The Pharmaceutical Manufacturers Association would later become the Pharmaceutical Research and Manufacturers Association.

74. Temple joined the FDA in 1972 and today is the agency's associate director for medical policy. He is highly regarded both inside and outside of the agency for his work in drug review.

75. Jeffords was a member of the Republican Party when he replaced Kassebaum.

76. See "Henney Resigns; Thompson to Review RU-486," *Scrip,* no. 2611 (January 2001): 17.

77. Approximately 74 percent of Americans are covered by private health insurance (OECD, 1994).

78. In the United States, the government accounts for 11 percent of the pharmaceutical market, whereas retail and wholesale pharmacies make up 75 percent of that market (Schwartzman, 1976).

79. Pharmaceutical Research and Manufacturers Association, www.phrma.org.

80. "The Power 25."

81. Center for Responsive Politics, 2002. The Center for Responsive Politics describes itself as a "non-partisan, non-profit research group based in Washington, D.C. that tracks money in politics, and its effect on elections and public policy." The CRP website is www.opensecrets.org. The $26.4 million figure represents a combination of contributions from individuals, political action committees (PACs), and soft money.

82. Johnson, of Connecticut, chairs the Health Subcommittee of the House Ways and Means Committee. At the time, Torricelli was a member of the Healthcare Subcommittee of the Senate Finance Committee and represented New Jersey, home to more than 60,000 pharmaceutical industry jobs.

83. *Fortune,* April 2002.

84. OTA (1994: 72). The Office of Technology Assessment was abolished as a part of a congressional reorganization in 1994.

85. Statement issued by Christopher Molineaux, PhRMA vice president for public affairs, in response to the "Rx R&D Myths" paper released by Public Citizen, July 23, 2001.

86. Families USA (2002). The nine companies included in the Families USA study were Merck and Co.; Pfizer, Inc.; Bristol-Myers Squibb Company; Abbott Laboratories; Wyeth; Pharmacia Corporation; Eli Lilly & Co.; Schering-Plough Corporation; and Allergan, Inc.

87. Currently, approximately 80 percent of the drugs approved in Japan originate outside of Japan and only 20 percent originate in Japan. The ratio was previously much closer to 60:40.

88. European-wide regulation of new drug approvals dates back as early as 1965 when EC Directive 65/65 was issued in the attempt to harmonize European drug safety regulations. While European-wide harmonization efforts moved glacially slow throughout the 1970s and 1980s, they were greatly accelerated in the mid-1990s.

89. For an overview of the current European system, see Abraham and Lewis (2000).

90. The EMEA's impact is largely twofold (USGAO, 1996). First, the EMEA has established a set of performance guidelines that must be met by individual regulatory authorities as well as those countries acting as rapporteurs. These performance guidelines are designed to ensure the timely review of company dossiers. Second, and most important, the decisions of the CPMP and the European Commission are now legally binding. Unlike the previous arrangement, all member states are required to comply with the decisions of the commission. Finally, unlike in the United States, patient access to medicines in Europe requires a two-step process. The regulatory approval phase naturally gathers the most attention. However, pricing remains the final phase to market access as each European member state determines a national pricing/profit policy.

91. "Five Agencies Do 59% of EMEA Reviews," *Scrip,* no. 2759 (June 2002): 2.

92. As one European industry observer told me, "The MCA will get stronger as a result of the EMEA because even more countries will rely on the MCA's expertise and excellent performance."

93. Given the difficulties associated with attempting to harmonize several distinctive regulatory standards (in addition to the more immediate logistical issues such as travel and language barriers), ICH meetings have generally taken place once every two to three years. The initial meeting took place in Brussels in 1991 and subsequent meetings have occurred in Orlando, Fla. (1993), Yokohama, Japan (1995), Brussels (1997), and San Diego, Calif. (2000). The next ICH meeting is scheduled for February 2003 in Tokyo, Japan.

94. A total of fourteen drugs were withdrawn between 1992 and 2001 (USGAO, 2002).

95. For a discussion, see Abraham (1995); Friedman et al. (1999); Fried (1998); and Willman (2000). For an interesting exchange over the safety concerns involving one of the drugs in Table 6.2—Lotronex—see Horton (2001a, 2001b) and Moynihan (2002).

96. For precise definitions of adverse drug reactions and a discussion of the implications of adverse drug reactions, see Goldman (1996); Goldman et al. (1995); Karch and Lasagna (1975); and Rawlins (1981).

97. In addition to the Lotronex case, *Los Angeles Times* investigative reporter David Willman won a Pulitzer Prize for his chronicling of agency decisionmaking during and in the aftermath of seven prescription drugs that were withdrawn from the market in the PDUFA era (see Willman, 2000).

98. Though the authors acknowledge that the list of withdrawals is not a comprehensive one, the list is useful for examining patterns of drug withdrawals over a four-decade period. For the benefit of the reader, Fung and colleagues make available the complete list of 121 withdrawn products, along with the relevant safety concerns, the year of withdrawal, and the countries where the drug was withdrawn.

99. As an interesting side note, of the 121 drugs identified by Fung and collaborators, 31.4 percent of those were drugs affecting the central nervous system (i.e., CNS drugs), 16.5 percent were musculoskeletal products, and 14.9 percent were cardiovascular agents. Further segmentation by therapeutic category revealed the three most common classes of drugs withdrawn were nonsteroidal anti-inflammatory drugs or NSAIDs (13.2 percent), analgesics (8.3

percent), and antidepressants (7.4 percent). In addition, the most common body toxicities for drug withdrawals were hepatic (i.e., liver toxicity) (26.2 percent), hematologic (10.5 percent), cardiovascular (8.7 percent), dermatologic (6.3 percent), and carcinogenic (6.3 percent).

100. "Pfizer Holds Largest Share," 16–17.

101. See 21 CFR 201.5 and 201.128.

102. For reviews on off-label prescribing and promotion, see Christopher (1993); Kessler (1978, 1991); USGAO (1991); Shapiro (1978); U.S. House (1991); and Kessler and Pines (1990).

103. See 65 FR 14286 and 14287 (March 16, 2000); 61 FR 52800 (October 8, 1996); and 62 FR 64093 (December 3, 1997).

104. Joseph DiMasi, testimony before the Subcommittee on Health and the Environment, Committee on Commerce, U.S. House of Representatives, April 23, 1997.

105. Ibid.

106. Interestingly, in several European countries, study designs on healthy volunteers are not controlled. In Britain, for example, the administration of substances to healthy volunteers is not covered under the 1968 Medicines Act. As such, studies administering the substance in question to human volunteers are self-regulated by the medical profession and its various ethics committees (MCA, 1996). Later-phase trials determine critical factors such as dosage and efficacy.

107. Dr. Janet Woodcock, CDER director, testimony before the Subcommittee on Health, Committee on Energy and Commerce, U.S. House of Representatives, March 6, 2002.

108. CDER was commended by an Institute of Medicine Review Committee in 1991 for the clarity of issues that may be brought before the attention of an advisory committee (IOM, 1992). These included the approvability of specific drugs, general drug development and the design of clinical trials, and issues pertaining to marketed drugs (e.g., safety, efficacy, proper indication, etc.).

109. Provisions in PDUFA III will rename the "approvable" and "not approvable" letters "complete response" letters.

# BIBLIOGRAPHY

Abraham, John. 1995. *Science, Politics, and the Pharmaceutical Industry.* London: UCL Press.

Abraham, John, and Graham Lewis. 2000. *Regulating Medicines in Europe: Competition, Experts and Public Health.* London: Routledge.

Anderson, Oscar. 1958. *The Health of a Nation: Harvey W. Wiley and the Fight for Pure Food.* Chicago: University of Chicago Press.

Andersson, Fredrick. 1992. "The Drug Lag Issue: The Debate from an International Perspective." *International Journal of Health Services* 22, no. 1: 53–72.

Arrow, Kenneth. 1951. *Social Choice and Individual Values.* New York: Wiley.

Arthur, Brian. 1994. *Increasing Returns and Path Dependence in the Economy.* Ann Arbor: University of Michigan Press.

Bakke, Olav, M. Manocchia, F. de Abajo, K. Kaitin, and L. Lasagna. 1995. "Drug Safety Discontinuations in the United Kingdom, the United States, and Spain from 1974 Through 1993: A Regulatory Perspective." *Clinical Pharmacology and Therapeutics* 58, no. 1: 108–117.

Bakke, Olav, W. Wardell, and L. Lasagna. 1984. "Drug Discontinuations in the United Kingdom and the United States, 1964 to 1983: Issues of Safety." *Clinical Pharmacology and Therapeutics* 35, no. 5: 559–567.

Ballentine, Carol. 1981. "Taste of Rasperries, Taste of Death: The 1937 Elixir Sulfanilamide Incident." *FDA Consumer* 15, no. 5 (June): 18–21.

Barnett, Samuel, and Jeffrey James. 1995. "Measuring the Clinical Development Process." *Applied Clinical Trials* (September): 44–54.

Barral, P. E. 1996. "20 Years of Pharmaceutical Research Results Throughout the World." Rhone-Poulenc Rorer Foundation, through the Pharmaceutical Research and Manufacturers web page, www.phrma.org/publications/backgrounders/world/12_global.phtml (May 23, 2001).

Bates, D., N. Spell, D. Cullen, E. Burdick, N. Laird, L. Petersen, S. Small, B. Sweitzer, and L. Leape. 1997. "The Costs of Adverse Drug Events in Hospitalized Patients." *Journal of the American Medical Association* 277, no. 4: 307–311.

Baumgartner, Frank, and Bryan Jones. 1993. *Agendas and Instability in American Politics.* Chicago: University of Chicago Press.

————. 2001. "Policy Dynamics." Paper presented at the Annual Meeting of the Midwest Political Science Association, Chicago, April 18–21.

Becker, Gary S. 1976. *The Economic Approach to Human Behavior.* Chicago: University of Chicago Press.

Behrman, Bradley. 1980. "Civil Aeronautics Board." In James Q. Wilson, ed., *The Politics of Regulation,* pp. 75–120. New York: Basic Books.

Belcher, Paul. 1995. "Medicines Licensing: A Case for Greater Transparency?" *Eurohealth* 1, no. 3 (December 1995): 6–8.

Bernstein, Marver. 1955. *Regulating Business by Independent Commission.* Princeton: Princeton University Press.

Birkland, Thomas. 1997. *After Disaster: Agenda Setting, Public Policy, and Focusing Events.* Washington, DC: Georgetown University Press.

Blake, John. 1968. *Education in the History of Medicine.* New York: Hafner Publishing Co.

Breyer, Stephen. 1982. *Regulation and Its Reform.* Cambridge, MA: Harvard University Press.

Brichachek, Andra, and L. J. Sellers. 2000. "Big Pharma Spend Trends." *Pharmaceutical Executive* (September): 96–116.

Burger, Alfred. 1986. *Drugs and People: Medications, Their History and Origins, and the Way They Act.* Charlottesville: University Press of Virginia.

Burkholz, Herbert. 1994. *The FDA Follies.* New York: Basic Books.

Campbell, Rita Ricardo. 1976. *Drug Lag: Federal Government Decision Making.* Stanford, CA: Hoover Institution Studies.

Canedy, Dana. 1997. "Claims and Counterclaims Fly as Two Giants Battle for Supremacy in the Antihistamine Market." *New York Times,* February 27, 1997, p. D4.

Carpenter, Daniel. 1996. "Adaptive Signal Processing, Hierarchy, and Budgetary Control in Federal Regulation." *American Political Science Review* 90, no. 2: 283–302.

————. 1999. "Bureaucratic Choice as a Stopping Problem: A Theoretical and Empirical Analysis of FDA Drug Review." Paper presented at the 1999 annual meeting of the Midwest Political Science Association, Chicago.

————. 2000. "Groups, the Media, and Agency Waiting Costs: The Political Economy of FDA Drug Approval." Paper presented at the 2000 annual meeting of the Midwest Political Science Association, Chicago.

————. 2001. "Protection Without Capture: Product Approval by a Politically Responsive, Bayesian Regulator." Unpublished manuscript, Univeristy of Michigan, Dept. of Political Science.

Carrier, Michael. 1996. "Federal Preemption of Common Law Tort Awards by the Federal Food, Drug, and Cosmetic Act." *Food and Drug Law Journal* 51, no. 4: 509–611.

Ceccoli, Stephen. 2002. "Divergent Paths to Drug Regulation in the U.S. and U.K." *Journal of Policy History* 14, no. 2: 135–169.

Center for Responsive Politics. 2002. "Pharmaceuticals/Health Products: Long-Term Contribution Trends." Available online at http://www.open secrets.org/industries/indus.asp?Ind=H04, March 2, 2003.

Christopher, William. 1993. "Off-Label Drug Prescription: Filling the Regulatory Vacuum." *Food and Drug Law Journal* 48, no. 2: 247–262.

Chubb, John. 1983. *Interest Groups and the Bureaucracy: The Politics of Energy.* Stanford: Stanford University Press.

Cimons, Marlene. 1997. "Seldane Pulled for a Safer Allergy Drug." *Los Angeles Times,* December 30.

Clark, Cheryl. 1989. "A Tenacious AIDS Activist Credited for Quicker OK of Drugs." *San Diego Union-Tribune,* November 12, 1989, p. A3.

CMR (Centre for Medicines Research). 1996. *CMR News* (Surrey, UK) 14, no. 1 (Spring 1996).

Coase, Ronald. 1937. "The Nature of the Firm." *Economica* 4: 386–405.

Cobb, Roger, and Charles Elder. 1983. *Participation in American Politics: The Dynamics of Agenda-Building.* Baltimore: Johns Hopkins University Press.

Coppin, Clayton, and Jack High. 1991. "Entrepreneurship and Competition in the Bureaucracy: Harvey Washington Wiley's Bureau of Chemistry, 1883–1903." In Jack High, ed., *Regulation: Economic Theory and History,* pp. 95–118. Ann Arbor: University of Michigan Press.

Coppinger, Paul, C. Peck, and R. Temple. 1989. "Understanding Comparisons of Drug Introductions Between the United States and United Kingdom." *Clinical Pharmacology and Therapeutics* 46, no. 2: 139–145.

*CQ (Congressional Quarterly) Almanac.* Various editions, 1960–2000. Washington, DC: Congressional Quarterly.

Davis, John. 2000. "From Penicillan to Viagara—A Century of Achievement." *Scrip Magazine* (January): 37–40.

de Haen, Paul. 1975. "The Drug Lag: Does It Exist in Europe?" *Drug Intelligence and Clinical Pharmacy* 9, no. 3: 144–150.

————. 1976. "Effect of Legislation on the Introduction of Drugs—Is There a Drug Lag?" *Drug Intelligence and Clinical Pharmacy* 10, no. 2: 86–93.

Denver Post Editorial. "Safer Medicine Chest." *Denver Post,* January 3, p. B7.

Derthick, Martha, and Paul Quirk. 1985. *The Politics of Deregulation.* Washington, DC: Brookings Institution.

DiMasi, Joseph, R. Hansen, and H. Grabowski. 1991. "The Cost of Innovation in the Pharmaceutical Industry." *Journal of Health Economics* 10, no. 2: 107–142.

————. 2003. "The Price of Innovation: New Estimates of Drug Development Costs." *Journal of Health Economics* 22: 151–185.

DiMasi, Joseph, Mark Seibring, and Louis Lasagna. 1994. "New Drug Development in the United States from 1963–1992." *Clinical Pharmacology and Therapeutics* 55, no. 6: 609–622.

Dranove, David, and David Meltzer. 1994. "Do Important Drugs Reach the Market Sooner?" *RAND Journal of Economics* 25, no. 3: 402–423.

Duffy, John. 1979. "The American Medical Profession and Public Health: From Support to Ambivalence." *Bulletin of the History of Medicine* 53, no. 1: 1–22.

Duggan, Paul. 1988. "1,000 Swarm FDA's Rockville Office to Demand Approval of AIDS Drugs." *Washington Post,* October 12, p. B1.

Dupree, A. Hunter. 1957. *Science in the Federal Government: A History of Policies and Activities to 1940.* Cambridge, MA: Harvard University Press.

Easton, David. 1965. *A Framework for Political Analysis.* Englewood Cliffs, NJ: Prentice Hall.

Eggertsson, Thrain. 1990. *Economic Behavior and Institutions*. New York: Cambridge University Press.

Eisner, Marc. 2000. *Regulatory Politics in Transition*. 2d ed. Baltimore: Johns Hopkins University Press.

Eisner, Marc, Jeff Worsham, and Evan Ringquist. 2000. *Contemporary Regulatory Policy*. Boulder: Lynne Rienner Publishers.

Epstein, David, and Sharyn O'Halloran. 1999. *Delegating Powers: A Transaction Cost Politics Approach to Policy Making Under Separate Powers*. New York: Cambridge University Press.

Epstein, Steven. 1996. *Impure Science: AIDS, Activism, and the Politics of Knowledge*. Berkeley: University of California Press.

Families USA. 2002. "Profiting from Pain: Where Prescription Drug Dollars Go." Publication no. 02-105. Washington, DC, July.

Ferejohn, John. 1987. "The Structure of Agency Decision Processes." In M. McCubbins and T. Sullivan, eds., *Congress: Structure and Policy*, pp. 441–461. New York: Cambridge University Press.

Fletcher, David. 1997. "Hayfever Drug Faces Sales Curb After 14 Sufferers Die." *Daily Telegraph* (London), April 25.

Fox, Daniel. 1986. *Health Policies, Health Politics*. Princeton: Princeton University Press.

Frech, H. E., and Richard Miller Jr. 1999. *The Productivity of Health Care and Pharmaceuticals: An International Comparison*. Washington, DC: AEI Press.

Fried, Stephen. 1998. *Bitter Pills*. New York: Bantam Doubleday.

Friedman, M., J. Woodcock, M. Lumpkin, J. Shuren, A. Hass, and L. Thompson. 1999. "The Safety of Newly Approved Medicines—Do Recent Market Removals Mean There Is a Problem?" *Journal of the American Medical Association* 281: 1728–1734.

Fritschler, A. Lee. 1989. *Smoking and Politics: Policy Making and the Federal Bureaucracy*. 4th ed. Englewood Cliffs, NJ: Prentice Hall.

Fumento, Michael. 1995. "Overdue Overhaul of Pesticide Limitations." *Washington Times*, December 13, p. A19.

Fung, M., A. Thornton, K. Mybeck, J. Wu, K. Hornbuckle, and E. Muniz. 2001. "Evaluation of the Characteristics of Safety Withdrawal from Prescription Drugs from Worldwide Pharmaceutical Markets, 1960 to 1999." *Drug Information Journal* 35, no. 1: 293–317.

Garrett, Laurie. 2001. *The Betrayal of Trust: The Collapse of Global Public Health*. New York: Hyperion.

Gieringer, Dale. 1985. "The Safety and Efficacy of New Drug Approval." *Cato Journal* 5 (Spring/Summer): 177–201.

Goldberg, Robert. 1996. "Untimely Access: An Analysis of America's 'Drug Lag.'" GWU Center on Neuroscience, Medical Progress, and Society. Washington, DC, February.

Goldman, S. A. 1996. "The Clinical Impact of Adverse Event Reporting." U.S. Food and Drug Administration. Rockville, MD, October.

Goldman, S. A., D. L. Kennedy, and R. Lieberman, eds. 1995. "Clinical Therapeutics and the Recognition of Drug-Induced Disease." U.S. Food and Drug Administration. Rockville, MD, June.

Gormley, William. 1983. *The Politics of Public Utility Regulation*. Pittsburgh: University of Pittsburgh Press.

———. 1986. "Regulatory Issue Networks in a Federal System." *Polity* 18, no. 4: 595–620.

Grabowski, Henry. 1976. *Drug Regulation and Innovation*. Washington, DC: American Enterprise Institute.

Grabowski, Henry, and John Vernon. 1983. *The Regulation of Pharmaceuticals*. Washington, DC: American Enterprise Institute.

Graig, Laurene. 1993. *Health of Nations*. 2d ed. Washington, DC: CQ Press.

Griffin, John. 2002. "Is Big Pharma Too Close to the Regulators?" *Scrip Magazine* (November): 18–19.

Hammond, Thomas, and Jack Knott. 1996. "Who Controls the Bureaucracy?: Presidential Power, Congressional Dominance, Legal Constraints, and Bureaucratic Autonomy in a Model of Multi-Institutional Policy Making." *Journal of Law, Economics, and Organization* 12, no. 1: 119–166.

Hancher, Leigh. 1989. "Regulating Drug Prices: The West German and British Experience." In L. Hancher and Michael Moran, eds., *Capitalism, Culture, and Regulation*, pp. 79–108. Oxford: Clarendon Press.

———. 1990. *Regulating for Competition*. Oxford: Clarendon Press.

Harris, Richard. 1964. *The Real Voice*. New York: Macmillan.

Harris, Richard, and Sidney Milkis. 1996. *The Politics of Regulatory Change: A Tale of Two Agencies*. New York: Oxford University Press.

Harvey, C., C. Lumley, and S. Walker. 1993. "A Comparison of the Review of a Cohort of NCEs by Four National Regulatory Authorities." *Journal of Pharmaceutical Medicine* 3: 65–75.

Heclo, Hugh. 1978. "Issue Networks in the Executive Establishment." In Anthony King, ed., *The New American Political System*, pp. 87–124. Washington, DC: American Enterprise Institute.

Heimann, C. F. Larry. 1997. *Acceptable Risks: Politics, Policy, and Risky Technologies*. Ann Arbor: University of Michigan Press.

Helms, Robert, ed. 1975. *Drug Development and Marketing*. Washington, DC: American Enterprise Institute.

Henkel, John. 1998. "Medwatch: FDA's 'Heads Up' on Medical Product Safety." *FDA Consumer* (November–December): 10–15.

Herring, Edward P. 1936. *Public Administration and the Public Interest*. New York: Russell and Russell.

Herrmann, Mark, and Geoffrey Ritts. 1996. "Preemption and Medical Devices: A Response to Adler and Mann." *Food and Drug Law Journal* 50, no.1: 1–19.

Hirschman, Albert. 1982. *Shifting Involvements*. Princeton: Princeton University Press.

Horn, Murray. 1995. *The Political Economy of Public Administration*. New York: Cambridge University Press.

Horton, Richard. 2001a. "Lotronex and the FDA: A Fatal Erosion of Integrity." *The Lancet* 357 (May 19): 1544–1555.

———. 2001b. "The FDA and *The Lancet:* An Exchange." *The Lancet* 358 (August 4): 415–418.

Hotelling, Harold. 1938. "The General Welfare in Relation to Problems of Taxation and Railway and Utility Rates." *Econometrica* 6, no. 3: 242–269.

Hult, Karen, and Charles Walcott. 1990. *Governing Public Organizations*. Belmont, CA: Brooks/Cole Wadsworth.

Huntington, Samuel. 1952. "The Marasmus of the Interstate Commerce Commission." *Yale Law Journal* 61, no. 4: 467–509.

———. 1968. *Political Order in Changing Societies*. New Haven: Yale University Press.

Insight Team of the Sunday Times of London. 1979. *Suffer the Children: The Story of Thalidomide*. New York: Viking Press.

IOM (Institute of Medicine). 1988. *The Future of Public Health*. Committee for the Study of the Future of Public Health. Washington, DC: National Academy Press.

———. 1992. *Food and Drug Administration Advisory Committees*. Committee to Study the Use of Advisory Committees by the Food and Drug Administration. Washington, DC: National Academy Press.

Jackson, Charles. 1970. *Food and Drug Legislation in the New Deal*. Princeton: Princeton University Press.

Jannsen, Wallace. 1981. "The Story of the Laws Behind the Labels." *FDA Consumer* 15, no. 5 (June 1981). Washington, DC: Food and Drug Administration.

Johnson, Jeffrey, and Lyle Bootman, 1995. "Drug-Related Morbidity and Mortality: A Cost of Illness Model." *Archives of Internal Medicine* 155, no. 18: 1949–1956.

Jones, Bryan, Frank Baumgartner, and James True. 1998. "Policy Punctuations: U.S. Budget Authority, 1947–1995." *Journal of Politics* 60, no. 1: 1–33.

Joskow, Paul. 1974. "Inflation and Environmental Concern: Structural Change in the Process of Public Utility Price Regulation." *Journal of Law and Economics* 17, no. 2: 291–327.

Kaitin, Kenneth. 1989. "Reply to 'Understanding Comparisons of Drug Introductions Between the United States and the United Kingdom.'" *Clinical Pharmacology and Therapeutics* 46, no. 2: 146–148.

Kaitin, K., P. DiCerbo, and L. Lasagna. 1991. "The New Drug Approvals of 1987, 1988, and 1989: Trends in Drug Development." *Journal of Clinical Pharmacology* 31, no. 2: 116–122.

Kaitin, Kenneth, and Elaine Healy. 2000. "The New Drug Approvals of 1996, 1997, and 1998: Drug Development Trends in the User Fee Area." *Drug Information Journal* 34, no. 1: 1–14.

Kaitin, K., M. Manocchia, M. Seibring, and L. Lasagna. 1994. "The New Drug Approvals of 1990, 1991, and 1992: Trends in Drug Development." *Journal of Clinical Pharmacology* 34, no. 2: 120–127.

Kaitin, K., N. Mattison, F. Northington, and L. Lasagna. 1989. "The Drug Lag: An Update of New Drug Introductions in the United States and the United Kingdom, 1977 Through 1987." *Clinical Pharmacology and Therapeutics* 46, no. 2: 121–138.

Kaitin, Kenneth, N. Phelan, D. Raidford, and B. Morris. 1991. "Therapeutic Ratings and End-of-Phase II Conferences: Initiatives to Accelerate the Availability of Important New Drugs." *Journal of Clinical Pharmacology* 31, no. 1: 17–24.

Kaitin, K., B. Richard, and L. Lasagna. 1987. "Trends in Drug Development: The 1985–86 New Drug Approvals." *Journal of Clinical Pharmacology* 27, no. 8: 542–548.

Kallet, Arthur, and F. J. Schlink. 1933. *100,000,000 Guinea Pigs: Dangers in Everyday Foods, Drugs, and Cosmetics.* New York: Vanguard Press.

Karch, F. E., and L. Lasagna, 1975. "Adverse Drug Reactions: A Critical Review." *Journal of the American Medical Association* 234: 1236–1241.

Kazman, Sam. 1991. "Death by Regulation." *Regulation* 14 (Fall): 18–22.

Kennedy, Donald. 1978. "A Calm Look at the Drug Lag." *Journal of the American Medical Association* 239, no. 5: 423–426.

Kessler, David, 1978. "Regulating the Prescribing of Human Drugs for Non-Approved Uses Under the Food, Drug, and Cosmetic Act." *Harvard Journal on Legislation* 15, no. 4: 693–760.

———. 1991. "Drug Promotion and Scientific Exchange." *New England Journal of Medicine* 325, no. 3: 201.

———. 1997. "Remarks to the Annual Educational Conference, Food and Drug Law Institute." Washington, DC, December 11.

———. 2001. *A Question of Intent.* New York: Public Affairs Press.

Kessler, David, and Wayne Pines. 1990. "The Federal Regulation of Prescription Drug Advertising and Promotion." *Journal of the American Medical Association* 264 (November 14): 2409–2415.

Kessler, David, A. Haas, K. Feiden, M. Lumpkin, and R. Temple. 1996. "Approval of New Drugs in the United States: Comparison with the United Kingdom, Germany, and Japan." *Journal of the American Medical Association* 276, no. 22: 1826–1831.

Kingdon, John. 1984. *Agendas, Alternatives, and Public Policies.* New York: Harper Collins.

Klotz, Robert, and Stephen Ceccoli. 2002. "Media Coverage of Drug Approvals." Paper presented at the annual meeting of the American Political Science Association, August 28–September 1, Boston.

Knight, Jack, and Itai Sened, eds. 1998. *Explaining Social Institutions.* Ann Arbor: University of Michigan Press.

Kohn, Linda, Janet Corrigan, and Molla Donaldson, eds. 1999. *To Err Is Human: Building a Safer Health System.* Institute of Medicine. Washington, DC: National Academy Press.

Kolko, Gabriel. 1963. *The Triumph of Conservatism: A Reinterpretation of American History, 1900–1916.* London: Free Press of Glencoe.

———. 1965. *Railroads and Regulation, 1877–1916.* Princeton: Princeton University Press.

Krause, George. 1999. *Two Way Street: The Institutional Dynamics of the Modern Administrative State.* Pittsburgh: University of Pittsburgh Press.

Kulynych, Jennifer. 1999. "Will FDA Relinquish the "Gold Standard" for New Drug Approval? Redefining 'Substantial Evidence' in the FDA Modernization Act of 1997." *Food and Drug Law Journal* 54, no. 1: 127–150.

Kwitny, Jonathan. 1992. *Acceptable Risks.* New York: Poseidon Press.

Landau, Richard, ed. 1973. *Regulating New Drugs.* Chicago: University of Chicago Press.

Lasser, Karen, Paul Allen, Steffie Woodhandler, David Himmelstein, Sidney Wolfe, and David Bar. 2002. "Timing of New Black Box Warnings and Withdrawals for Prescription Medications." *Journal of the American Medical Association* 287, no. 17: 2215–2220.

Law, Jacky. 2001. "Electronic Dossier Ushers in Global Information Age." *Scrip Magazine* (November): 5–7.

Lazarou, J., B. H. Pomeranz, and P. N. Corey. 1998. "Incidence of Adverse Drug Reactions in Hospital Patients." *Journal of the American Medical Association* 279, no. 15: 1200–1205.

Leape, L., T. Brennan, N. Laird, A. Lawthers, A. Localio, B. Barnes, L. Hebert, J. Newhouse, P. Weiller, and H. Hiatt. 1991. "The Nature of Adverse Events in Hospitalized Patients: Results of the Harvard Medical Practice Study II." *New England Journal of Medicine* 324, no. 6: 377–384.

Leary, Warren. 1988a. "FDA Pressed to Approve More AIDS Drugs." *New York Times,* October 11, p. C5.

———. 1988b. "FDA Announces Changes to Speed Testing of New Drugs." *New York Times,* October 20, p. A1.

Liebenau, Jonathan. 1987. *Medical Science and Medical Industry: The Formation of the American Pharmaceutical Industry.* Baltimore: Johns Hopkins University Press.

Lindblom, Charles. 1959. "The Science of 'Muddling Through.'" *Public Administration Review* 19, no. 2 (Spring): 79–88.

———. 1965. *The Intelligence of Democracy.* New York: Free Press.

———. 1977. *Politics and Markets.* New York: Basic Books.

Loewenberg, Gerhard, and Samuel Patterson. 1979. *Comparing Legislatures.* Boston: Little, Brown.

Lowrance, William. 1976. *Of Acceptable Risk: Science and the Determination of Safety.* Los Altos, CA: W. Kaufmamn.

Lowry, William. 1994. *The Capacity for Wonder.* Washington, DC: Brookings Institution.

Mashaw, Jerry. 1985. *Due Process in the Administrative State.* New Haven: Yale University Press.

MCA (Medicines Control Agency) (UK Department of Health). 1996. *Agency Framework Document, 1995/96.* London: MCA.

McCubbins, Matthew. 1985. "The Legislative Design of Regulatory Structure." *American Journal of Political Science* 29, no. 4: 721–748.

McCubbins, Matthew, Roger Noll, and Barry Weingast. 1987. "Administrative Procedures as Instruments of Political Control." *Journal of Law, Economics, and Organization* 3, no. 2: 243–277.

———. 1989. "Structure and Process, Politics and Policy: Administrative Arrangements and the Political Control of Agencies." *Virginia Law Review* 75, no. 2: 431–482.

McCubbins, Matthew, and Thomas Schwartz. 1984. "Congressional Oversight Overlooked: Police Patrols Versus Fire Alarms." *American Journal of Political Science* 28 (March): 165–169.

McDonald, Tom. 2002. "New View on Pharmacovigilance." *Scrip World Pharmaceutical News* (May 17).

McFayden, Richard. 1976. "Thalidomide in America: A Brush with Tragedy." *Clio Medica* 11, no. 2: 79–93.

McNollgast. 1999. "The Political Origins of the Administrative Procedures Act." *Journal of Law, Economics, and Organization* 15, no. 1: 180–221.

McPhee, William. 1963. *Formal Theories of Mass Behavior.* New York: Free Press/Glencoe.

Medical Industry Today. 1997. "FDA Approves Allegra-D; Hoechst Agrees to Pull Seldane." *Drug and Biotechnology News* (December 31).

Meier, Kenneth. 1988. *The Political Economy of Regulation: The Case of Insurance.* Albany: SUNY Press.

Michaels, Adrian. 2001. "When Sweetening the Pill Is Illegal: US Regulators Are Taking a Close Look at the Methods Used by Drug Companies to Sell Their Products to Doctors." *Financial Times* (London), March 29, p. 13.

Miller, Gary. 1992. *Managerial Dilemmas: The Political Economy of Hierarchy.* Cambridge: Cambridge University Press.

Mitnick, Barry. 1980. *The Political Economy of Regulation.* New York: Columbia University Press.

Moe, Terry. 1982. "Regulatory Performance and Presidential Administration." *American Journal of Political Science* 26, no. 2 (May 1982): 197–224.

———. 1984. "The New Economics of Organization." *American Journal of Political Science* 28, no. 4: 739–777.

———. 1985. "Control and Feedback in Economic Regulation: The Case of the NLRB." *American Political Science Review* 79, no. 4 (December): 1094–1117.

———. 1987. "An Assessment of the Positive Theory of Congressional Dominance." *Legislative Studies Quarterly* 12, no. 4 (November): 475–520.

———. 1989. "The Politics of Bureaucratic Structure." In John Chubb and Paul Peterson, eds., *Can the Government Govern?* pp. 267–329. Washington, DC: Brookings Institution.

———. 1998. "The Presidency and the Bureaucracy: The Presidential Advantage." In Michael Nelson, ed., *The Presidency and the Political System,* pp. 437–468. 5th ed. Washington, DC: CQ Press.

Morris, Lou. 1999. "Reminder and Help Seeking Ads: Alive and Well." *DTC Times* (July): 14.

Moynihan, Ray. 2002. "Alosetron: A Case Study in Regulatory Capture, or a Victory for Patients' Rights?" *British Medical Journal* 325 (September 14): 592–595.

Mulcahy, Neal. 1995. Remarks at the annual meeting of the Food and Drug Law Institute. Washington, DC, December 12.

National Center for Health Statistics. 2001. "Deaths: Preliminary Data for 2000." *National Vital Statistics Reports* 49, no. 12. Centers for Disease Control and Prevention.

———. 2002. "Health, United States, 2002, with Chartbook on Trends in the Health of Americans." Hyattsville, MD.

NIHCM (National Institute for Health Care Management Research and Educational Foundation). 2001. "Prescription Drugs and Mass Media Advertising, 2000." November.

———. 2002. "Prescription Drug Expenditures in 2001: Another Year of Escalating Costs." Revised report, May 6.

Niskanen, William. 1971. *Bureaucracy and Representative Government.* Chicago: Aldine-Atherton.

———. 1973. *Bureaucracy: Servant or Master?* London: Institute for Economic Affairs.

Noll, Roger. 1971. "The Behavior of Regulatory Agencies." *Review of Social Economy* 29, no. 1: 15–19.

———. 1985. "Government Regulatory Behavior: A Multidisciplinary Survey and Synthesis." In R. Noll, ed., *Regulatory Policy and the Social Sciences,* pp. 1253–1282. Berkeley: University of California Press.

North, Douglass. 1981. *Structure and Change in Economic History.* New York: Norton.

———. 1990. *Institutions, Institutional Change, and Economic Performance.* Cambridge: Cambridge University Press.

Numbers, Ronald. 1978. *Almost Persuaded: American Physicians and Compulsory Health Insurance, 1912–1920.* Baltimore: Johns Hopkins University Press.

OECD (Organization for Economic Cooperation and Development). 1994. *The Reform of Health Care Systems.* Paris: OECD.

———. 1995. *Internal Markets in the Making: Health Systems in Canada, Iceland, and the U.K.* Paris: OECD.

Okun, Arthur. 1975. *Equality and Efficiency: The Big Tradeoff.* Washington, DC: Brookings Institution.

Olson, Mary. 1995. "Regulatory Agency Discretion Among Competing Industries: Inside the FDA." *Journal of Law Economics and Organization* 11, no. 2: 379–405.

———. 1996. "Substitution in Regulatory Agencies: FDA Enforcement Alternatives." *Journal of Law, Economics, and Organization* 12, no. 2: 376–407.

———. 1997. "Firm Characteristics and the Speed of FDA Approval." *Journal of Economics and Management Strategy* 6, no. 2: 377–401.

OMB (Office of Management and Budget). 1991–2001. *Budget of the United States Government.* Washington, DC: U.S. Government Printing Office.

OTA (Office of Technology Assessment, U.S. Congress). 1982. "Post Marketing Surveillance of Prescription Drugs." OTA-H-189. Washington, DC: Government Printing Office, November.

———. 1993. "Pharmaceutical R&D: Costs, Risks, and Rewards." OTA-H-522. Washington, DC: Government Printing Office, February.

Parker, J.E.S. 1977. "Regulating Pharmaceutical Innovation: An Economist's View." *Food, Drug, Cosmetic Law Journal* 32, no. 4: 160–181.

Peacock, Alan. 1984. *The Regulation Game.* Oxford: Basil Blackwell.

Peck, Carl. 1995. Remarks at the annual meeting of the Food and Drug Law Institute. Washington, DC, December 12.

———. 1996. "Revitalizing New Product Development from Clinical Trials Through FDA Review." Testimony before Senate Committee on Labor and Human Resources, 104th Congress, 2nd sess., S.Hrg. 104–444, February 21.

Peltzman, Sam. 1973. "An Evaluation of Consumer Protection Legislation: The 1962 Drug Amendments." *Journal of Political Economy* 81, no. 5: 1049–1091.

———. 1974. *Regulation of Pharmaceutical Innovation.* Washington, DC: American Enterprise Institute.

———. 1976. "Toward a More General Theory of Regulation." *Journal of Law and Economics* 19 (August): 211–240.

Perrow, Charles. 1986. "Economic Theories of Organization." *Theory and Society* 15: 1–2.

———. 1993. *Complex Organizations: A Critical Essay.* 3d ed. New York: McGraw-Hill.

Petersen, Melody. 2002. "Heartfelt Advice, Hefty Fees." *New York Times,* August 11, p. C1.

Pew Internet and American Life. 2002. "Vital Decisions: How Internet Users Decide What Information to Trust When They or Their Loved Ones Are Sick." May 22. Available online at www.pewinternet.org/reports/toc.asp? report=59, June 18, 2003.

*Pharmaceutical Journal.* 1962. 188 (21 April).

———. 1966. 198 (July 23): 86.

———. 1967. 199 (July 15): 59.

———. 1968. 200 (March 9): 274.

Phillips, David, Nicholas Christenfeld, and Laura Glynn, 1998. "Increase in U.S. Medication-Error Deaths Between 1983 and 1993." *The Lancet* 351 (February 28): 643–644.

Posner, Richard. 1974. "Theories of Economic Regulation." *Bell Journal of Economics and Management Science* 5 (Autumn): 337–352.

Porter, Roy. 1997. *The Greatest Benefit to Mankind: A Medical History of Humanity.* New York: Norton.

Price, Deb. 1990. "'ACT UP' Group Uses Rage to Fight AIDS Complacency." Gannett News Service, November 23.

PPSSCC (President's Private Sector Survey on Cost Control). 1983. "Report on User Charges." Washington, DC, Spring–Fall.

Public Citizen. 1998. "HRG Report: Lower Standards Permit Dangerous Drug Approvals—FDA Medical Officers Report." Health Research Group report no. 1466, December.

Public Citizen, Congress Watch. 2001. "Rx R&D Myths: The Case Against the Drug Industry's R&D 'Scare Card.'" Washington, DC, July.

———. 2002. "Pharmaceuticals Rank as Most Profitable Industry, Again." Washington, DC, April 17.

Quirk, Paul. 1980. "The Food and Drug Administration." In James Q. Wilson, ed., *The Politics of Regulation.* New York: Basic Books.

———. 1981. *Industry Influence in Federal Regulatory Agencies.* Princeton: Princeton University Press.

Rawlins, M.D. 1981. "Clinical Pharmacology: Adverse Reactions to Drugs." *British Medical Journal* 282 (March 21): 974–976.

Rawson, Nigel, K. Kaitin, K. Thomas, G. Perry. 1998. "Drug Review in Canada: A Comparison with Australia, Sweden, the United Kingdom, and the United States." *Drug Information Journal* 32, no. 4: 1133–1141.

Redford, Emmette. 1969. *Democracy in the Administrative State.* New York: Oxford University Press.

Redwood, Heinz. 1993. *Price Regulation and Pharmaceutical Research: The Limits of Co-Existence.* Suffolk, UK: Oldwicks Press.

Reekie, W. Duncan. 1975. *The Economics of the Pharmaceutical Industry.* London: Macmillan.

———. 1988. "Legislative Change and Industrial Performance: A Case Study." *Scottish Journal of Political Economy,* 27, no. 2 (June 1980): 107–129.

Review Panel, Department of Health, Education, and Welfare. 1977. "Review Panel on New Drug Regulation, Final Report." Report (Norman Dorsen, chairman), May.

Rhein, Reginald. 2000. "Henney Ushers in a Modernised FDA." *Scrip Magazine* (February): 25.

———. 2001. "FDA Comes Under Fire from All Directions." *Scrip Magazine* (February): 20–22.

Rienzo, David. 1998. "About-Face: How FDA Changed Its Mind, Took on the Tobacco Companies in Their Own Back Yard, and Won." *Food and Drug Law Journal* 53, no. 2: 243–266.

Ripley, Randall, and Grace Franklin. 1984. *Congress, the Bureaucracy, and Public Policy.* 3d ed. Homewood, IL: Dorsey Press.

Robinson, Glen. 1991. *American Bureaucracy: Public Choice and Public Law.* Ann Arbor: University of Michigan Press.

Roemer, Milton. 1991. *National Health Systems of the World.* New York: Oxford University Press.

Rosenbloom, David. 2000. *Building a Legislative-Centered Public Administration: Congress and the Administrative State, 1946–1999.* Tuscaloosa: University of Alabama Press.

Rothenberg, Lawrence. 1994. *Regulation, Organization, and Politics: Motor Freight Policy at the Interstate Commerce Commission.* Ann Arbor: University of Michigan Press.

Rothstein, William. 1995. "Pharmaceuticals and Public Policy in America: A History." In W. G. Rothstein, ed., *Readings in American Health Care: Current Issues in Socio-Historical Perspective.* Madison: University of Wisconsin Press.

Rourke, Francis. 1976. *Bureaucracy, Politics, and Policy.* 2d ed. Boston: Little, Brown.

———. 1984. *Bureaucracy, Politics, and Policy.* 3d ed. Boston: Little, Brown.

Rubin, R. 1998. "Policy Speeds Approval, but Some Say It's Risky." *USA Today,* July 10–12, pp. 1–2.

Sabatier, Paul, and Hank Jenkins-Smith. 1999. "The Advocacy Coalition Framework: An Assessment." In Paul Sabatier, ed., *Theories of the Policy Process,* pp. 117–166. Boulder: Westview Press.

Sager, Alan, and Deborah Socolar. 2001. "Drug Industry Marketing Staff Soars While Research Staffing Stagnates." Unpublished paper, Health Reform Program, Boston University School of Public Health, December 6.

Sarett, L. H. 1974. Testimony for "Examination of the Pharmaceutical Industry, 1973–74." Joint Hearings before the Subcommittee on Health, Committee on Labor and Public Welfare, and the Subcommittee on Administrative Practice and Procedure, Judiciary Committee, U.S. Senate. Part 7, August 15–16.

Sargent, Jane. 1985. "The Politics of the Pharmaceutical Price Regulation Scheme." In Wolfgang Streeck and Phillipe Schmitter, eds., *Private Interest Government,* pp. 105–127. London: Sage.

Schifrin, Leonard, and Jack Tayan. 1977. "The Drug Lag: An Interpretative Review of the Literature." *International Journal of Health Services* 7, no. 3: 359–381.

Schlozman, Kay Lehman, and John Tierney. 1986. *Organized Interests and American Democracy.* New York: Harper and Row.

Schmidt, Alexander. 1975. Testimony for "Congressional Oversight of Administrative Agencies (FDA & EPA)." Hearings before the Subcommittee on Separation of Powers, Judiciary Committee, U.S. Senate. July 21 and 23.

Schuck, Peter, ed. 1994. *Foundations of Administrative Law.* New York: Oxford University Press.

Schultz, Stacey. 2002. "The Drug That Could Have Been." *U.S. News and World Report,* August 19, pp. 18–23.

Schultze, Charles. 1977. *The Public Use of Private Interest.* Washington, DC: Brookings Institution.

Schwab, David, and Susan Todd. 2002. "FDA Nominee Facing a Full Slate of Issues." *Newark Star Ledger,* September 29, Business section, p. 1.

Schwartzman, David. 1976. *Innovation in the Pharmaceutical Industry.* Baltimore: Johns Hopkins University Press.

Seachrist, Lisa. 1997. "Sen. Jeffords PDUFA/FDA Reform Bill Dodges Contentious Issues." *Bioworld Today* 8, no. 103 (May 29): 1.

Seidman, David. 1977. "The Politics and Economics of Pharmaceutical Regulation." In John Gardiner, ed., *Public Law and Public Policy,* pp. 177–203. New York: Praeger Publishers.

Shapiro, Martin. 1994. "APA: Past, Present, and Future." In Peter Schuck, ed., *Foundations of Administrative Law,* pp. 60–68. New York: Oxford University Press.

Shapiro, Sidney. 1978. "Limiting Physician Freedom to Prescribe a Drug for Any Purpose: The Need for FDA Regulation." *Northwestern University Law Review* 73, no. 5 (December 1978): 801–872.

Shepsle, Kenneth. 1979. "Institutional Arrangements and Equilibrium in Multidimensional Voting Models." *American Journal of Political Science* 23, no. 1: 27–59.

Shulman, Sheila, Peg Hewitt, and Michael Manocchia. 1995. "Studies and Inquiries into the FDA Regulatory Process: An Historical Review." *Drug Information Journal* 29, no. 2: 385–413.

Silverman, Milton, and Philip Lee. 1974. *Pills, Profits, and Politics.* Berkeley: University of California Press.

Simon, Herbert. 1957. *Administrative Behavior.* 2d ed. New York: Free Press.

Skocpol, Theda, and Kenneth Finegold. 1982. "State Capacity and Economic Intervention in the Early New Deal." *Political Science Quarterly* 92, no. 2 (Summer): 255–278.

Skowronek, Stephen. 1982. *Building a New American State: The Expansion of National Administrative Capacities, 1877–1920.* Cambridge: Cambridge University Press.

Slinn, Judy. 1995. "Research and Development in the UK Pharmaceutical Industry from the Nineteenth Century to the 1960s." In Roy Porter and Mikulas Teich, eds., *Drugs and Narcotics in History,* pp. 168–186. Cambridge: Cambridge University Press.

Sneader, Walter. 1985. *Drug Discovery: The Evolution of Modern Medicines.* New York: Wiley.

Stephens, Trent, and Rock Brynner. 2001. *Dark Remedy: The Impact of Thalidomide and Its Revival as a Vital Medicine.* Cambridge, MA: Perseus Publishing.

Stigler, George. 1971. "The Theory of Economic Regulation." *Bell Journal of Economic and Management Science* 2, no. 1 (Spring): 2–21.

Stigler, George, and Claire Friedland. 1962. "What Can Regulators Regulate? The Case of Electricity." *Journal of Law and Economics* 5, no. 1: 1–17.

Tan, Lorna. 2000. "Global Drug Sales to Rise 8% to $638b(S)." *The Straits Times* (Singapore), October 21, p. 84.

Teff, Harvey, and C. Munro. 1976. *Thalidomide: The Legal Aftermath*. London: Saxon House.

Temin, Peter. 1980. *Taking Your Medicine: Drug Regulation in the United States*. Cambridge: Harvard University Press.

Temple, Robert, and Martin Himmel. 2002. "Safety of Newly Approved Drugs: Implications for Prescribing." *Journal of the American Medical Association* 287, no. 17: 2273–2275.

True, James. 1999. "Attention, Inertia, and Equity in the Social Security Program." *Journal of Public Administration Research and Theory* 9, no. 4: 571–596.

Truman, David. 1951. *The Governmental Process*. New York: Knopf.

UNAIDS. 2002. "Report on the Global HIV/AIDS Epidemic 2002." Joint United Nations Program on HIV/AIDS. Geneva, Switzerland: UNAIDS.

U.S. Bureau of the Census. *Statistical Abstract of the United States*. 1997, 2001. Washington, DC.

U.S. Congress, Committee on Government Operations. 1970. "The British Drug Safety System." Washington, DC.

U.S. Congress, Congressional Budget Office. 1993. "The Growth of Federal User Charges." Washington, DC, August.

USFDA (U.S. Food and Drug Administration). 1976. "Annual Reports, 1950–1974, on the Administration of the Federal Food, Drug, and Cosmetic Act and Related Laws." Washington, DC.

———. 1995a. "A Guide to Resources on the History of the Food and Drug Administration." Food and Drug Administration History Office. Washington, DC.

———. 1995b. "From Test Tube to Patient: New Drug Development in the United States." FDA Consumer Special Report. 2d ed. Washington, DC, January.

———. 1995c. "Timely Access to New Drugs in the 1990s: An International Comparison." Washington, DC, December.

———. 1995d. "Third Annual Performance Report: Prescription Drug User Fee Act of 1992." Washington, DC, December 1.

———. 1998. "Guidance for Industry: Providing Clinical Evidence of Effectiveness for Human Drug and Biological Products." Washington, DC, May.

———. 1999. "Managing the Risks from Medical Product Use: Creating a Risk Management Framework." Report to the FDA Commissioner from the Task Force on Risk Management. Washington, DC, May.

———. 2000. "FDAMA: Report on FDA Plan for Statutory Compliance." Washington, DC: FDA, September.

USGAO (U.S. General Accounting Office). 1980. "FDA Drug Approval—A Lengthy Process That Delays the Availability of Important New Drugs." GAO Report HRD 80-64. Washington, DC, May 28.

———. 1991. "Off-Label Drugs: Reimbursement Policies Constrain Physicians in Their Choice of Cancer Therapies." GAO/PEMD-91-14. Washington, DC, September 27.

———. 1995. "FDA Drug Approval: Review Time Has Decreased in Recent Years." GAO/PEMD-96-1. Washington, DC, October 1995.

———. 1996. "European Union Drug Approval: Overview of New Medicines Evaluation Agency and Approval Process." GAO/HEHS-96-71. Washington, DC, April.

———. 1997. "Consumer Product Safety Commission: Better Data Needed to Help Identify and Analyze Potential Hazards." T-HEHS-98-23. Washington, DC, October 23.

——— 2002. "Effect of User Fees on Drug Approval Times, Withdrawals, and Other Agency Activities." GAO-02-958. Washington, DC, September 17.

USHHS (U.S. Department of Health and Human Services). 1991. "Final Report of the Advisory Committee on the Food and Drug Administration." Washington, DC, May.

———. 1999. "Health, United States, 1999." PHS 99-1232, 9-0475. Washington, DC, July.

U.S. House of Representatives. 1980. "Volume I: Drug Regulation Reform— Oversight: New Drug Approval Process." Hearing before the Subcommittee on Health and the Environment, Committee on Interstate and Foreign Commerce. Serial no. 96-170, June 25.

———. 1982. "The Regulation of New Drugs by the Food and Drug Administration: The New Drug Review Process." Hearings before a subcommittee on Intergovernmental Relations and Human Resources, 97th Congress, 2nd Session, August 3–4.

———. 1991. "Promotion of Drugs and Medical Devices for Unapproved Uses." Hearings before the Committee on Government Operations, Subcommittee on Human Resources and Intergovernmental Relations, June 11.

———. 1992a. "Council on Competitiveness and FDA Plans to Alter the Drug Approval Process at FDA." Hearing before the Committee on Government Operations, Subcommittee on Human Resources and Intergovernmental Relations. Washington, DC, March 19.

———. 1992b. "User Fees for Prescription Drugs." Hearing before the Subcommittee on Health and the Environment, Committee on Energy and Commerce. Serial no. 102-161, August 10.

———. 1997. "Prescription Drug User Fee Reauthorization and Drug Regulatory Modernization Act of 1997." House Report 105-310, October 7.

———. 2002. "Reauthorization of the Prescription Drug User Fee Act." Subcommittee on Health, Committee on Energy and Commerce. House Report 107-93, March 6.

U.S. Senate. 1974. "Regulation of New Drug R&D by the Food and Drug Administration, 1974." Joint hearings before the Subcommittee on Health, Committee on Labor and Public Welfare, and the Subcommittee on Administrative Practice and Procedure, Judiciary Committee, September 25 and 27.

———. 1991. "Advisory Committee on the FDA: Final Report." Senate Committee on Labor and Human Resources. S. Hrg. 102-1164, May 15.

———. 1996. "Food and Drug Administration Performance and Accountability Act of 1995." Report 104-284. 104th Congress, 2d session, June 20.

———. 1998. "President Clinton's Budget for 1999: Summary and Analysis." Prepared by Senate Budget Committee, Democratic Staff, February 3.

Usborne, David, 2002. "How Imclone's Dirty Dealings Soiled America's Diva of Domestic Perfection." *The Independent* (London), June 21, p. 18.

Vogel, David. 1986. *National Styles of Regulation.* Ithaca: Cornell University Press.

———. 1989. *Fluctuating Fortunes.* New York: Basic Books.

Vogel, Steven. 1996. *Freer Markets, More Rules: Regulatory Reform in Advanced Industrial Countries.* Ithaca: Cornell University Press.

Ward, Michael. 1992. "Drug Approval Overregulation." *Regulation* (Fall): 47–53.

Wardell, William. 1973. "Introduction of New Therapeutic Drugs in the U.S. and Great Britain: An International Comparison." *Clinical Pharmacology and Therapeutics* 14, no. 5: 773–790.

———. 1974. "Therapeutic Implication of the Drug Lag." *Clinical Pharmacology and Therapeutics* 15, no. 1: 73–96.

———. 1978a. "A Close Inspection at the 'Calm Look.'" *Journal of the American Medical Association* 239, no. 19: 2004–2011.

———. 1978b. "The Drug Lag Revisited: Comparison by Therapeutic Area of Patterns of Drugs Marketed in the United States and Great Britain from 1972 Through 1976." *Clinical Pharmacology and Therapeutics* 24, no. 5: 499–524.

———, ed. 1978c. *Controlling the Use of Therapeutic Drugs: An International Comparison.* Washington: AEI Press.

Wardell, William, and Louis Lasagna. 1975. *Regulation and Drug Development.* Washington, DC: American Enterprise Institute.

Weaver, R. Kent, and Bert Rockman, eds. 1993. *Do Institutions Matter? Government Capabilities in the United States and Abroad.* Washington, DC: Brookings Institution.

Weingast, Barry, and Mark Moran. 1987. "Bureaucratic Discretion or Congressional Control? Regulatory Policy Making by the Federal Trade Commission." In R. Mackay, J. Miller, and B. Yandle, eds., *Public Choice and Regulation: A View from the Federal Trade Commission.* Stanford, CA: Hoover Institution.

Weiss, Rick. 2001. "Thompson Signals He'll Initiate New HHS Review of Abortion Drug." *Washington Post,* January 20, A8.

White, Ben, and Justin Gillis, 2002. "Former ImClone Chief Indicted; Grand Jury Acts After Plea-Deal Talks Fail." *Washington Post,* August 8, E1.

Wierenga, Dale, and John Beary. 1995. "The Drug Development and Approval Process." In *New Medicines in Development for Cancer,* p. 27. Pharmaceutical Research and Manufacturers Association, Washington, DC, May.

Wildavsky, Aaron. 1964. *The Politics of the Budgetary Process.* Boston: Little, Brown.

Williamson, Oliver. 1975. *Markets and Hierarchies.* New York: Free Press.

———. 1985. *The Economic Institutions of Capitalism.* New York: Free Press.

Willman, David. 2000. "The New FDA." *Los Angeles Times,* December 20, p. A1.

Wilson, James Q. 1980. *The Politics of Regulation.* New York: Basic Books.

———. 1989. *Bureaucracy: What Government Agencies Do and Why They Do It.* New York: Basic Books.

Wlezian, Christopher. 1995. "The Public as Thermostat: Dynamics of Preferences for Spending." *American Journal of Political Science* 39, no. 4: 981–1000.

Wood, B. Dan, and Richard Waterman. 1991. "The Dynamics of Political Control of the Bureaucracy." *American Political Science Review* 85, no. 3:
801–828.

————. 1994. *Bureaucratic Dynamics: The Role of Bureaucracy in a Democracy.* Boulder: Westview.

Worsham, Jeff, Marc Eisner, and Evan Ringquist. 1997. "Assessing the Assumptions: A Critical Analysis of Agency Theory." *Administration and Society* 28
(February): 419–440.

Young, James Harvey. 1961. *The Toadstool Millionaires: A Social History of
Patent Medicines in America Before Federal Regulation.* Princeton:
Princeton University Press.

————. 1967. *The Medical Messiahs: A Social History of Health Quackery in
Twentieth Century America.* Princeton: Princeton University Press.

————. 1981. "The Long Struggle for the 1906 Law." *FDA Consumer* 15, no.
5 (June): 12–16.

Zegart, Amy. 1999. *Flawed by Design: The Evolution of the CIA, JSC, and
NSC.* Stanford, CA: Stanford University Press.

Zuger, Abagail. 1997. "How Grapefruit Juice Makes Some Pills More Powerful." *New York Times,* October 7, Science Times section.

# INDEX

# ABOUT THE BOOK

From aspirin to Viagra to the latest cancer treatment, the Food and Drug Administration acts as a gatekeeper determining what medicines are legally available in the United States. But in fulfilling that regulatory role, Stephen Ceccoli argues, the FDA may inadvertently be promoting new drugs at the expense of public health.

The FDA's initial mandate to protect health grew out of pharmaceutical-related disasters in the early 1900s. Later criticisms that the agency's approach impeded industry competitiveness and failed to meet public need, however, led to a political compromise on its mission. The new FDA has cut its review time nearly in half and allows direct-to-consumer advertising, off-label promotion of drugs, and the "fast-tracking" of treatments. Ceccoli convincingly shows that this approval process, while redressing valid complaints, is also creating a new complex of problems that must be resolved.

**Stephen J. Ceccoli** is assistant professor of international studies and J. S. Seidman Research Fellow at Rhodes College.